TOVRAINE ET BLESOIS

Châteaudun

ORLEANS

VENDOME

Talcy

Sully-sur-Loire

Gien

Menars

BLOIS

Chambord

Bury

Villesavin

La Cisse

Cheverny

Chaumont

Amboise

Le Moulin

Chanteloup

Manoir de Beauregard

Chenonceau

Le Cher

Valençay

Loches

Brißac

OF THE LOIRE

CHATEAUX OF THE LOIRE

By the same Author

VERSAILLES
PALACES AND PROGRESSES OF ELIZABETH I

CHÂTEAU DE MONTGEOFFROY

Châteaux of the Loire

IAN DUNLOP

WITH A PREFACE BY
THE DUC DE BRISSAC

HAMISH HAMILTON
LONDON

First published in Great Britain, 1969
by Hamish Hamilton Ltd.
90 Great Russell Street London W.C.1
Copyright © 1969 by Ian Dunlop

SBN 241 01627 4

Printed in Great Britain by
Western Printing Services Ltd. Bristol

CONTENTS

LIST OF ILLUSTRATIONS

ILLUSTRATIONS IN THE TEXT

B.N.	Bibliothèque Nationale
B.M.	British Museum
T.C. de F.	Touring Club de France
Arch: Phot:	Archives Photographiques
F.G.T.O.	French Government Tourist Office
Bib: de Tours	Bibliothèque de Tours
C. Life	Country Life

Endpapers

The Châteaux of the Loire

ACKNOWLEDGMENTS

I would like to express my gratitude to Mr. Charles de Winton, British Council Representative and Cultural Attaché to the British Embassy in Paris for his unfailing help and hospitality; to Colonel and Mrs. Robert Dawson, formerly of the British Embassy, Paris, for their hospitality, and to M. Jacques Dupont of the Affaires Culturelles whose letters of introduction have opened so many doors.

I am most grateful also to the duc de Brissac for his help and encouragement and for writing the preface to this book; to his son the marquis de Brissac, to the marquis de Contades and to Princess Maria-Pia d'Orléans-Bragance, comtesse de Nicolay, for their help and hospitality; to the duc de Luynes and to M. François Carvallo for the special facilities which they have allowed me; to Prince Jacques de Broglie and the Prince de Ligne for providing the photographs for plates 10 and 20b; to the marquis de Vibraye for plates 9b, 27, and 32b; to M. de la Morandière and M. François Pion for privileged access to Chenonceau and Chambord. Finally I would like to thank the marquise de Boisséson for her charming hospitality in Paris, and Mrs. Rosemary Rutt for typing the manuscript.

IAN DUNLOP

PREFACE

Par le Duc de Brissac

Président de l'Association 'Les Amis des Châteaux de la Loire'

Voici un ouvrage qui s'adresse à des lecteurs avertis; je veux dire ayant déjà quelques connaissances du Val de Loire, quelques lumières en architecture et quelques notions de l'histoire de la France depuis le quinzième siècle. Il faudra se rappeler de nos rois et nos reines, quitte à consulter un ouvrage élémentaire. On devra également se souvenir des favorites, car celles-ci jouent souvent le premier rôle dans les modes et les arts de la monarchie: ainsi Agnès Sorel à la fin de la Guerre de Cent Ans, et la Marquise de Pompadour sous le règne de Louis XV.

Aussi n'est-il pas inutile, je crois, de 'cadrer' le sujet dès l'abord; de le placer en peu de mots, dans son temps et dans son site; bref de faire de cette préface une introduction, une introduction à la visite, sur les lieux ou par ce livre, des châteaux de la Loire.

*

La Loire, d'abord. Ce fleuve, le plus long de France (600 milles), ce fleuve, la Loire, ne sert à rien. A rien. A notre époque, quelle richesse! On a essayé jadis de la rendre navigable, mais Dieu merci! on n'y est point parvenu. Ni remorqueurs, ni chalands, ni grues de port; sur son cours, seulement quelques canoës au fil de l'eau et les barques des passeurs et des pêcheurs. La Loire estivale s'en va d'un cours sableux et paresseux, mais sa gloire est de parapher la constellation, la guirlande, le cortège de ces fameux châteaux qui profilent, dans les ciels de l'Orléanais, du Blésois, de la Touraine et de l'Anjou, leurs blanches pierres et leurs ardoises bleues.

Ce n'est pas que tous les châteaux de la Loire soient au bord du fleuve; beaucoup se reflètent dans les rivières affluentes: ainsi Chenonceau sur le Cher, Azay-le-Rideau sur l'Indre, Chinon sur la Vienne. Chambord, l'extravagant palais de François Ier, se trouve sur moins encore: sur le Cosson, qui alimente l'eau des douves. D'autres enfin, Valençay, Beauregard, Cheverny, Montgeoffroy, ne sont sur rien du tout, ou si peu que rien, en eau courante s'entend.

Si leur situation nous interdit une définition, l'histoire peut-elle nous en fournir une?

xi

Retiendrons-nous seulement les châteaux de la Renaissance? Ceci est tentant, car régnaient, à la grande époque du val, les Valois. Mais ce serait faire fi des féodaux: Chinon, Loches, Saumur, Angers, Luynes; ce serait biffer le siècle XV où l'ogival français, le gothique, comme on l'appelle (je ne m'y ferai jamais), mûrit ses plus beaux fruits civils: Montsoreau, Montreuil-Bellay, Ussé, Le Plessis-Bourré, Blois (l'aile de Charles), Talcy, les tours de Brissac, la chapelle d'Amboise; ce serait oublier le XVIIe siècle, car malgré l'aveuglant attrait du Roi-Soleil à Versailles, on a construit ici sous Louis XIV: Cheverny, Blois (l'aile de Gaston), la Ferté Saint-Aubin, l'aile sud de Valençay, le grand logis de Brissac, la chapelle de Serrant.

Ce serait, et combien grave! s'interdire le sourire du XVIIIe devant la Tour Neuve de Valençay, le château de Montgeoffroy, la pagode de Chanteloup, et refuser le souvenir de la Marquise à Ménars, Ménars avec ses escaliers, ses terrasses, son orangerie, son Temple de l'Amour, ses rampes, ses jardins bas, sa grotte, ses griffons à buste de femme, ses futaies qui fuient vers le nord et son reflet qui fuit dans l'eau vers l'occident, vers l'Océan. . . .

A défaut de définition, nous nous en remettrons au commun consentement: les châteaux de la Loire vont de Gien à Angers, parsemant le val sur 120 milles, et sont au nombre d'une trentaine. Je parle ici des plus connus, des étoiles de première grandeur. Car si le touriste s'en donne la peine, il découvrira dans les environs une multitude de demeures seigneuriales plus modestes, manoirs, gentilhommières, qui certes 'méritent le détour', comme disent les guides.

Le R. P. Dunlop a classé son ouvrage par époques historiques. Il descend le cours du temps. Les touristes, eux, descendent en général le cours du fleuve, quitte à zigzaguer parmi les siècles. Mais quant à l'histoire, tous les historiens du val commencent leur narration par la célèbre entrevue de Jeanne d'Arc et du dauphin Charles, qui se situe à Chinon en 1429. On y voit encore les débris de la salle qui fut le théâtre d'une rencontre grave de tant d'évènements.

Tout en retraçant la grande et la petite histoire, l'auteur met l'accent sur l'architecture des édifices qu'il décrit. Il faut dire qu'il eut, grâce à la munificence du marquis de Salisbury, libre accès à la bibliothèque du château de Hatfield, dont les riches éléments lui donnèrent licence d'écrire un livre sur les châteaux anglais disparus au XVIe siècle, oeuvre qui lui valut de siéger à la Société des Antiquaires de Londres. Son goût et sa science de l'architecture lui permettent de suivre pas à pas l'évolution des châteaux de la Loire, passionnante évolution, car ils vont du médiéval aux temps modernes.

La Renaissance attire particulièrement le R. P. Dunlop, et quoique son ouvrage soit consacré à la Loire, il nous parle souvent du château de Gaillon, lequel se trouve en Normandie. Effectivement, c'est à Gaillon que les érudits fixent le début de la Renaissance, en 1509, dans les édifices tout au moins, car c'est là que des artistes et artisans venus d'Italie ont laissé leur témoignage dans les pierres sculptées du portail. La Renaissance irait de cette date, 1509, jusqu'à l'assassinat d'Henri III, le dernier Valois, en 1589. Elle aurait duré 80 ans, couvrant presque entièrement le seizième siècle. Notion un peu pédagogique, donc simplifiée, mais qu'on peut retenir en première instance.

La Renaissance, c'est l'italianisant. La France eut toujours la nostalgie de l'Italie, et le grand siècle classique, le XVIIe, devait y revenir avec Versailles, qui est italianisant, encore que les maisons sans toits s'accommodent mal du régime pluvieux de l'Ile de France, ce que me fit remarquer un jour un ami anglais à qui je faisais visiter le palais de Louis XIV, et qui me dit froidement: 'Il ne va pas dans le paysage'. . . .

*

On s'instruira en lisant l'ouvrage du R. P. Dunlop. Je souhaite qu'il incite les visiteurs à venir toujours plus nombreux dans la vallée ligérienne. Que n'a-t-on écrit, et à juste titre, sur le Val de Loire, sur sa douceur, son accueil, son charme!

Non loin du Paris, voici des édifices voulus par l'orgueil ou par l'amour, désirés par le goût du faste, parfois aussi imposés par la force obsédante d'un rêve, comme Chambord ou Chenonceau; des monuments élevés par l'homme, non à ses dieux, mais à lui-même, pour le jeu de ses loisirs et l'éclatante sanction de sa réussite; greffés sur des forteresses abolies, ou édifiés sur un site élu, afin d'en jouir en l'interprétant; cherchant l'eau pour se mirer dans le naturel miroir avec une coquette complaisance; riches de souvenirs tragiques, la conjuration d'Amboise ou l'assassinat du duc de Guise à Blois, mais le plus souvent galants, car la Loire est une région féminine, toute de grâce et de distinction, et ce n'est pas fortuitement que les Valois, eux-mêmes un peu féminins, ont tant aimé ses rives.

Témoins d'heures néfastes, mais plus souvent d'époques de félicité, souvenirs émouvants de nos arts et de nos annales, toujours vus et revus avec l'émotion d'une première surprise, tels sont les châteaux du Val de Loire, et tels nous les fait revivre avec une érudite affection le présent ouvrage auquel je souhaite toute audience et tout succès.

PREFACE

Translation by the Author

Here is a book which is aimed at the educated reader; by which I mean one who has already some familiarity with the Loire Valley, some enlightenment as regards architecture and some rudiments of French History since the fifteenth century. We must hold in remembrance our Kings and Queens, without having to look them up in an elementary textbook. We need also to remember the Mistresses, for these often play the leading role in the world of fashion and of art under the monarchy—as did Agnès Sorel at the end of the Hundred Years War and the marquise de Pompadour in the reign of Louis XV.

Therefore I think it might be useful to outline the whole subject at the very start; to give it its place, both architectural and geographical, as briefly as possible; in fact to make this Preface an Introduction—an introduction to our visit, either on the spot, or through the medium of this book, to the Châteaux of the Loire.

*

First—the Loire. This river, the longest in France (six hundred miles)—this river, the Loire, is of no utility. None whatever. In these days, how precious! An attempt was once made to render it navigable, but, thank heavens, it did not succeed. No tug-boats, no barges, no dockside cranes; along its course only a few canoes, going with the current, and the small boats of the ferry or the fisherman. In summer the Loire dwindles to a lazy trickle in a sandy bed. But its glory is that it underlines with an appropriate flourish the procession, the garland, the galaxy of famous châteaux which cut their silhouettes of white stone and blue slate against the skies of Orléanais, Blésois, Touraine and Anjou.

But this does not mean that all the 'Châteaux of the Loire' are on this river; many cast their reflections upon the waters of its tributaries; Chenonceau on the Cher, Azay-le-Rideau on the Indre, Chinon on the Vienne. Chambord, palatial extravaganza of François I, stands on an even smaller stream, the Cosson, which supplies its moats with water. Others, even, such as Valençay, Beauregard, Cheverny and Montgeoffroy

*possess no running stream, or none worth mentioning. If their position
makes the term difficult to define, perhaps History will provide the answer.*

It is a great temptation to restrict ourselves to the châteaux of the
Renaissance, for during the great period of the Valley's history the
Valois were on the throne. But this would be to turn one's back on
the feudal castles—on Chinon, Loches, Saumur, Angers and Luynes; it
would be to strike off the list the whole fifteenth century, when the French
Pointed, which some call Gothic (though I can never reconcile myself
to that term), produced its ripest fruit in domestic architecture: Montsoreau,
Montreuil-Bellay, Ussé, Le Plessis-Bourré, Blois (Charles' wing),
Talcy, the towers at Brissac, the Chapel at Amboise; it would be to forget
the seventeenth century for, despite the dazzling attraction of the Sun
King at Versailles, there was building here under Louis XIV: Cheverny,
Blois (Gaston's wing), La Ferté Saint-Aubin, the south wing of Valençay,
the main block of Brissac, the Chapel at Serrant.

Worse still, it would be to renounce the graciousness of the eighteenth
century in the face of the New Tower at Valençay, the château de Montgeoffroy, the Pagoda at Chanteloup, and to refuse the memory of the
Pompadour at Ménars—Ménars, with its flights of steps, its terraces,
its orangery, its Temple of Love, its Lower Gardens, its Grotto, its
Sphinxes; the lines of tall trees vanishing towards the north; the reflections
losing themselves in the water towards the west, towards the sea. . . .

For want of a better definition we will start again with the accepted
convention: the 'Châteaux of the Loire' lie between Gien and Angers,
dotted about the valley for a hundred and twenty miles, and they number
about thirty. I am speaking now of the best known, the brightest stars in
the galaxy. For if the visitor will take the trouble he will discover in the
neighbourhood a multitude of more modest seigneurial lodgings—the
Manors and smaller Country Houses which are certainly, as the guide
books say, 'worth the detour'.

The Reverend Ian Dunlop classifies his subjects by the period of history
to which they belong; he follows the course of history. Visitors, however,
not restricted to the meanderings of Time, follow more often the course
of the river. But when it comes to History, all historians of the Valley
begin their account with the famous interview between Joan of Arc and
the Dauphin Charles which took place at Chinon in 1429. One can still
see here the ruins of the room which was the scene of an encounter so charged
with consequences.

While he follows the course of history, both at national and at domestic
level, Mr. Dunlop focuses attention on the architecture of the buildings
which he describes. I may say that he once had, thanks to the generosity of

*Lord Salisbury, free access to the library at Hatfield House, and from the
wealth of material there was able to produce a book on the English Palaces
of the sixteenth century which have disappeared—a work which earned
him, no doubt, his Fellowship of the Society of Antiquaries of London.
His taste and his knowledge of architecture enable him to follow step by
step the development of the Châteaux of the Loire, a development of
absorbing interest, for they range from the Middle Ages right up to the
present day.*

*The Renaissance particularly attracts Mr. Dunlop, and although his
book is devoted to the Loire, he talks much of the Château de Gaillon
which is in Normandy. It is in fact at Gaillon that scholars place the
beginnings of the Renaissance, in 1509, at least for architecture, for it
was here that artists and craftsmen who had come from Italy first left
their mark in the sculptured stonework of the gatehouse. The Renaissance
proceeds from this date, 1509, right up till the murder of Henri III, last
of the Valois, in 1589. That would make it last for eighty years, covering
almost the whole of the sixteenth century. Such an idea has a textbook
simplicity about it, but one which need not be discarded just at first.*

*The Renaissance—it means italianisation. France has always been
nostalgic about Italy, and the great classical age, the seventeenth century,
was to return to it with Versailles, which is an italianisation, although
buildings with flat roofs do not really come to terms with the rainfall of
the Ile de France, a circumstance which caused an English friend of
mine, to whom I was once showing the palace of Louis XIV, to say coldly
'it does not fit into the landscape'.*

*

*One will learn a lot from reading Mr. Dunlop's book. I hope that it will
stimulate visitors to come in ever greater numbers to the Ligerian Valley.
How much has been written, and deservedly, on the Valley of the Loire
and its gentle, hospitable charm!*

*Here, not far from Paris, stand these buildings, created by the require-
ments of pride or of love, necessitated by the taste for display, sometimes
even imposed by the obsessive power of a dream—like Chambord or
Chenonceau; monuments raised by Man, not to his gods, but to Man,
for the exercise of his leisure and as the crowning symbol of his success.
Grafted on to the stock of some dismantled fortress, or built on some selected
site to enjoy its beauties while at the same time giving to them a new
significance; seeking the waterside in order to admire themselves, Narcissus-
like, in Nature's mirror; rich in memories of tragedy—the conspiracy of
Amboise or the murder of the duc de Guise at Blois—but more often of*

gallantry, for there is something essentially feminine about the elegance and refinement of the Loire region, and it is not by chance that the Valois —themselves inclined to be effeminate—should have been so attracted to its banks.

Witnesses of inauspicious events, but more often of periods of felicity, moving memorials of our art and of our history, always viewed and reviewed with the same feelings of astonishment of their first impact, such are the châteaux of the Loire Valley, and as such they are brought to life by the sympathetic scholarship of this book. I hope that it will get a good reception and wish it every success.

Brissac

TO
DEIRDRE
WITH ALL MY LOVE

INTRODUCTION

BENEATH the ruins of the medieval castle which disposes its enormous length of crumbled masonry along the high ridge that overtops the river Vienne at Chinon there is a statue of Rabelais—born here towards the end of the fifteenth century. It would perhaps have been more appropriate to have placed him in front of a ruined monastery, but a medieval ruin is symbolic enough.

For Rabelais typifies the age of the renaissance. Having broken loose from the cloister and all that it stood for, he had by no means abandoned Christianity. But his was no longer a religion that based itself upon the text 'deny thyself' but rather on the saying 'I am come that they might have life and have it abundantly'. It was the God-given abundance of life that intoxicated Rabelais. There was no corner of the whole vast field which was tabu; the physical, sensual, intellectual, aesthetic and spiritual experiences of the human animal were there for the plucking. In his first books, published in 1532, he exults over the ripening fruit of the French renaissance.

'Now every form of study is restored,' writes Gargantua to Pantagruel; 'the whole world is full of learned men, of very erudite tutors and most extensive libraries.' Thanks to the art of printing the age of the renaissance will surpass even that of Plato; 'no one will in future risk appearing in public who is not well polished in the workshop of Minerva'.

Rabelais packs a lot of his preaching between the capacious walls of a Utopian institution, the Abbey of Thelema. It is significant that this *château idéal* should have been sited on the banks of the Loire. One could hardly imagine it being anywhere else.

The Abbey and its grounds were designed for the satisfaction of cultivated and catholic appetites. On the one hand lay the gardens and the park; the exercises of hunting, hawking, tennis, *ballon*, tilting at the ring and shooting with bow and arquebus kept the men in a state of exuberant virility. On the other hand were the libraries and galleries; 'so nobly were they instructed that there was not a man or woman amongst them who could not read and write, sing, play musical instruments, speak five or six languages and compose in them both verse and prose'.

The Abbey was a club and the condition of membership was a lust for living. All lived for pleasure, but their pleasures were those of men who thirsted after knowledge as keenly as they thirsted after wine.

The architecture of Thelema need not detain us: Bonnivet, Chantilly, Chambord were all in the author's mind, but the Abbey was to be 'a hundred times more magnificent'. Of its domestic comforts he says but little. It is perhaps disappointing that Rabelais, of all people, should have omitted to pass on to posterity any information about contemporary sanitation, for it was a way of life that he was preaching and not a style of architecture. That is why he typifies the renaissance.

It is easy for the art historian to create the impression that the great movement called the renaissance was essentially a matter of cornices and pilasters, of the correct use of the orders and of the proper proportions of a façade. Volumes have been devoted to recording the spread of this fashion from Italy and to tracing the influence, real or conjectural, of one artist upon another.

Style is, of course, a proper subject in its own right, with its own interest and its own methods of scholarship: it does not exhaust the study of architecture. A man who knows everything about the Gothic style and nothing of the Christian religion will be in no position to understand a cathedral. He has only studied one facet of it, and that, from the point of view of the original builders, not the most important. Style is the manner in which something is done. A consideration of style leaves unanswered the more fundamental questions *what* is being done and *why*. Practically no buildings are put up as an essay in style.

Any study of the Châteaux of the Loire, or indeed of any other region, must start by asking the question: what is a château?

For the Englishman there is no ambiguity about the word

'castle'. It conjures up an impressive compendium of towers, turrets, battlements, machicolations, moats and barbicans: it is synonymous with 'fortress' and appears something of a misnomer when we stand confronted by the domes and porticoes of *Castle* Howard or Mereworth *Castle*. One would not, in fact, expect a single term to embrace both Harlech and Hatfield, Bodiam and Boughton, Kenilworth and Petworth.

And yet in French the word *château* spans precisely this gap; it applies to the baroque palace as well as to the feudal fortress. In some cases, it is true, the distinction architecturally is not so clean cut as in England. While there is no hint of fortification at Chatsworth, for instance, there is a deep moat and a pair of vestigial towers at the contemporary Dampierre. It was the distinction of the French renaissance to have made the tower into one of its most successful ornaments. Later styles found it more difficult to assimilate; the remarkable fact is that they should have attempted to do so. 'What is extraordinary,' wrote André Félibien of Chambord, 'is that in those days men were still accustomed to provide their châteaux with the complement of towers and turrets that, although these caused great irregularities in the distribution of the rooms, and great inconvenience in certain places, none the less they suffered all these faults; they were less concerned with external elegance and internal communications than to preserve this ancient use of towers and *donjons*, which used to be the strength and beauty of the castle.' Even in Félibien's time the tower was by no means obsolete.

The fact is that the tower had become a sort of hall-mark to the aristocracy. As late as 1770 we find the bailli de Mirabeau writing to the marquis: 'I have always felt, on seeing a château with towers at its corners, a sort of respect for the owner, unknown though he be; a fine house deprived of these ornaments has never seemed to me to be more than the dwelling place of a wealthy bourgeois.'

For the tower was not just an instrument of fortification; it was a safe, a repository for title deeds. The feudal rights were said to appertain to the *Tour* du Louvre, the *Tour* d'Issoudun, and as the dignity of the owner depended on the rights secured

by these deeds, so the stronghouse in which they were kept
became the status symbol of nobility.

It was precisely this aspect which attracted the wrath of the
Revolutionaries. Where their intention was incendiary—'*de
porter la flamme dans les châteaux*'—their objective was the
chartrier, the muniment room—'*pour y brûler les titres*'.

One unfortunate result of the bonfires of the Revolution was
that much was destroyed which might have greatly increased
our knowledge of the châteaux. Building accounts from which
the dates of construction, the names of the craftsmen and even
of the architects, could have been established; inventories in
which the particulars of tapestries and furnishings would have
been recorded; contracts for repairs from which details of
vanished buildings could have been reconstructed, and a mass
of other miscellaneous material all fed the flames, with the
result that the historian of the Châteaux of the Loire is often
faced with an acute shortage of documentation.

There is, however, both in the fabric of those which survive,
and in the writings of those who knew them in their prime,
enough information to see a significant difference between the
French château and the English country house.

This difference in architecture reveals a distinction between
the aristocracies of the two countries. In England it moved with
the times: in France it remained tied to the past. 'The true
strength of the English aristocracy,' wrote the comte de Montalembert in 1856, 'abides in the many thousands of families of
landed proprietors, who, in virtue of their property, are the
magistrates and administrators of the country. They do not dis-
dain, as the old French nobility did, to accept administrative,
legislative and judicial functions.' Richard Rush, American
Ambassador during the Regency, makes the same point: 'they
have *houses* in London,' he writes, 'but their *homes* are in the
country . . . the permanent interests and affections of the most
opulent classes centre almost universally in the country.'

As the result of this marriage between the great families and
the countryside, the stately homes of England were an integral
and a vital part of English life. These bland palladian palaces
and their vast grounds, thrown open to the countryside by a

Bridgeman, a Kent or a Capability Brown, are part and parcel of the land. They dominate, but they belong. The sweeping lines of their quadrant colonnades, the serene proportions of their main façades and the austere economy of their ornament may have been borrowed from Vicenza, but scarcely one of them could be mistaken for an Italian house. They remain as firmly but undefinably English as the clustered irregularities of their Tudor forerunners.

Hand in hand with the embellishment of the domain went the improvement of agriculture. The Earl of Scarsdale at Kedleston 'not only ornamented the country in a very noble manner, by raising a very magnificent mansion,' wrote Arthur Young; 'but in the disposition of his park and environs, he has at the same time worked a vast improvement in the soil.' This was a thing most dear to Young's heart. 'It is one great national advantage of the nobility and gentry improving the environs of their houses—they are excellent farmers, whether they design it or not.'

The English house enriched the countryside. The château, as often as not, bled it dry. Perhaps the most convincing evidence of the normally oppressive rôle of the château comes from the annals of Brissac during the Revolution. It is convincing because it is hostile to the Republic as well as to the Ancien Régime. It is a letter addressed by the citizens to the Département of Maine-et-Loire. 'Republicans,' it begins; 'under the Ancien Régime the Château de Brissac was the bane of the inhabitants of this land; under the New it seems that this monument of tyranny and pride will finally crush the most unfortunate citizens of this town. It has always been our stumbling block.' Under the Old Régime they had to have 'slaves and parasites to maintain their odious rights and usurpations'; under the New the situation had not noticeably improved. The soldiers of the Republic had no more respect for the rights and welfare of the people than had their feudal predecessors. '*Oh! Fatalité inconcevable! Il faut donc des esclaves, des satellites et des sbires pour conserver une propriété jadis féodale.*'

As with the Monarchy, it was the system rather than the individual which was at fault. Louis-Hercule, eighth duc de

Brissac, who lost his life in the Revolution, was a kindly and considerate man. His great work of draining the mosquito-infested marshes on the banks of the Aubance was carried out with a scrupulous regard to the rights of the inhabitants, and he had a soft spot for foundlings—so soft that one suspects that the Château de Brissac became a favourite dumping ground for unwanted children. They were brought up at the Duke's expense. In his accounts there figure such items as 'for the little girl of the park: six chemises'.

A château was more often a stumbling block to its locality because of the absence of the owner than because of his character. These absences were often so prolonged as to constitute normality and led, among other evils, to neglect of the fabric. In the seventeenth century France was liberally supplied with châteaux, some of them in the last stages of disrepair. Mlle de Montpensier, visiting for the first time her Château of St. Fargeau, was obliged to accomplish the last lap of the journey on foot, the bridge being unsafe for vehicles. '*J'entrai dans une vieille maison,*' she wrote, '*où il n'y avait ni portes ni fenêtres et de l'herbe jusqu'aux genoux dans la cour.*'

Such cannot have been the destiny intended by the builder. The great houses of the renaissance were designed as residences, and had it not been for the wars of religion they would doubtless have been lived in.

When the troubles were over, Henri IV and Sully did all that they could to encourage the landlord to live on his land. 'It has been from time immemorial the honour of the Gentlemen of France to live in the country,' said the King, 'and only to go to the towns to do their service to the King or to see to affairs of importance.' The great work of Olivier de Serres, *Le Théâtre d'Agriculture et Ménage des Champs*, was both the product and the instrument of this policy. And of course if they were to live in the country they must expect to be suitably housed. 'His Majesty,' wrote Guillaume Girard in his *Histoire d'Epernon*, 'urged the greater part of the most wealthy members of the nobility to plan the erection of fine houses.'

But the dagger of Ravaillac and the uncertain minority of Louis XIII put an end to the work of Henri IV and Sully. When

a firm government at last was established it was in the hands of
a man who was no lover of feudal rights or feudal castles.

Armand du Plessis, Cardinal and duc de Richelieu, was both
a builder and a destroyer of buildings. The château from which
he took his name he made into one of the architectural wonders
of his age, but to secure its supremacy in the district he decreed
the destruction of another château whose loss is incalculable to
the architectural historian—Champigny-sur-Veude, renaissance
palace of the great family of Bourbon-Montpensier.

The history of Champigny is largely unknown. It may have
been as important as Gaillon in its influence on the châteaux of
the Loire, but its dates are uncertain and its appearance is
largely conjectural. At least it is reasonable to suppose that the
Sainte Chapelle, which, together with the Stable court, alone
survives, had at least been started in June of 1507. For in that
month Louis de Bourbon, Prince de la Roche-sur-Yon, drew up
the statutes.

They are somewhat curious. The establishment was to con-
sist of a Dean and ten other Clergy, and none was to be admitted
to the Chapter who had not first undergone examination. It was
required that he should be 'honest, but not lame nor hunch-
backed, nor one-eyed, nor deficient in any limb, and not a bastard'. If he fulfilled these moral and physical requirements he
had to undertake not to wear clothes 'of divers colours', nor
was his gown to have anything so modish as a slit up the back
(*fendue par derrière*). He must not wear red shoes, nor yellow,
nor even 'Persian', and he must not allow his hair to grow too
long. On the day that the Dean was saying the Offices he was to
shave both chin and tonsure.

Unfortunately the lords of Richelieu owed allegiance to the
lords of Champigny. It was unthinkable that the Cardinal
should owe allegiance to anyone, especially to Gaston
d'Orléans. Gaston d'Orléans, by virtue of his marriage with
Marie de Bourbon-Montpensier, was lord of Champigny. He
was forced to exchange the estate against that of Bois-le-
Vicomte, and the Château was demolished. Richelieu would have
demolished the Sainte Chapelle also, and applied to the Pope
for permission to do so, claiming that it was ruinous. The Pope,

who had once celebrated the Mass there, sent his legate to inspect the building, who found it *'magnifique et en fort bon état'*. Permission was refused.

Cardinal Richelieu has been called a great destructor of châteaux, but it was not so much the country house as the right to private fortification at which he aimed his blow. He did not discourage the residence of the landlord on his estates.

Undoubtedly the greatest factor in the decline of the château was the creation of Versailles. Louis XIV obliged the majority of great landowners to reside at Court. Their country estates were reduced to mere sources of revenue from which every *sou* had to be wrung to support their extravagant living and their suicidal gambling. 'The consequences of this,' wrote Saint-Simon in a prophetic passage, 'are without end and will lead to nothing less than total ruin and collapse.' In the meantime the Courtier became, like the Palace he frequented, a thing of marble—hard but highly polished. 'The Court does not make one happy,' observed La Bruyère; 'it merely prevents one from being happy elsewhere.'

The abandoning of interest in the land for the glamour of life at Versailles is spotlit by Saint-Simon in his own inimitable manner. In 1699 the comtesse de Fiesque died at a ripe old age; 'she possessed virtually nothing,' he wrote, 'because she had either squandered it or allowed her agents to fleece her. In the early days of these magnificent mirrors—then extremely rare and extremely dear—she purchased a perfectly beautiful mirror.

' "Ah, comtesse," her friends would say; "where did you get that mirror?"

' "I had a nasty bit of land which yielded nothing but corn; I sold it and bought this mirror. Don't you think I have done well? Corn—or this mirror?" '

There were of course honourable exceptions to this rule, men and women of noble rank and great possessions who lived among their tenants on the land and wisely furthered the interests of local enterprise. Perhaps the most outstanding of these was Jeanne Duplessis, duchesse de Liancourt.

'Made to be one of the principal ornaments of the Court of Louis XIV,' writes the Abbé Boileau, 'she preferred to live in retirement, occupied with the cares of her household and the education of her children.' Her husband, First Gentleman to the King, was obliged by his office to remain at Versailles, to the ever increasing peril of his soul and to the intense discomfiture of his wife. For Jeanne was a sincerely religious woman.

It is refreshingly unexpected to find a French duchess in the days of Louis XIV preaching social equality. In her book of household rules, drawn up for the instruction of her daughter, she says of the treatment of servants: 'men are all of the same nature and the same quality before God . . . you ought to regard them as equals in your heart.'

Little by little she managed to withdraw her husband from the Court and to invite him first to taste the pleasures of country life, and from these more innocent amusements, to the duties of devotion. The building of Liancourt and the lay-out of its famous gardens were part of her all-embracing scheme to compass the salvation of the Duke.

It was at Liancourt, a century later, that Arthur Young was to find the first and most striking evidence of a return to country life by the French aristocracy. 'The mode of living and the pursuits,' he noted, 'approach much nearer the habits of a great nobleman's house in England than would commonly be conceived.'

Life at Liancourt was the same compound of outdoor exercise, learned conversation and delicious dinners that might have been found at a Chatsworth or a Stowe. Apart from the sport of deer-shooting, which Young found to be 'like angling, incessant expectation and perpetual disappointment', the regimen was robustly satisfying. Riding, gardening and shooting alternated with music, chess and conversation, or with retreat to the library—spacious, elegant and equipped with its eight thousand volumes 'well calculated to make the time pass agreeably'. All these converged and culminated in 'the festivity of the dinner at the close of the day'. Sometimes these meals were quite informal 'with no other dressing but the refreshment of clean linen; and these were not the repasts', he added, 'at which the dutchess's champaigne had the worst flavour!'

On one occasion he accompanied the Duke to a Provincial Assembly where he could meet with some local farmers. 'I watched their carriage narrowly to see their behaviour in the presence of a great Lord of the first rank,' he wrote, 'and it was with pleasure that I found them behaving with becoming ease and freedom ... without any obsequiousness offensive to English ideas.'

His whole stay at Liancourt—he came for three days and stayed for three weeks—is one of the finest examples of the *vie de château* for which France has always been so abundantly equipped, and for which the fashion now once more flourished. But it came too late. It was this same duc de Liancourt to whom it fell to inform Louis XVI of the taking of the Bastille.

'But this is a revolt,' said Louis.

'No, Sire,' corrected Liancourt; 'it is a revolution.'

The Revolution did little in the way of direct destruction, but it put an end to the movement back to the land which might have restored the château to its proper place in the life of the country. In the early days of the nineteenth century, the *vie de château* was at a low ebb.

To this general rule the Valley of the Loire saw one short but brilliant exception: for the summer of 1810 the Château de Chaumont was occupied by Madame de Staël. She hastened to fill the place with her friends; 'you will find Mme Récamier here,' she wrote to Gaudet, 'who could well give this dwelling the air of an enchanted castle.'

It is a typical lack of appreciation: Chaumont is enchanting without Mme Récamier. 'He who has not seen the sun set at Chaumont,' wrote the Prince de Broglie, 'has not experienced one of nature's most lovely spectacles.'

Nature, however, was of no great interest to Mme de Staël. 'I wouldn't open my window to see the bay of Naples for the first time,' she confessed; 'whereas I would go five hundred leagues to talk to one intelligent man whom I have never met.' Like so many of the French, she suffered, when not in Paris, from a *'mal de la capitale'*. The superb setting of Chaumont left her unmoved. When Benjamin Constant asked her if she did not admire the magnificent scene, she admitted: 'I was thinking of Paris, and in truth I confess I prefer the black trickle that I see there to the clear and limpid waters of the Loire here.'

Mme de Staël is representative of the general attitude of her countrymen. In 1833, when Elizabeth Strutt made her leisurely tour of the Loire Valley, she found that the duc de Duras came but once a year to Ussé—and then only to collect his rent. 'Nothing can be a greater proof of the total distaste of the French for country life,' she wrote, 'than to see a residence like this, so exquisitely situated, possessing everything to make the country delightful—wood, streams, noble terraces, winding walks and cultivated gardens, so totally neglected.'

There is no escaping the conclusion: the great country houses of France represent an ideal that was never fully realized. Their proud and beautiful façades had to be insulated from the countryside by acres of formal garden; some of them have retained the stiff discomfort of clothes that have been seldom worn. There are, of course, significant exceptions. Brissac, Cheverny, Montgeoffroy and Le Lude are homes that have been loved and lived in, but whether they have survived as habitations or whether they have ended their days as elegant museums, they are never without interest. They are as fascinating to study as they are delightful to look upon.

Any study of the French château must lead us sooner or later to the valley of the Loire, for it was here, during the critical period which saw the transition from fortress to palace, from Gothic to renaissance style, that the Court of France was chiefly in residence. It was a happy coincidence which united the most beautiful of buildings with the loveliest of landscapes.

CHAPTER I

The Happy Valley

'TOURAINE, THAT Pleasure Garden of Delight, enjoys so sweet an air that it invites its inhabitants to divert themselves by all manner of pastimes, with the result that the Tourangeaux are a happy, gay, good-natured people.'

Thus wrote Martin Marteau, himself a Tourangeau, who published in 1661 a book of eulogy about his native land. In his view the man who chanced to inhabit this region was indeed a favourite of Fortune. A pure air gave him health and length of days; a temperate climate and a fertile soil furnished him with abundance of food and wine, and with a wealthy industry in silk; a confluence of rivers added to these both trade and irrigation, and the four combined to make the Tourangeau a man of honest work and pleasant conversation. To this *bon naturel* the frequent resort of Royalty had lent the refinement of courtly manners.

One of the favourite occupations of this plain and unsophisticated age was to go for walks. 'On summer evenings after supper,' wrote Elie Brackenhoffer in 1643, 'men and women, old and young, go walking arm in arm together, in long chains, conversing with each other, amusing themselves and taking the air.' For this purpose they made at Tours a Pall Mall of incomparable beauty, and so cherished by the City Magistrates that in wet weather no one was permitted to walk in it, under penalty of a heavy fine.

But for the more adventuresome, the City gates gave access to gardens and woods and orchards and to the great open spaces, the most notable of which was called the Prairie de Gloriette. Beside these the Château of Le Plessis-lès-Tours, the Abbey Marmoutiers, the Priory of St. Côme-en-l'Isle and the ruins of Rochecorbon invited the inhabitants of Tours to make frequent excursions along the valley of the Loire.

The touch of time has been gentle with this region, and the valley which so much delighted Martin Marteau, La Fontaine, Mme de Sévigné and countless others, was recognizably the same as that described two centuries later by Alfred de Vigny. He was in fact writing of the seventeenth century.

'Do you know that country which has been called the Garden of France?' he asked, and in case his reader was not familiar with the scenery, he gave a thumbnail sketch; 'little valleys peopled with pretty white houses encompassed by woods; hill-sides golden with vines or white with cherry blossom; old walls covered with budding honeysuckle; gardens of roses from which slender towers rise unexpectedly; everything speaks of the fertility of the soil or of the antiquity of its monuments.' Vigny was one of a long line of eulogists who have given the valley of the Loire pride of place in the landscape of France. They form the Great Tradition.

Against them is the voice of Victor Hugo. 'The Loire and Touraine have been far too highly praised,' he wrote; 'it is time justice is done. The Seine is far more beautiful than the Loire; Normandy is a much more charming garden than Touraine. A broad and yellow river, flat banks, poplars everywhere—and there you have the Loire.' Hugo bases his dislike of the Loire on his distaste for poplars—'one of the classical forms of bore-dom'. One may agree or disagree with his taste; it in no way discounts the Great Tradition, for in the eighteenth century, and before, the poplar was not so much in evidence. The set of views near Amboise painted in the 1760's by Jean-Pierre Houel for the decoration of Chanteloup show a valley not unlike that of the Seine.

But the Seine could never have been what the Loire was to France, the cradle of its monarchy—with all that that meant in terms of patronage of art. Normandy lies uncomfortably close to England, and England was the enemy of France.

In any case, poplars, or no poplars, the voice of Victor Hugo is shouted down by the verdict of history. 'This is the most delightful and most pleasant province in the Kingdom,' wrote Pierre Duval in 1680. 'I have never seen anything to equal the beauty of this route,' enthused Mme de Sévigné, travelling by barge to Blois; 'I heard a thousand nightingales.' 'I have one complaint,' noted La Fontaine, 'which is that having seen this, I cannot imagine that there is anything left worth seeing.' 'I walked through vineyards as far as Roche Corbé,' wrote John Evelyn from Tours, 'from whence the country and river yield a most incomparable prospect.'

'It might be called the Arcadia of France,' said Cardinal Bentivoglio in 1619, 'but if it has not the name of Arcadia at least it deserves that of Garden of France, and (in truth) not without reason, especially when one considers the beautiful Loire which waters it—that happy valley, that fertile land, those lovely views.'

At least it is certain that there has been no time in history when the valley of the Loire has not inspired the admiration of its visitors and the devotion of its inhabitants; both have been moved to lyricism and nostalgia in their writings. Guillaume le Breton may speak for the Middle Ages: 'No situation is more beautiful; no countryside more fertile; clear springs, orchards furnished with delicious fruits . . . and all round, the sunny slopes laden with vineyards and woodlands.'

But perhaps the most moving of all the eulogies is the most ancient, the lament of Alcuin, called to abandon Touraine for preferment at Rome. It is addressed to the valley itself. 'A river wandering at will, bordered with meadows and flowers, encircles you with her stream into which the fisherman never casts his net in vain; orchards and gardens, lilies and roses fill the cloisters with their sweetest perfumes, and at morning dawn the melodious song is heard of innumerable birds vying with one another to sing the praise of God their maker.' One can almost feel the tears rising to his eyes as he turns his back on the familiar landscape; *'douce demeure que j'aimerai toujours, adieu!'*

Naturally they were mostly Frenchmen, men who knew and loved the land, who praised it, but it seems to have been an Italian, a Florentine named Florio, who, in 1477, first gave to Touraine its name 'The Garden of France'. In a letter to Jacopo Tarlatti he confesses himself so delighted with the place that he has resolved to end his days there, and to exchange the banks of the Arno for those of the Loire. The comparison was prophetic.

It was not long before the Loire was to become for France what the Arno had been for Italy—the nursery of the renaissance.

But when the eulogists call Touraine a garden, we must remember what that word meant to them—a landscape to which the hand of man had given a new shape and a new embellishment. It was not the 'unspoilt' oases where Nature reigned supreme, but the more 'built up areas'—those 'decorated with large and opulent cities and superb châteaux, and with an infinity of fine houses'—which made the countryside a garden. The admiration of the sixteenth century for landscape increased in direct proportion to the number of buildings on it. The highest praise that de Vieilleville could find for the Loire valley (and he meant to praise it highly) was to say that from Paris to Nantes was 'just one suburb'.

For the large and opulent cities, no less than the châteaux and the *gentilhommières*, were the ornaments of the countryside.

'Blois, like Orléans, is on the side of a hill,' wrote La Fontaine; 'the roofs of the houses are disposed in such a way as to resemble the steps of an amphitheatre. That struck me as most beautiful, and I think it would be difficult to find a happier and more pleasing aspect.' This irregular amphitheatre was enclosed by a wall, buttressed and embattled; above the walls and towers rose the tiers of rooftops, and above the rooftops projected the salient features of the city. To the west, St. Nicolas and St. Sauveur stood sentinels to the Château, and to the east the Cathedral of St. Louis dominated that quarter of the town.

But Blois held architectural surprises that did not thus impose upon the skyline. Frequently, amid the maze of steep and narrow streets whose timbered fronts almost shut out the light, one came upon some great renaissance porch, of freestone finely carved, whose round arched doors gave access to a spacious court. Here were tall, pilastered windows, shady Italian loggias and walls adorned with terra cotta busts; here, in the imitation of his architecture, the courtiers paid their sincerest flattery to the King. Supreme among these houses was Florimond Robertet's Hôtel d'Alluye, the town house to his magnificent Château de Bury.

But the demands of a luxuriant age were not to be contained within the curtain wall of a medieval city. Already in the sixteenth century the gardens of the Château had overflowed to the west, while to the east the Promenade du Mail was planted outside the line of fortifications along the Quay St. Jean. It was the Mail which most attracted Evelyn, who found it 'very long and so noble shaded with tall trees (being in the midst of a great wood) that, unless that of Tours, I had not seen a statelier'.

From Blois Evelyn made an excursion into the forest 'to see if we could meet with any wolves'. The search was appropriate, for the name Blois derives from the celtic *Bleiz*, a wolf. Even at this period they were so numerous, Evelyn was assured, that they took the very children from the streets. In spite of this the Duke, Gaston d'Orléans, would not permit the beasts to be destroyed.

Evelyn came at the height of spring, when the fruit trees were in full blossom and the nightingales in full song. On April 28 he came down the river from Orléans, dining at Beaugency and sleeping at St. Dyé. Here he hired horses to take him to Blois by way of Chambord.

Rumours of this great Château 'set in the middle of a solitary park', on which eighteen hundred workmen had wrought for twelve years, led him to expect something even more remarkable. He found it 'no greater than divers gentlemen's houses in England, both for room and circuit'. Evelyn was of course familiar with such palatial labyrinths as New Hall and Audley End; to a contemporary Frenchman, le Sieur Coulon, Chambord seemed 'by reason of its size capable of lodging all the Princes in Europe'. Evelyn praised the carvings as 'very full and rich', found the spiral staircase 'an extraordinary work, but of far greater expense than use or beauty'; noted the large, deep moat and the chimneys standing 'like so many towers' against the sky, and finally rode off to Blois through a countryside 'full of corn and wine, with many fair gentlemen's houses'.

On May 2 he continued his journey downstream. 'We took boat again, passing by Chaumont, a proud castle on the left hand; before it is a sweet island deliciously shaded with tall trees.' They halted at Amboise, where they proceeded at once to the Château, passing over a drawbridge 'which has an invention to let one fall unless premonished'. Evelyn saw Amboise in its pristine glory, a building ten times larger than it is today. He admired the two great towers with their spiral ramps, but what interested him most was a stag's head 'consisting of twenty brow antlers, the beam bigger than a man's middle, of incredible length'.

There is evidence that in these ancient forests there were stags that had grown to a prodigious size. Andrea Navigero reported one at Blois in 1528 with monstrous antlers, which no one was permitted to hunt, for the beast was revered *'comme pour une merveille véritable'*. Elie Brackenhoffer, in 1643, had convinced himself that the Amboise antlers were genuine, claiming that princes from all over Europe had sent their most experienced huntsmen to inspect them, and all had owned their authenticity. It seems, however, that these were the antlers carved in wood by Jean de Launay in 1496 for a figure of a stag ornamenting the Logis des Sept Vertus.

From Amboise, Evelyn visited Montlouis, 'a village having no houses above ground, but such only as were hewn out of the main rocks of excellent freestone'. This was his introduction to the troglodite dwellings of Touraine. 'Here and there the funnel of a chimney appears on the surface amongst the vineyards, and in this manner they inhabit the caves . . . on one side of the river for many miles.' Their existence was a tribute to the climate of the valley; as Arthur Young remarked a century and a half later 'in England the rheumatism would be the chief inhabitant'.

At last they came to Tours—*'Cité blanche et bleue'*. The medieval town had been greatly enriched during the renaissance by the wealth of its noble families, and the names of Briçonnet and Berthelot, Bohier and de Beaune were enshrined in its architecture and in its fountains. Evelyn and his party were immediately captivated; 'No city in France,' they declared, 'exceeds it in beauty or delight.' They found it 'spacious, well built and exceeding clean'. This was on account of the fountains, which were so numerous that to Thibault Lepleigny, a century earlier, the whole town appeared to be crossed and recrossed by little rivulets, *'qui est une chose fort délectable et de grand plaisir'*.

But to Evelyn the greatest attraction was the Mall—'without comparison the noblest in Europe for length and shade, having seven rows of the tallest and goodliest elms I had ever beheld, the innermost of which embrace each other, and at such height that nothing can be more solemn and majestical'. The Mall at Tours, like the Cathedral of Bourges, consisted of a central nave with two supporting aisles on either side.

From Tours they made the obvious excursions; the Abbey of Marmoutiers, the caves of Colombiers, the ruins of Roche-corbon and the Château of Le Plessis-lès-Tours. 'It has many pretty gardens full of nightingales,' noted Evelyn, 'and in the Chapel lies buried the famous poet Ronsard.'

Ronsard. The very name is redolent of the combined charms of rural life and learned taste which typified the French renaissance.

> *J'aime fort les jardins qui sentent le sauvage,*
> *J'aime le flot de l'eau qui gazouille au rivage,*
> *Là, devisant sur l'herbe avec un mien ami*
> *Je me suis par les fleurs souvent endormi.*

His poetry is strongly autobiographical and reveals an epicurean existence, at once vigorous and refined. We can see him in all the varied activities of a country gentleman—now reading his Ovid beneath some willow's shade; now gathering herbs with meticulous precision for a salad or picnicking on cheese and milk and *fraises des bois*; he was a great huntsman and a lover of violent exercise; he was fond of society, music and dancing were his delight, and these brought him into contact with the ladies to whom he wrote amorous verses. In this he was in no way inhibited by the fact that he was a Churchman, and when in residence at his Priory of St. Côme-en-l'Isle he would attend the full round of Prime, Tierce, Sext and None with unflagging zeal. Although it is expressed with a delicacy unknown to Rabelais, there was a full-blooded comprehensiveness about this regimen which is not far from that of Pantagruel.

La Possonnière, the Ronsard family home in the valley of the Loir, was one of the first of the smaller houses, or *gentilhommières*, to show the impact of the renaissance. Built originally

in the style of Le Plessis-lès-Tours, it received in about 1514
a decoration of pilasters which may have been derived direct
from Gaillon.

It is interesting to compare La Possonnière with Talcy, the
home of Barnard Salviati, father of Ronsard's Cassandre. For
whereas La Possonnière was decorated by a Frenchman in a
modern Italian style, Talcy was built by an Italian in a style
resolutely medieval and French.

On September 12, 1520, Salviati applied to his feudal over-
lord for permission to fortify his house 'for the security of his
person and possessions'. Towers, drawbridge, battlements,
barbicans, machicolations and all the paraphernalia of the fortress were included in the application. It was granted on the
significant condition—'provided always that he shall not be
entitled by reason of the said fortifications, in any manner or
means, to style himself the "Seigneur Châtelain" '.

It would appear that Salviati was more concerned to identify
himself with the French nobility than to be up to date with the
architectural fashion of his own country, and he built accordingly. Towers were status symbols; pilasters were not. So
Talcy is a charming anachronism; looking at the turrets and
chemin de ronde of the gatehouse, or at the gables and cloisters
of the court, one has to remind oneself that this building is later
than Chenonceau or Azay-le-Rideau. A sharp eye will detect
that most of the machicolations are dummies.

There were in fact two potent forces which combined to give
the French renaissance its vigour and its charm; a flourishing
native tradition greatly strengthened by its identification with
nobility, and a growing interest in things Italian. But if France
was beginning to admire the architecture of Italy, it must not be
forgotten that Italians were full of praise for what they saw in
France. Chambord, Gaillon and Chantilly were among the
palaces admired by Jerome Lippomano, as well as the more
classical Ecouen and Verneuil.

It is often assumed that at this period the architects of Europe
looked only to Italy for inspiration. If the Maréchal de Vieilleville is to be believed, architects came from all countries to
study the châteaux of the Loire. 'France,' he claimed, 'can pride

itself on being of all Kingdoms under the sun, the best adorned with fine and splendid houses'; as for the Royal Palaces—'there is neither king nor monarch upon earth who is housed in so great a splendour as the King of France'.

His own Château of Durtal on the Loir was honoured by Royalty when Henri II spent four days there in 1550. A Royal visit was a challenge to the hospitality of the châtelain; it was a challenge to which de Vieilleville made most liberal response: 'It was as if the wine rose from a spring,' he boasted, 'so vast a quantity was produced. Four *sommeliers* were kept at work, and at each repast two bottles, one of white and one of *clairet*, were placed before each of the more distinguished guests.'

In principle the wines of the Loire were the same in the sixteenth century as they are today. Thibault Lepleigny, writing in 1541, claimed that 'it is impossible to find better wines than we have in Touraine, for as regards the white wines Vouvray has the renown, and as regards *clairet*, Montrichard'. The red wines of Chinon and Bourgeuil were known as 'Breton' and drunk, then as now, slightly chilled.

Detailed information appears in the Administration Accounts of Chenonceau; they show that the science of viticulture was far from being in its infancy. Nevertheless the period was one of great experiment in trying the vines of one area in the soil of another.

The Abbé Chevalier gives a charming picture of the life of Denis Briçonnet, the brother of Catherine the builder of Chenonceau. He was Abbot of Cormery and had taken the Manor of Montchenin on the advice of his physician *'qui lui blasonnait hautement les délices'*. It was a place, the Cartulary informs us, 'most agreeable, being surrounded on all sides with beautiful fountains, and situated on a steep slope, at the foot of which runs the little stream known as the Echandon, full of goodly fish'. Briçonnet had embellished it further with a small villa, and here he devoted his retirement to the importing of vines from all over France. His devotion of wine, however, did not impair his attention to charity, and he earned himself the title *'le Père des Pauvres'*. His brother-in-law continued his experiments, transplanting vines from Orléans, Anjou, Beaune and Arbois to the vineyards of Chenonceau.

The Vin d'Abois from Chenonceau became the favourite of Diane de Poitiers, and every autumn great barrels of it were sent to Anet to await the arrival of the Court. Not all of it survived for its intended use, for a cellar served for other purposes than the storage of wine. The register of André Bérau tells the tale; 'there were also expended two casks of wine, old and of the best quality, by the Valets de Cuisine, because those who larded her Grace's meat larded it in the cellar'.

Already in the sixteenth century France has acquired her reputation for good and gracious living. Antonio de Beatis, secretary to the Cardinal of Aragon, has left an important picture of the country in the early days of François I.

The food, he found, was good and varied, though he chiefly admired the French ability to make the best of something simple. 'For a roast shoulder of mutton with the little onions which are served with it throughout France, I would willingly forego the most delicate cheer.' But although the standard of gastronomy was high it did not span the gulf between the classes. There were, Beatis noted, more gentlemen living *'en vrais Seigneurs'* than in Italy, but the peasants were 'chivvied and exploited worse than dogs or slaves'. It was the first who earned his final censure—'all the French are avid for their own amusement, and live in gaiety. They abandon themselves to food and drink and gallant pastimes to such an extent that I do not know how they will ever again do anything worth while.'

The artistic, architectural and literary achievements of post-renaissance France are perhaps the best answer to Beatis.

CHAPTER II

The Fortresses

I T WOULD be impossible to imagine such a flowering of Royal and domestic architecture as is implicit in the term 'Châteaux of the Loire' apart from a strong and centralized régime. The first important step in this direction was the achievement of Joan of Arc; the movement started in March of 1429 with her visit to the Dauphin, Charles VII, at Chinon. With Chinon the story of the Châteaux of the Loire begins.

'In that time,' writes the chronicler Jehan Chartier, 'there came news of a certain Maid near Vaucouleurs, on the borders of Barrois, which Maid was twenty years of age, or thereabouts, and many times did say to one named Robert de Beaudricourt, Captain of the said Vaucouleurs, and to many others, that it was necessary that they should take her to the King of France, and that she would do him great service in the wars.' Her words were met with laughter and contempt, and she herself was thought a simpleton, but such was her persistence that the escort she required was provided, and on March 6 her little cavalcade arrived at Chinon.

Years later, in the prisons of Rouen, when Cauchon's net was closing in upon her, and she was subjected to persistent and repeated interrogations, the memory of Chinon was fresh and clear before her mind; from her answers we can reconstruct the details of her visit.

She had taken lodgings, she told her inquisitors, *'chez une bonne femme, près du Château'*. While waiting for her summons to the King she had spent much time in prayer, but as she went about the humdrum business of the day, she cannot have failed to see, towering above the little town, the walls and bastions of one of France's proudest castles.

It is today a most substantial ruin. A water colour by Gaignières, done in 1699, shows little more than we can see ourselves.

11

The high pitched gable ends that mark the Royal Lodgings need only their roofs and dormers to complete the scene. The other punctuations to the 1,200-foot expanse of curtain wall are still the same; the Tour du Moulin, marking like some extinguished lighthouse the westernmost extremity of the headland; the Tour de Boissy, a clean-cut work of masonry set solidly astride the curtain wall; the Tour du Coudray, a massive cylinder of stone which was the *donjon*, set back behind the outer ring of towers. Next came the Royal Lodgings, whose walls display the only windows of the front. To the east of these the Tour du Trésor, square and low and powerfully abutted from the south, provides the last significant projection until the Tour de l'Horloge, or gatehouse tower, presents its slender profile, like the spine of a book, towards the river and the town.

The site of Chinon is a natural redoubt. From the south it is protected by the high cliff on which it perches; from the north and west encircled by a steep re-entrant; but from the east it is approachable and thereby vulnerable along the ridge that overtops the Vienne. It is from the east, therefore, that the system of fortification must be considered.

It formed a suite of three defensive units; the Fort St. Georges, a separate enclosure to the east; the Château du Milieu, in which the Royal Lodgings stood, and the Château du Coudray, the ultimate resort which centred on the keep. Each of these defensive units was separated from the next by a deep, dry moat.

The castle of Chinon represents, as well as any other building, the divided loyalties of the feudal age. It had been since 1044 in the hands of the Counts of Anjou, and since 1154 the Counts of Anjou had been the Kings of England. In 1205 Philippe-Auguste had successfully laid siege to Chinon, and united Touraine to the house of France. But he had made few additions; Chinon, like Château Gaillard, was English-built.

And now the English were advancing once again towards the valley of the Loire; Orléans was besieged, and the Dauphin, as yet uncrowned, lingered somewhat fecklessly at Chinon.

Joan had boldly declared that she would be able to distinguish the King from any other man, and she was taken at her word.

After much enquiry, the King sent the comte de Vendôme, Grand Maître de l'Hôtel du Roi, to accompany the Maid to his presence.

It was already night when they began to mount the steep ascent that led from the town of Chinon to the Fort St. Georges. The great hulks of the castle buildings loomed in massive silhouette, dark against dark, save where the occasional flambeau cast its uncertain patch of light against the grey stone wall.

From the Fort St. Georges they crossed the first moat and entered the Château du Milieu, passing beneath the archway of the tall, slim Tour de l'Horloge. In front the Royal Lodgings were now plainly visible; they surrounded three sides of a narrow court. To the left, and overlooking the town, was the Grande Salle, recently added by Charles VII, and linked by a wooden gallery to the older Royal Apartments. To the right was the Chapelle St. Mélaine.

In front of the Grande Salle stood a well, its mouth protected by a canopy of roof. This well may once have served for water, but it also communicated with the exterior of the curtain wall. Its pulley mechanism was used for hoisting up the blocks of stone which were quarried on the south slopes of the promontory.

The Grande Salle itself was a large hall, eighty-one feet long by twenty-seven broad. It will not bear comparison with the Great Hall at Kenilworth, a building measuring ninety feet by forty-five, but none the less it was impressive. Its only known feature was the great fireplace which still adheres to the western wall—large, simple and clean-cut, its tall hood rising, like the steep roof of a French pavilion, to a height where the gable end began to taper between the great rafters of the open timbered roof.

Fifty flaming torches—Joan could remember the number—were lit at sundown, filling the hall with light and all the crannies of the roof with smoke, and there was a great press of people.

Somehow Joan found her way to the Dauphin, for he had mingled with the crowd. A man of mean attire and undistinguished looks, he had placed himself, according to Jehan Chartier, in a group of nobles 'pompously and richly dressed'.

It did not deceive Joan, who knelt before him 'a lance's length away', and discharged her embassy.

'*Gentil Dauphin,*' she began; '*j'ai nom Jeanne la Pucelle, et vous mande le Roi des Cieux par moi que vous serez sacré et couronné à Reims et serez le lieutenant du Roi des Cieux, qui est le Roi de France.*' Brave words in which we can see a foreshadowing of the doctrine of Divine Right, developed by the Valois and taken to its logical conclusion by Louis XIV. 'God,' he told his son, 'is a superior Power, of which our Royal power is part.'

The two conversed in private for some time, while the Court watched and wondered; then the Dauphin summoned the Sire de Gaucourt and confided to him the news; 'she had told me,' he said, 'that she has been sent by God to help me recover my Kingdom.' Gaucourt now led her to an apartment in the Château. Turning left from the Royal Lodgings they came to the second moat, a vast and artificial chasm as broad as it was deep. Here was a stone bridge which crossed its cavity in three unequal vaults. The bridge gave access to the inmost sanctuary of Chinon, the Tour du Coudray, where Joan was placed in the charge of Mistress Anne de Maillé. Here, in the Chapel of St. Martin, she passed the greater part of the next three days; here her page, Louis de Coutes, noted that she spent most of her time in prayer, and that as she prayed she wept.

The sequel is well known. Joan was burnt; Charles regained his Kingdom and returned to the valley of the Loire, this time in company with another woman who was not a Maid—Agnès Sorel. They were sometimes at Chinon; he installed her in a house, the maison du Roberdeau, across the dry valley to the north, and he had a subterranean passage to link the château with the house.

It is not, however, at Chinon that the memory of Agnès Sorel is best evoked, but at Loches—another fortress which the Counts of Anjou had built from which to launch their ceaseless brigandage against their feudal neighbours.

There can be little doubt that the Donjon of Loches was the building of Foulque Nerra, who succeeded to the County of Anjou in 987. It can be placed by the cut of its masonry and by the details of its architecture later than the castle of Langeais

(989) and of Montbazon (999) and contemporary with the Abbaye de Beaulieu (1007).

Most of what was good and all of what was bad about the Dark Ages was combined in the turbulent figure of Foulque Nerra. He was a man of conflict and of conflicting passions; his life was an impetuous alternation between cruelty and Christianity, pillage and pilgrimage, sacrilegious destruction and pious foundation. He had his own wife Elizabeth burnt alive at Angers; he had himself flogged on the steps of the Holy Sepulchre at Jerusalem. In forty-three years of unremitting warfare, he built eight castles, eleven religious foundations and fortified at least a dozen towns.

It is the castles which chiefly concern us here. Langeais, Montbazon, Montrichard, Montrésor, La Haye, Mirabeau, Sainte-Maure, and in the middle of the network, Loches, the focal point of his defensive system.

As in England, so in Anjou, the art of castle building had been learnt from the Norman invader. The lofty, square Keep, which derives a rugged elegance from the tall half-cylinders of stone by which it is abutted, is probably more dignified in its present ruins than in its former prime. Its parapet was once encumbered with wooden excrescences called hordes which gave the defenders the necessary overhang later supplied by the stone machicolations and *chemin de ronde*.

The Keep was backed by a smaller building, the Petit Donjon with which it only communicated at first-floor level. The Grand'salle on this floor commanded the whole system of corridors and stairways throughout the Keep. He who was master of this room was master also of the Castle.

In spite of its solid strength and subtle network of approaches, Loches appears to have been fairly easily taken. In 1189 Richard Cœur de Lion, in revolt against his father, Henry II, and in alliance with Philippe-Auguste of France, laid siege to Loches and took the citadel within a week. With Tours and Loches in their hands and Henry in his last stronghold of Chinon, they called a parley, and it was at Colombiers, now known as Villandry, that the humiliating peace was signed which brought the proud Plantagenet down in sorrow to his grave; he died at Chinon on July 6.

Five years later Loches was in the hands of Philippe-Auguste when Richard escaped from his prison at Dürnstein. This time Richard captured Loches in the space of three hours, 'which was incredible to be seen,' wrote the Chronicler of Anjou, 'since Loches is the strongest and most heavily defended place, both by nature and by artifice.'

By the fifteenth century, the Donjon was considered out of date, and the Castle was reinforced by the building of the Tour Ronde. But the valley of the Loire was already ceasing to be the scene of military operations; the Tour Ronde was destined to be more famous as a prison than as a fortress.

As early as the sixteenth century the name of Loches had become associated with the gruesome stories of its oubliettes. François de Pontbriant—a name important in the annals of Blois and Chambord—became the governor of Loches in 1500. According to Gruget, who wrote in 1565, the new governor had the curiosity to explore the warren of subterranean tunnels and passages with which Loches, like other fortresses, was lavishly supplied. Having had two massive iron doors forced, he found himself in a long passage, hewn out of the solid rock, which opened at last into a wide chamber. Here, to his horror, he saw the figure of a man seated on a stone, his head supported on his hands. How long he had sat thus, history does not relate, for on contact with the air, the figure fell into dust.

It has been shown by Edmond Gautier that many of the so-called oubliettes of Loches were made for strictly sanitary reasons, but the inscriptions on the walls of the Tour Ronde and Martelet tell their own story. Some are the result of infinite labour, for the letters are in embossed relief. They tell, both in their words and in their painful workmanship of the heavy passage of a useless time: '*Trop ennuie à qui attend*'. They tell of the bitter memories of bygone happiness:

> *Il n'y a au monde plus grande detstresse*
> *Du bon tempts soy souvenir en la tristesse.*

There is something infinitely moving about the graffiti of the prisoner in solitary confinement. If Loches cannot evoke its pathos, Roland de Pury's *Journal de Cellule* will. 'This man,' he writes, 'reaches despair. He goes down living into the land of the dead, where the passage of time is a passage to nowhere. He tries to prepare himself, to create some diversion, to immerse himself in memories and day dreams. He musters his pathetic little armoury—but now his own weapons inflict a further wound upon him: his thoughts, wandering here and there, come round at last to the dear familiar home . . .

'He has scaled the rock face of a day of suffering; he has clung to it, he has held on; he has lain down at eight o'clock exhausted; but the next day looms identical, inexorable, with all its minutes, all its hours. He has scaled the rock face of these eight hundred and forty minutes; but tomorrow he will awaken at the foot of the same ascent.'

One prisoner who has left a most impressive memorial of his confinement was Ludovico Sforza, Duke of Milan. He had poisoned his nephew in order to obtain the Dukedom, and was therefore treated not only as a prisoner of war, but as an assassin. He was, however, a man of broad vision and accustomed to vigorous action. Confined to a *cachot* in the Martelet of Loches, he found an outlet to his energies in painting.

His resources were limited. Yellow ochre, red-brown and blue-black were his only pigments; the four walls of his cell his only canvas. But with an untrained hand and a determined mind he managed to achieve a striking and original décor. His numerous inscriptions speak more of resignation than despair— a resignation which was not misplaced, for when he died, some eight years after his capture at Novara, he was still a prisoner at Loches.

As far removed as possible from these distressing prisons and occupying the uttermost extremity of the spur of ground on which the fortress stands, the Royal Lodgings evoke the softer memories of Agnès Sorel, who from the title of her Seigneurie could style herself Dame de Beauté.

Her epitaph records her 'pitiful loving kindness to all men, especially to the poor and the religious'; her few surviving letters confirm the claim. One, written from Coucy, begs on behalf of a victim of the wars with England; another intercedes for one caught helping himself to wood in a Royal forest; a third,

from Candé, tells of her cherishing of 'little Robin' who had been
wounded by accident in the course of a boar hunt. There is great
charm and gentleness in all that we know of Agnès Sorel which
is delightfully expressed in her memorial. Two lambs nestle
securely at her feet; two angels bend attentively towards her
head. Between these emblems of innocence and protective care
Agnès Sorel sleeps.

If Loches provides her last resting place it is because she left
endowments to the Castle Church, rather than because this,
more than any other place, was associated with her.

In 1425 Agnès and Charles VII spent some time at Saumur,
a château of far greater architectural importance than the Royal
Lodgings of Loches.

It was at Saumur that the influence of the Louvre of Charles
V made its most impressive appearance in the Valley of the
Loire. It is unfortunate that so little is known of the date and
builders of Saumur, but if there is little in the way of docu-
mentation, there is, in the *Très Riches Heures* of the duc de
Berri, the most admirable portrait.

Here is a building entirely different from Loches, for at
Loches there was a palace within a fortress; at Saumur, fortress
and palace are superimposed. The lower walls are solidly robust,
but in the upper parts strength yields to gracefulness. Crenel-
lation and machicolation, the current formula of parapet defence,
serve here for ornament as well, the former being crowned with
fleurs de lys. Above these battlements the crowd of slender
chimney shafts, the tapering roofs and bulbous weather vanes,
the crocketted dormers, gables and pinnacles, unite to form a
brilliant array of blue and white and gold against the sky. The
single aristocratic figure beneath the castle walls is dressed as
a dandy and not as a soldier; the tiltyard stands empty, but the
vineyard is busy with labourers. The scene, far from evoking the
art of war, gives infinite promise of 'a summer of roses and
wine'.

In these miniatures and in the tapestries of the age we have
a vivid and accurate record of the buildings and scenes of seigneurial life of the fifteenth century. They could be used as
illustrations to a vivid and detailed description of the visit of

Dom Pedro Niño, Ambassador from the King of Castile, to Renaud de Trie, Admiral of France. His castle, Sérifontaine, was in Normandy, but the *vie de château* of the Loire valley would have followed the same pattern.

The Admiral was a man of advancing years and failing health; his Lady—'*la plus belle dame qui fût alors en France*'. Within the one enclosure of the ward they lived their largely independent lives, an independence expressed architecturally by a draw-bridge between their twin establishments.

Their standard of living was clearly high, and often idyllic. For the Admiral there were fifty hounds and twenty horses and all the personnel required for hunting; for the household, the riverside was lined with orchards and gardens, and there was a great lake, walled in and locked and plentifully supplied with fish.

The Lady had as many as ten Maids of Honour; their function in the household was purely ornamental. 'They had no cares, but for their own persons and to keep company with the Lady.' Their day to day routine is carefully listed. First thing in the morning they walked in silence to a little coppice and accomplished there their personal devotions; next they gathered 'flowers and violets' before returning to hear the Mass, after which they broke their fast on 'chicken, larks and other roasted fowls' washed down with wine.

They now called for horses and rode out into the countryside; here was fixed some rendezvous with the Gentlemen, and time was passed in singing lays and roundelays and ballads—'*toutes sortes de chansons que les Français savent composer avec grand art*'. Returning to the Château, they found the Grande Salle set with tables which wanted for no delicacy or variety of dishes. During the dinner 'he who could talk of love or war, with courtesy and moderation, was sure of an audience'. Musicians were in atten-dance, and after the repast the Lady of the house stood up to dance with Pedro Niño, and each Knight likewise with his damoiselle. Then wines were served, and each retired for the siesta.

This emphasis on colourful and gracious living immediately expressed itself in an ornate and opulent approach to building.

Until the fifteenth century the châteaux of the Loire had formed an offensive and defensive system.

The mighty fortresses of Loches and Chinon guarded the southern approaches, while to the north a chain of minor strongholds linked Angers to Saumur, Saumur to Tours, Tours to Blois. Naturally, local traditions and local materials made for similarities of style. Great round bastions, massive curtain walls and tall, white cylinders of stone rose from the moats and precipices that were the outworks of their defence; designed for strength, they were confined to simplicity, and from this simplicity derived a beauty that was probably neither intended by their builders nor appreciated by their owners. Nevertheless men were learning, deep down, to value round shapes and smooth surfaces, and they were to use them with effect when a purely domestic style of building was in demand.

At the close of the fourteenth century the military castles, such as Philippe-Auguste had built, began to take on a more ornamental aspect. At a safer altitude, or within the protected precincts of a court, the art of architecture was freely and deliberately indulged. Towers, already tapering in pepperbox roofs, gave birth to smaller towers that raised their pointed cones among the weather vanes and chimneys, indenting the skyline. Windows, arranged in vertical ascents, rose above the eaves in lofty dormers, spiked and pinnacled, that cut their open patterns like white stone lace against the blue-tiled roof. The Chapel, bulging eastward in a many-sided apse, gave to the courtyard its architectural climax—a focal point of bright, flamboyant Gothic. Here, in contrast to the smooth round drums, were complex shapes and conscious ornament; the rich effect of tracery upon a blind stone wall, the narrow lancets glowing with kaleidoscopic glass; the upward movement of the ribs and buttresses, and crowning all, the slender open fretwork of the flèche that stood dramatically against the sky.

The French, in fact, possessed that happy gift which marries use with beauty. The châteaux painted in the *Très Riches Heures* show the state of architecture on the eve of the hundred years war, and show it to have been magnificent. Lusignan, redoubtable stronghold near Poitiers, which even in the age of gunpowder 'cost so much to ravish', rose from its concentric walls a proud and graceful lodging that reserved its richest architecture for the topmost storey of its inmost tower; slighted in 1575, it received its epitaph from Brantôme—'the most beautiful of the antique fortresses; the most noble of the ancient ornaments of France'.

If Lusignan had any rival in beauty it was the Château of Mehun-sur-Yèvre. Pol de Limbourg, in his exquisite miniature, depicts the castle with great accuracy, but he has set it against a chimerical and mountainous background which is most misleading. 'It stands in a wide-extended plain,' wrote the English traveller Wraxall, 'sheltered by deep woods, and at its foot flows the little river Yèvre which, dividing at the spot into several streams, forms a number of marshy islands covered with willows.'

Wraxall wrote in 1776, long after the place had been abandoned to decay. 'Though the castle of Mehun has been burnt by lightning, as well as greatly injured by time and the depredations of neighbouring peasants, yet its remains are even now inexpressibly august and beautiful.' When in its glory, as Pol de Limbourg painted it, the Château had presented a striking contrast between the lacelike tracery upon the topmost storeys and the solid base of fortification. Enough remained for Wraxall to admire; 'in the centre stands the Chapel,' he noted, 'the workmanship and delicacy of which are astonishing.'

Another of Jean de Berri's buildings where the line of demarcation between the military and the domestic was pronounced was Poitiers itself; up to the battlements it was a blind, unwindowed prison. Above it was a castle from fairyland—a group of slender towers, like delicately sharpened pencils, each with its ring of pinnacled dormers whose spacious mullioned windows gave ample prospects to the rooms within.

The marriage of an impregnable base to a delicate and decorative superstructure was not of long duration; the advent of gunpowder precipitated a divorce. The airy pinnacles of Saumur had on several occasions been blown away by the wind. The mere threat of high trajectory artillery rendered such baubles obsolete.

In Louis XI's reign domestic and military architecture
emerge distinct. Le Plessis-lès-Tours was his country house—
the greatest of hunting lodges, the least of palaces—inviting
and vulnerable, though somewhat inaccessible, in the narrow
tongue of land formed by the confluence of the Loire and the
Cher. The approach from the west was guarded, on the opposite
bank of the river, by the Château de Langeais, a building aus-
terely innocent of the frivolous adornments of the châteaux of
the duc de Berri.

It is unfortunate that le Plessis-lès-Tours, if known at all to
the British, is only known from Sir Walter Scott's description in
Quentin Durward. By his readers it is thought of as the quin-
tessence of medieval fortification, a compendium of every known
device of the feudal castle.

'There were three external walls,' wrote Scott, 'battlemented
and turretted from space to space and at each angle, the second
enclosure rising higher than the first, and being built so as to
command the exterior defence in case it was won by the enemy;
and being again, in the same manner, itself commanded by the
third and innermost barrier.' Each wall was insulated by a moat;
each moat defended by *chevaux de frises*. Within the inner sanctuary the Palace buildings clustered round 'an ancient and grim-
looking donjon-keep' with which Louis XI's additions were
made to harmonize by the use of blackened brick and mortar
mixed with soot—'so as to give the whole castle the same uni-
form tinge of extreme and rude antiquity'.

It is stark nonsense. It is evident that Scott had never set eyes
upon a picture, print or plan of the Château, nor can he have
inspected the remains. He seems to have read Philippe de
Commines and to have supplied the rest from his own copious
source of Gothic knowledge.

Before the imagination of the Romantic era got to work on it,
le Plessis-lès-Tours was known as a *château de plaisance*—a
Royal villa on the outskirts of Tours famous for its beautiful
gardens and numerous nightingales. The house itself, a most
unmilitary group of buildings with spacious lights and handsome brick façades, could not have stood a moment's siege, nor
was it ever designed to. 'It lends itself to every sort of pleasure,'

Florio wrote in 1477, 'and is convenient for every form of hunting.' Unlike Scott, Florio knew at first hand what he was talking
about. It may have had a gatehouse and a moat—but so did
every noble house in France. It may have had a gibbet, as every
feudal lordship had its *Justice Patibulaire.* It may even have been
set about with man-traps; we have Louis's order to Jehan
Forgier, for two hundred *chausse-trapes* for the Château des
Forges. But Les Forges was a hunting lodge deep in the forests
of Chinon; Louis was a fanatic for the chase, and there is little
doubt that the traps were for the protection of his game and
not his person.

In fact, as the nobility devoted themselves more to hunting
and less to private warfare, the locus of conflict soon transferred itself from the château to the gamekeeper's house.
Charles Estienne recommended that this should be fortified
against poachers. Over the doors and windows he prescribes
'little loopholes, through which the keeper may either shoot,
cast stones or scalding water to make them avoid from the
same'.

But if Le Plessis was not fortified it was most strictly guarded.
Towards the end of his life Louis became more and more afraid
of some coup d'état against his person, and his house was ringed
around with iron palissades; iron look-out posts supplied the
want of fortification, and the company of crossbowmen had
orders to fire on uninvited guests who came before the gates
were opened; the whole place, Commines asserted, was 'like a
frontier station, closely guarded'.

He was in fact his own imprisoner. Philippe de Commines
compared him with his unhappy victims who were locked up in
iron cages; these had living room 'some eight foot square,
while he who was so great a King, had but a tiny castle ward
to walk in'. Louis XI was a man of simple tastes, but with a lust
for power which greatly strengthened the position of the Crown.
He was not himself a great builder, but under him men rose to
positions of power and wealth which enabled them to adorn the
broad acres of their domains with châteaux proportionate to the
dignity of their rank.

CHAPTER III

The Buildings of Jean Bourré. Le Plessis-Bourré, Langeais, Jarzé, Le Moulin

IF THERE is any one man to whom we owe the first flowering of domestic architecture in Anjou and Touraine, it is to Jean Bourré. Born in 1424 and educated at Paris University, he took his degree in law and entered, at the age of eighteen, the service of the Dauphin, later Louis XI. In 1451 his master became the King of France.

Few kings have been less regal in their tastes or appearance than Louis XI. A man of mean attire and undistinguished looks, his whole interest was in the reality of power and never in its trappings. He was the midwife who enabled France to be reborn after the long travail of the English wars. Distrustful, and with reason, of the old nobility, Louis knew how to make use of the competence, diligence and loyalty of the bourgeoisie. 'Jean Bourré,' writes his biographer Georges Bricard, 'seems to personify this bourgeoisie which attaches itself to the King and serves him faithfully while the *grands seigneurs* betray him and fight among themselves; who reach the highest honours and the highest charges of the State, while the nobility is losing its prestige and ancient function with the King; who becomes rich at the moment when the nobility is becoming poor, even to ruin; who acquires what had been the real strength of the old lords—the possession of great estates; and who in the end receives from the King ennoblement—the last privilege which the feudal lords cannot lose, but whose importance they see everyday diminished.'

The most trusted minister of a most untrusting king, Bourré held a plurality of high and lucrative positions, which gave him a unique opportunity to patronize the costly art of building; and when in 1506 he died, he had given to the architecture of the Loire valley a character specifically its own. A whole constellation of private châteaux, part fortress and part stately home, derived their form and drew their inspiration from Jean Bourré's constructions. Three of the first and finest were his own design: Langeais for the King, Le Plessis-Bourré and Jarzé for himself. To these Ussé, Le Coudray-Montpensier and Le Verger are patently indebted, and from Le Verger descended Bury, the first renaissance château on the Loire. Durtal, Boumois, Montsoreau and Le Lude were all connected with this galaxy. It is seldom that a single man can have exercised an influence so decisive on so important a group of buildings.

The Marechal de Gié, busy with construction at the near-by Le Verger, was a frequent visitor to Le Plessis. Jacques de Daillon wrote Bourré a friendly rebuke for failing to call in at Le Lude in passing; *'je me attends que vous y passerez au retour pour voir ma belle chaussée et aussi mon édiffice qui se avance fort'*; Louis de Graville, Admiral of France, who was a regular guest of Bourré's, wrote to ask for some of his tapestry at cost price, adding with the greatest coolness; 'I know well that they are worth much more than this', but offering to oblige Bourré in the same way if occasion should serve. It is not known if the offer was accepted.

It would be typical of Bourré's open-handed generosity to have complied with every wish of his old friend and *compère*. Looking through the many letters which have survived one is struck by the warmth and friendliness of Bourré's relationships. He was happy in his work with the King; he was happy in his friends, but most especially was he happy in his marriage.

On November 12, 1463, he married Marguerite de Feschal, a union that was to last for thirty years and was to be blessed by a tender and reciprocal affection. Her letters to him, usually starting with the address *'Monsieur mon ami'*, are full of delicate allusions to their relationship. When, after eight years, Marguerite was at last with child and first felt its movement in her womb, she wrote at once to her husband: 'God send us joy through it to you and me; and please God that you might be here so that you might also feel it moving, as my sister doth every day.' Her one complaint was of her husband's protracted absences at Court.

It was because of the absence of Jean Bourré that the building of his Château of Le Plessis was conducted by his wife. By 1471, as the above letter discloses, she had private reasons for urging the speedy expedition of the work; 'I have great haste that the said house should be completed,' she writes, 'because I hope, if that would be your pleasure, to have there your little child.' At the time of this letter Le Plessis-Bourré was complete but unglazed. In January a contract had been signed with Jean Belotin, glazier at Tours, for glass for the whole *'grand corps de maison'*.

The buildings of the forecourt had not been started; 'I have not yet touched that,' explains Marguerite, 'but the stone will hardly suffice for the lake, and I am still waiting for the lake to be finished before I start work on the court; it would be folly to start on it without a plentiful supply of stone.'

It is this stone, the hard, white *pierre de Boulay*, to which Le Plessis owes the secret of eternal youth. For seen today from the distance dictated by the ample moat, the stonework has the chiselled freshness of a new-built house.

The moat, or rather lake, was so extensive as to cause a problem to local agriculture. 'Your farmers,' continues Marguerite, 'whose land is drowned by the lake, have come to me to ask me to buy them hay against the coming year.'

Her letter is the most delightful reading; it furnishes invaluable information about the building of Le Plessis and a charming picture of her domestic happiness. It ends on a typical note, wishing that her Lord might come over, even if it were only for a day, to see his Château—*'car il me semble que vous seriez bien joyeulx'*.

It is indeed a most attractive building. The first sight of Le Plessis from the main approach to the east is an exciting architectural experience. In spite of his obvious concern for fastness, Bourré did not hesitate to fill his rooms with light and air, piercing the substantial walls with large and frequent windows. He also placed his living-rooms high and his forecourt buildings low so as to provide the windows with extensive views of the surrounding plain. This disposition produced an ensemble which is most impressive—the build-up of towers, gables and dormers above a lower range of towers, roofs and dormers, which reaches its climax in the stately *donjon* at the south-east corner of the Château. It was this contrivance which was Jean Bourré's distinctive contribution to the development of the renaissance château. It was reproduced at Le Coudray, enlarged upon at Le Verger, italianized at Bury and became the basis of the whole design of Chambord. It found its way to England where it was adapted for the vast palaces of Theobalds, Holdenby and Audley End.

One is in some doubt whether beauty or security was foremost in the builder's mind. The Château was set in a labyrinth of moats; the moats enclosed a series of islands, and the islands were laid out as gardens. These gardens, together with the beauty of the buildings, continually and delightfully reflected in the water, created the impression of a *maison de plaisance*.

And yet the place was a fortress. It was a fortress by virtue of the thickness of its walls, by the disposition of its towers and by the communication of a *chemin de ronde* between them. In later years these features were put to a purely decorative use, but that Jean Bourré was seriously interested in fortification there can be no doubt, for on the south front he has omitted the machicolations—a military expedient which lent itself most readily to becoming a merely ornamental cornice—and replaced them with tall slots which somewhat mar the beauty of this front, but would certainly have enabled defenders to cover the foot of the castle with a devastating fire.

The provision was prudent, but, as it turned out, redundant. The annals of Le Plessis-Bourré are a peaceful record of domestic ease and abundant hospitality. Three sons and a daughter were born to the Bourrés and were brought up here, and when their father was absent at Amboise or Le Plessis-lès-Tours, he was kept informed of their health and happiness. '*Madame et tout le beau ménage,*' writes one of the domestics, '*font bonne chère et sont, Dieu merci, en bon point.*'

Marguerite de Feschal transmitted to her daughter Anne the peculiar gifts which made her a wife and mother of the first quality and a worthy mistress of one of the finest homes in France. In 1489 Anne Bourré was married to François de la Jaille and became the châtelaine of Durtal. 'Monseigneur,' wrote François to his father-in-law, 'if it should please you to ask me of my news you would receive the answer that your daughter is all that I hold most dear in all the world—*elle est toute mon désennuye et félicité.*'

The family seem to have radiated happiness to all around. Even the city of Angers had occasion to be grateful that they had so highly placed a neighbour as Jean Bourré. In 1485 the aldermen voted the dispatch of 'ten pipes of wine to Monsieur du Plessis-Bourré in consideration of certain great services done by him to the said city'. It was followed by a sturgeon, a gift of torches, another of candles, with always a pipe or two of wine for good measure, and in 1493, learning that the great Minister 'was to keep Christmas at the said place of Plessis-Bourré', they delivered a present of fish 'for the vigil of the said feast'.

It was a house to which the King could invite himself at a moment's notice and expect to be royally entertained. He would not be ashamed to summon Ambassadors to see him there. In June of 1487 Louis de Graville wrote to Bourré announcing the immediate arrival of the King. 'You will have to do the best you can,' he adds, 'for the Embassy will be with you tomorrow for dinner.' The Embassy, which was from Hungary, arrived with a cavalcade of nearly two hundred horses and forty-five mules, with their own trumpeters and musicians. Bourré had to slaughter 'one large ox and two sheep' for their refreshment.

The interior of the Château, in which these distinguished visitors were so lavishly entertained, has been largely redecorated. The eighteenth-century salons of the ground floor are fine, but out of place. Two important rooms, however, have happily conserved their original aspect, and from them may be inferred the magnificence of Jean Bourré's apartments.

The Salle du Parlement, occupying most of the west wing, is an architect's achievement. It derives its beauty from its finely-cut stonework and the crisp, prismatic profiles of the shallow vaulting. At the far end of the room, the north wall is almost entirely taken up by a monumental fireplace, typical of the times. Its massive hood, enlivened with two bands of delicate floral carving and a somewhat deeper band of tracery, is the focal point to the whole apartment.

The Salle des Gardes, on the first floor of the main block, is the work of the painter and the joiner; its panelled ceiling is its most conspicuous feature. Its twenty-four compartments are devoted to the weird, symbolic figures of the alchemist. They form a subject worth a study of its own. Suffice it here to mention *Chicheface*, the demon wolf-bitch whose lean and hungry looks reveal her want of nourishment. This was because she would only eat that great rarity 'the wife who obeys her husband's every command'.

One cannot resist the reflection that Marguerite de Feschal deserved the attentions of *Chicheface*. The normal ending to her letters was *'votre humble, obeyssante fille et amie'*. It was no empty formula, as her continual reference of all matters to her husband's wishes bears witness. Even in her last will and testament, in which she desires to be buried at Jarzé, there is the proviso: 'or anywhere else that my husband may direct.' He did, in fact, respect her wish.

It may seem at first sight odd that a woman whose life was so deeply involved with the Château du Plessis should have desired her mortal remains to be interred elsewhere. The explanation is probably that there is no Parish Church to Le Plessis, although there is of course a private chapel.

Jarzé, the second Château built by Jean Bourré, has unfortunately been virtually destroyed. It was sacked and burnt by the soldiers of the Vendée in 1793, after which its owner, Pierre-Jean Deurbrouck, a munitions manufacturer from Nantes, converted the ruins into a villa in which it is difficult to see the hand of its original builder.

Fortunately for posterity, Gaignières did several water colours of Jarzé at the end of the seventeenth century from which its architecture may be plainly known. It occupied a wonderful position, high above its town. To the north and west stretched the immense park; to the south and west unfolded the magnificent panorama of the Loire valley. From the town Jarzé resembed a smaller version of Langeais, but in white stone; from the courtyard it appeared as a somewhat more ornate elaboration of Le Plessis. The interstices between the windows of each floor are filled with blind tracery, making each flight of windows

a vertical unit in the design. It thus announces the theme developed, in more Italian idiom, at Le Lude. The staircase tower,
having the greatest number of windows, presents the greatest
intricacy of carving, and is a possible prototype of the exuber-
ance of Meillant and of the inner courtyard at Le Verger.

Jarzé and Le Plessis exercised, as has been seen, an important
influence upon the architecture of the time, especially in the
Loire valley. Both of them reflect the general *ordonnance* of
Langeais. It is stated in the preamble to his will that Jean
Bourré *'a édifyé et fait construire'* a number of châteaux, of which
Langeais is the first mentioned. But here he worked in colla-
boration with Jean Briçonnet, Général des Finances and Mayor
of Tours, to whom was committed, in 1465, 'the payment of the
works and buildings of the Château de Langeais'.

A most instructive letter survives from Briçonnet to Bourré.
It is undated, but can be placed with confidence in the year 1467.
It is clear that the Château is, at the time of the letter, more or
less complete up to and including the first of the great towers
which guard the entrance. Its façade would thus have resembled
closely those of Le Plessis or Jarzé. The feature which distin-
guishes it from both is the gatehouse and *donjon* tower, which
are the subject of this letter.

There are two possible inferences to be drawn. One is that the
original intention had been to leave Langeais without this
entrance from the town. This theory is supported by the irregular manner in which the masonry of the gatehouse joins on to
that of the left-hand tower; it does not suggest that the addition
had been foreseeen. The other possibility is that the gatehouse
and *donjon* formed part of the original design, but that the work
was divided, perhaps for financial reasons, into two phases. The
letter does suggest that payments have not been all they
should.

Briçonnet shows himself a cautious treasurer, and will not
start the work until he is sure of his funds. As soon as the works
begin, he reminds Bourré, *'il faudra avoir l'argent au poing'*. The
most interesting aspect of the letter is the light which it sheds
on the authorship of the design. Briçonnet undertakes to build
the wall down into the cellars *'ainsi que [vous] m'avez dit'*. In

other words he has received architectural instructions from Bourré. But he also makes some quite important changes in the design on his own inspiration. He is building the *donjon* larger than the other towers, as befitted its function. The tower is backed by a square projection forming the *retraictz* for purposes of sanitation and an octagonal turret containing the staircase. The design of this he discusses in the letter; 'it will be convenient that this spiral staircase, when it reaches the first floor, should come out and overhang on corbels, in such a manner that one may enter both the gatehouse and the said tower, without the rooms of one being subject to those of the other.'

The visitor today, standing on the terrace beneath the old fortress of Foulque Nerra, and looking at the court façade of the new Château, will see precisely this division of the staircase to the left of the entrance archway.

It is interesting that the paymaster, and not the master mason, should be determining such adjustments as are often necessary in the course of the constructions. It does not alter the fact that the broad outlines of the whole seem to have come from Bourré—and there is little enough at Langeais which is not comprehended in the term 'broad outlines'.

It might have been expected in a building which was half palace and half fortress, that the more protected and domestic façades of the courtyard would be the more ornamented, but this is not the case. For while the Royal rooms are barely embellished with slender mouldings to the window frames, the *chemin de ronde* on the outer façades, whose function was severely military and lethal, is treated as a decorative theme. Each cavity of the machicolation is surmounted by a slightly recessed panel; each panel printed with a delicately embossed trefoil. This, together with the regular rhythm of square-cut openings and narrow bow slits, makes the *chemin de ronde* the principal ornament to Langeais, taking the place of frieze and cornice in the design, and binding the breaks and towers to the façade.

It is interesting to contrast the buildings of Jean Bourré with another contemporary house in the region, the Château du Moulin, near Lassay. This delightful architectural jewel was started in 1480 by Philippe du Moulin under the direction of the master mason Jacques de Persigny. It owes nothing to the group of buildings which have already been considered.

In the first place it is built of brick, with diaper patterns and stone dressings, following the more economical example of Louis XI at Le Plessis-lès-Tours, but previous to the very similar buildings of Anne de Beaujeu at Gien. Secondly its plan is not compact. An ample court, encircled by a wall and moat, encloses an area which is mostly free of buildings. The Château proper is free standing and extremely small—a rectangle containing only two rooms on each of four storeys, with a square staircase tower towards the court and an apsidal projection towards the moat which provides a further room to each of the floors. To the ground-floor salon is appended a charming little oratory.

The rest of the lodgings, including the Salle des Gardes and Kitchens, adjoin the gatehouse and link it with the north-east corner tower. This tower, it must be admitted, has certain affinities with the surviving towers of Le Verger, but once again the brickwork is distinctive. The whole of Le Moulin forms a picturesque ensemble, derived from this haphazard distribution. It represents a secondary theme to the main development of architecture in the region, which recurs in many delightful variations in the smaller manor houses or *gentilhommières*. These smaller houses are as much a part of the architectural and historical heritage of the Loire valley as the great stone châteaux of Jean Bourré.

Philippe du Moulin was companion at arms to Charles VIII and managed to save the King's life during the disaster at Fornova. This naturally raised him still further in the esteem and affection of his Prince, who made him Governor of Langres, Chamberlain of France and a member of the King's council. To these were added, in 1498, the sad duty of being one of the pallbearers at his Royal master's untimely funeral.

In December of 1491 Charles had married Anne, the Duchess of Brittany, thus uniting her important territory to the throne of France. The marriage took place at Langeais. They were not exactly a good-looking couple. Zacharie Contarini, Venetian Ambassador in France, is harsh in his descriptions: 'The King

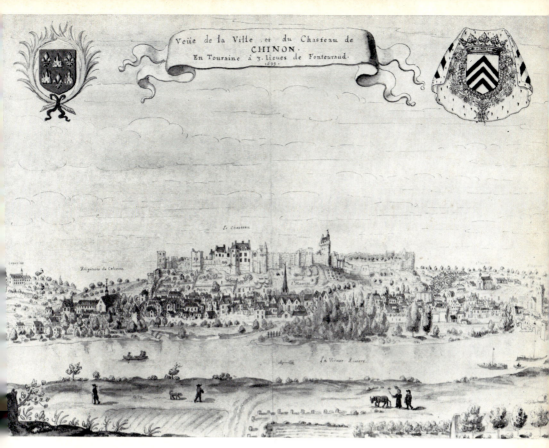

Veüe de la Ville et du Chasteau de
CHINON.
En Touraine à 7. lieues de Fontevraud.
1699.

CHINON: from a watercolour by Gaignières
CHINON: the same view today

CHINON: ruins of the
Grande Salle,
by Gaignières

LOCHES: Château
and town in 1699,
by Gaignières

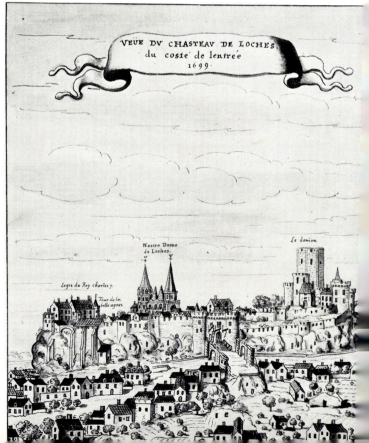

SAUMUR: miniature from *Très Riches Heures de duc de Berri* in the Musée de Condé at Chantilly

THE TOMB OF AGNÈS SOREL: from *Promenades Pittoresques en Touraine* by C. Chevalier

LE PLESSIS-BOURRÉ: the Donjon

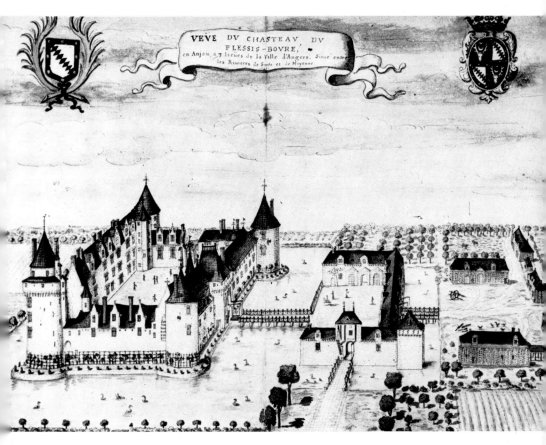

LE PLESSIS-BOURRÉ: watercolour by Gaignières

LE PLESSIS-BOURRÉ: view from the north-east

JARZÉ: watercolour by Gaignières

LANGEAIS: from the old donjon

AMBOISE: aerial view from across the Loire; drawing by
du Cerceau

AMBOISE: from across the Loire downstream; an anonymous
watercolour of the seventeenth century

AMBOISE: from across the Amasse; reconstruction by
Ian Dunlop

AMBOISE: from across the Loire; reconstruction by
Ian Dunlop

is small and has a poor presence, an ugly face with large, white eyes, more apt to see badly than to see well; a hooked nose, also large and fatter than is becoming; the lips also are large and they are always hanging open.' He had certain nervous gestures of the hand which Contarini found displeasing, and he was slow in his speech.

Anne de Bretagne, also small and thin, limped noticeably on one leg, but if her physical attractions were few they were amply compensated by her mental and spiritual endowments. Contarini found her to be 'most sagacious for her age'. In contrast to Charles she was full of vitality and charm—'*jeune et pleine de si bonne grâce qu'on prenait plaisir à la regarder*'.

Her wedding dress was the richest possible, of cloth of gold entirely embroidered with designs 'traced in high relief in gold'. It was December and she used the cold as a pretext for an impressive display of sable and otter furs. She had brought her own bed with her by barge from Nantes; curtains and tester were of cloth of gold, lined with crimson and violet silk and heavily fringed with black. Her attendants had all been provided with dresses of silk and velvet, and her horses were arrayed in black and crimson.

The marriage ceremony took place in the Grande Salle of the Château, and a magnificent banquet rounded off the festivities. The food was brought in ritual procession from the *cuisine de bouche*. 'Trumpets and clarions went before, sounding melodiously; next the Kings at Arms and Heralds; after these six ordinary Maîtres d'Hôtel, two by two, and after them the Grand Maître d'Hôtel; behind him the Ecuyer who carried the meat.'

The food for the Royal table consisted of 'one sucking pig served whole with a pear between its teeth; one peacock with the tail displayed; several swans, geese and pheasants; then pies which contained live birds which sang '*moult mélodieusement*', and finally a set piece of sugar dishes representing all sorts of figures.'

The next day the Royal couple left Langeais for Le Plessis-lès-Tours, but neither Langeais nor Le Plessis-lès-Tours was to be their principal residence. It was to the old Château at Amboise that the young King now turned his thoughts.

CHAPTER IV

Amboise

I T IS not surprising that a young King, brought up under the able tutelage of so great a builder as Jean Bourré, should have become himself a great enthusiast for buildings.

Charles VIII had spent most of his childhood at Amboise. He must have retained happy memories of his early days, for when he came of age he determined to make Amboise his principal residence, and to enlarge and embellish it accordingly. In the autumn of 1493 Gentile Becchi, Ambassador from Florence, was received by the King at Le Plessis-lès-Tours. 'He showed us a model for a château at Amboise,' the Ambassador wrote, 'which he is erecting into a city.'

It lent itself in many ways to such an undertaking. The ample space enclosed within the curtain wall afforded room for an ambitious project, and combined the security of a natural strong-hold with the attractions of commanding one of the finest views in France. The letters of Charles VIII show that he appreciated landscape, and no doubt this was one of the determining factors of his choice.

Built on the high spur of rock which separates the valley of the Amasse from that of the Loire, the castle enjoyed a sweet air and a pleasant prospect. 'The position is superb,' wrote Andrea Navigero; 'the country round about, the loveliest in France.' A century later La Fontaine was to echo his praise. '*Ce qu'il y a de beau*', he wrote, '*c'est la vue.*' It was grand; it was majestic and of vast extent; 'the eye finds nothing to obstruct it, and no object that may not entertain it in the most agreeable manner possible. You have before you a riverside of the happiest and most varied aspect that I have ever yet beheld.'

To the delights afforded by a free air and a fine view were added the attractions of a large and game-infested forest. The hunting was so good that Louis XI had exempted the citizens from the *taille*—'provided always that they swear and promise on the Holy Gospels of God that they will not hunt in the said forest'.

Amboise, in fact, had everything that could commend a site to Royal use. Catherine de' Medici described it as a 'residence so beautiful, so healthy and so convenient for the lodging of one's children'. Charles VIII, François I and her own three sons all spent their childhood here, and from its towers and terraces had first surveyed the land they were to rule.

Thus, La Fontaine could call Amboise 'the cradle of the Kings of France'. He might have added 'the nursery, also, of her renaissance'. For Amboise only emerges from the obscurity of its feudal foundations with the coming of Charles VIII.

In 1494 Charles was in Italy. The country round about Naples made the most immediate impact upon him. 'You cannot believe the beautiful gardens which I have [seen] in this city,' he wrote to his brother-in-law. Arbours, fountains, orange trees and singing birds filled his heart with envy and all his senses with delight, so that it seemed as if only 'Adam and Eve were wanting to make it a terrestrial Paradise'.

In order to recreate his own terrestrial Paradise on the banks of the Loire, Charles set about the purchasing of works of art, which, his letters show, were destined for Amboise. Not all of them arrived. On July 6 his cavalcade of 6,000 pack horses was ambushed at Fornova and almost all his collection had to be abandoned. He did not, however, come home empty-handed. He brought with him twenty-two *hommes de métier* who were to work for him 'after the manner of Italy'.

The term *homme de métier* covered a wide field, as his wages book reveals. At the head of the list were Guido Paganino, painter and illuminator; Jean Jocundus (Fra Giocondo) 'deviser of buildings'; Dom Passello, gardener; Jerome Passerot, mason; Domenico de Courtonne, *faiseur de chasteaulx* (which almost certainly means a maker of architectural models); Alphonse Damasso, turner of alabaster, who had to go back to Naples in search of his wife, and Bernadin de Brissia, worker of ceilings, who was a specialist in marquetry.

The rest were a somewhat more miscellaneous group. One was

a goldsmith 'newly baptised'; another was a confectioner of perfumes; several were tailors and couturiers—*'faiseurs d'habille-
ments de dames à l'italienne'*. One was a builder of organs, and
one, Lascaris, a scholar of Greek. Some combined an odd assort-
ment of roles, such as Luc Becjeame who was at once a jeweller,
a deviser of buildings and a 'subtle inventor for the incubation
and hatching of chickens'. The art of living, in its most varied
aspects, was to be enriched and refined by the activities of this
team of experts.

The Château on which so many distinguished artisans were
to work 'in the Italian manner', remained, however, firmly
French. The first problem of converting a fortress into a palace
was one of communication. A *château fort* is by definition inaccessible, and Amboise was only connected with its town either by
devious or by abrupt and narrow means. The problem was
tackled by Charles in the boldest and most dramatic way. Two
enormous towers, each like the shaft of some gigantic well, were
built out from the plateau on which the castle stood, and within
their capacious drums were spiral ramps down which a coach
and horses could safely go. On state occasions the walls were
hung with tapestries and perilously lit with flaming torches. A
more impressive and original means of access has seldom been
devised. They were not, however, without their hazards.

In 1539 the Emperor Charles V passed through France, and
François I was determined to dazzle him with the brilliance of
his Court. On December 8 the cortège was due at Amboise. It
was arranged that it should not arrive until after dark, for darkness provided François with opportunities for showing off his
architectural splendours in the dramatic and flattering light of
artificial illuminations.

'In order that the Emperor's arrival should be the more
magnificent,' wrote Du Bellay in his memoirs, 'the King ordained that it should be by night, by means of one of the said
towers, adorned with every embellishment that could be
devised, and so furnished with flambeaux and other lights that
one could see as clearly as at high noon in the open country.'

It was certainly an inspired conception, this winding corridor
of light that opened out on to the galaxy of illuminated archi-

tectural devices which surrounded the courtyard—the glowing colours of the tapestries that lined the walls, the glittering reflections from every polished sconce and candlestick, the constellations of the candelabra and the broad flare of the torches combined to dazzle and delight the Imperial visitor.

But there was one thing which François had overlooked. This form of illumination is as dangerous as it is beautiful, and on this occasion it was nearly fatal. 'When the Emperor was half way up,' continues Du Bellay, 'a certain ill-fated torch bearer set fire to it, so that the whole tower was in flames, and because of the tapestries which caught fire, the smoke was so dense, being unable to find an outlet, that there was great doubt but that the Emperor would suffocate.' There was an ugly rush for the exit; what had been planned as the most magnificent and dignified arrival degenerated into a stampede. When they finally emerged, choking and spluttering, into the courtyard of the Château, François's rage and disappointment knew no bounds. He ordered the instant arrest of those responsible and would have hanged them then and there had not the Emperor intervened and begged their pardon. Charles, one cannot help feeling, may have privately enjoyed his rival's discomfiture.

It is certain that the original plan for Amboise made provision for a third *escalier de carosse* at the north-east corner of the gardens, but it was never built. Nevertheless, in the few years of Charles VIII's reign, the constructions went forward at an astonishing speed. One hundred and seventy masons were set to the task simultaneously. They worked in winter: there were payments for fuel 'to unfreeze the stones that the masons could work in the winter time'. They worked at night: the accounts record the purchase of candles for the craftsmen *'qui ont besogné de nuit à la chandelle'*. In less than three years the greater part of the Château was completed: it presented a very impressive ensemble. From the narrow streets of the town the façades could only be seen in towering perspective; it was the distant prospect of Amboise that was the most magnificent.

There exists today, in the Cabinet des Estampes, a remote view of the town and castle as they appeared in the middle of the seventeenth century. It gives an admirable impression of the first, unforgettable *coup d'œil* obtained by the visitor who approached by river from Tours. The whole Château rides superbly above the rooftops of the town, as a mountain range rides above the gathered foothills at its base. We must picture the scene in the soft, clear light that is so lovely a feature of the landscape of Touraine, the gilded points of its pinnacles and *poivrières* all sparkling together in the sun. 'This mass of pavilions, galleries, towers, spires and roofs of varying heights,' wrote Dr. Bruneau, 'lent much animation to the scene.'

Dr. Bruneau was a local antiquary of Louis XIV's time. He knew Amboise when most of it was still intact, and he had access to the full building accounts, now long since vanished from the Chapter Library. But his description would mean little to us today had not Du Cerceau left the most confident and comprehensive record of the whole vast lay-out in two bird's-eye views preserved in the British Museum.

Du Cerceau, however, must be treated with circumspection. His drawings are an unlikely combination of exact detail and quite unaccountable error. He has got his ground plan wrong, making a pronounced angle in the middle of the south range, near the Chapelle St. Blaise, where in fact the walls are almost straight. At the same place he has introduced two towers with conical roofs where there was certainly only one. It is as if he had drawn the same tower from widely different angles, and never realized that it was the same tower. Anyone who has tried to draw a detailed bird's-eye view of a large and irregular building will sympathize with Du Cerceau's predicament.

Subject to these limitations, his view from the north is a magnificent introduction to Amboise. Along the north range that overlooks the Loire were the King's Apartments and the great Salle des Gardes adjoining them. The huge Tour des Minimes, containing the *escalier de carosse*, gave access to this portion of the palace.

Along the south range, overlooking the Amasse, were the Queen's Apartments—the *Logis des Sept Vertus*, so named, Dr. Bruneau informs us, from the terra cotta statues which adorned its inward façade. The Tour Hurtault, the other *escalier de carosse*, connected the Queen's Apartments with the town. Next to the Queen's rooms came those of the Enfants de France, and from this range projected the Chapelle St. Blaise, the only surviving fragment today of the whole southern range of the Château.

At the westernmost extremity of the spur were the oldest buildings, known archaically as La Maison Neuve. The most distinctive feature of this block was the tall tower with *chemin de ronde* and *poivrière* identical to those at Langeais. In this it is easy to detect the authorship of Jean Bourré.

The King's Apartments were linked to those of the Queen by a long, moated gallery, so that the ground plan of the whole resembled a capital A, with this gallery as the cross bar. East of the gallery, and standing in its own cloisters, was the Collegial Church of St. Florentin, whose spire provided the highest point in the silhouette of Amboise.

It was from the southern range that the magnificent panorama for which Amboise was justly famous was best enjoyed. From the King's rooms one could walk out on to a flat, terraced roof, bordered by balustrades, and look out across the broad stream of the Loire to Nazelles and Noisay and the distant Coteaux de Vouvray. On the other side of the terrace one could look down into the inner courtyard of the Palace, round which there ran a colonnade of two storeys providing a covered corridor to most of the lodgings of the Court. These superimposed colonnades were the most striking and original features of Amboise. 'The spectator standing in the middle of the courtyard,' wrote Dr. Bruneau, 'saw nothing but arcades, colonnades and pilasters all around him, which, in an age when simple forms and beautiful proportions were unknown, certainly created an effect of the greatest richness and magnificence.' Bruneau, who speaks with some of the condescension of the classical age, had seen at least the debris of these galleries, and knew that they had been richly polychromed and gilded.

One after another these buildings on the south and west of the Château fell into disrepair and were demolished. By the nineteenth century the Chapel of St. Blaise was the sole survivor. Originally this would only have been visible from some of the windows and from a narrow terrace immediately behind it; but from the town it was plainly conspicuous, delicately perched like a rather elaborate howdah on the top of an elephantine bastion.

It was undoubtedly the most beautiful of Charles VIII's additions, and it is evidence of the broadness of his taste that while he was embellishing his rooms and gardens in a style luxuriously Italian, he was adorning his Château with a Chapel that was flamboyantly Flemish. His taste was both catholic and eclectic; as Philippe de Commines observed, 'he assembled here all the lovely things that he had seen when he was welcomed in any land, were it in France, in Italy, or in Flanders'.

The purely French contribution was in the general outlines of the architecture and in the beautiful quality of the stonework. Three master masons—Colin Biart, Guillaume Senault and Louis Amangeart, names which figure also in the annals of Le Verger, Gaillon and Blois—were at the head of the team. Among their assistants were names later to be famous: Jacques Sourdeau and Pierre Nepveu, both of whom were to play an important role at Chambord; Martin and Bastien François, who later built Semblançay's house at Tours, and Pierre Gadier, the future master mason at Madrid—a château built by François I in the Bois de Boulogne. Many of the great renaissance houses of France owed the excellence of their stonework to craftsmen who had learnt their skill at Amboise.

There is no knowing what the place might have become had Charles been able to accomplish his intention, for the models of the Grand Design, which Gentile Becchi and Philippe de Commines had inspected—models *de merveilleuse entreprinse et despense*'—have not survived. Commines assures us that it was the far-reaching plan of a young man who had most of his life to look forward to.

Unfortunately Charles had nothing of the sort. In April 1498, he died suddenly and tragically of concussion. Passing from the Queen's Apartment to watch the tennis in the dry moat of the *donjon*, he entered a gallery named Haquelebac—a disagreeable place for '*tout le monde y pissait*'—and, stooping to enter by the low archway, he cracked his head against the lintel of the door. Shortly afterwards he collapsed, and lay there on a poor palliasse until nine in the morning when he died. Philippe de Commines gives his epitaph; 'thus departed this life so mighty and so great a King in so miserable a place; he who had so many fine houses and was building so fine a house.'

After the death of Charles VIII, Amboise became the home of Louise de Savoie and her two remarkable children—the duc d'Angoulême, later François I, and Marguerite, later Queen of Navarre. Louise was placed under the supervision of the Maréchal de Gié, who was at this time just completing his magnificent château of Le Verger in Anjou. Once again, one of the most important builders of the age was to be found in close association with Amboise.

The boyhood of François I is described for posterity by the child who shared it with him, Robert de la Marck, Seigneur de Florange. His story, an autobiography in which he styles himself 'the Young Adventurer', reads like a children's tale come true. He was only eight when he left his paternal Château de l'Ecluse in Flanders to offer his services to Louis XII, who was then in residence at Blois. 'My son,' said the King, when the diminutive Knight Errant was presented to him, 'you are very welcome. You are too young to be in my service, and for this reason I am going to send you to Monsieur d'Angoulême at Amboise; he is your age; I think you will get on very well together.'

The next day his little cavalcade took the road along the *levée* of the Loire from Blois to Amboise, where they lay at the Sign of the Holy Beard on the island opposite the town. Great stores of wine and other gifts arrived from Louise de Savoie, and across the river they could see the royal castle raising its towers and bastions high above the rooftops of the town.

Here Florange was to spend his formative years as close companion to François. Together they learnt to draw the bow; together they were initiated into the mysteries of the hunt. They played Italian games such as *la grosse boulle* with an inflatable ball 'as large as the bottom of a barrel'; they played at soldiers, having miniature castles constructed in the tennis court which one defended and the other attacked; and when they were a little older they learnt to ride at tilts and jousts.

Here also François received the education that led him to

become a patron of the arts and lover of learning when he succeeded to the throne. One of his first moves as King was to invite Leonardo da Vinci, one of the greatest all-rounders of the renaissance, to come to France, where he was installed in the little Château du Clos Lucé at Amboise. Unfortunately Leonardo had a stroke the following year which deprived him of the use of his right arm. 'Although the said Master can no longer lay on the colours,' wrote Antonio Beatis, *'avec la douceur qui lui était particulière'*—yet he was still training an apprentice, Francesco Melzi, 'who works excellently under his directions'.

Beatis came with the Cardinal of Aragon on October 8, 1517. Eighteen months later Leonardo was dead. On August 12 his remains were laid in the cloisters of the Chapel Royal of St. Florentin. The *acte de décès* describes him as *'noble millanois, premier peintre et ingénieur et architecte du Roy, meschanischien d'Etat, et anchien directeur de peinture du duc de Milan'*.

In the summer of 1864, Arsène Houssaye, Inspecteur des Beaux Arts under Napoleon III, arranged for the excavation of the site of the Eglise St. Florentin, demolished in 1808. His object was to discover the tomb of Leonardo.

On June 23 the first dig was made. They had to go deep, for the ground level had been built up, and there were few vestiges of foundations left to guide them. On the second day bones and skeletons began to come to light, and a multitude of small architectural fragments. In the course of the next weeks they made some interesting discoveries. Beneath the High Altar they found the body of an infant one year old—perhaps a child of Charles VIII. Only one tomb was found intact, that of the Demoiselle de Cast *'fille de noble homme Alphon de Cast'*. Could this have been a daughter of one of the murderers of the duc de Guise, Olphant de Gast?

In August they were working for the second time over the site of the Choir, and on August 20 they came upon another tomb. Carefully and with reverence they began to uncover the skeleton, and after a few handfuls of earth had been cleared away a skull was revealed of the most noble proportions—*'une grande physionomie dans la majesté de la mort'*. The figure was lying, as if asleep, the left hand pillowing the head. It was an unusual position for a burial. To the expectant mind there was a suggestion about the whole scene of a thinker at rest from his labours.

It immediately occurred to everyone present that they had found the object of their search, but in the absence of any proof no one cared to say so. The details were corroborative; a coin found was of the earliest François I mintage; the height was correct and the contours of the skull corresponded with the self-portrait of the great artist; medical opinion confirmed that the man had died in his seventies. Above all, the excavators were impressed with the sense of powerful intellect about the high dome of the forehead.

It was the gardener who found the first circumstantial evidence—a fragment of tombstone on which were legible the letters N.C. A careful washing of the stone revealed the further initial I. The search was renewed and duly produced another fragment with the letters LEO. Already the jig-saw was becoming exciting. Pieces of another inscription in different lettering now came to light: EO . . . DUS . . . VINC.

The discovery of the inscription only confirms what was in any case beyond doubt, and since the *acte de décès* states specifically that Leonardo was interred in the cloister and not in the Choir, one may remain sceptical about the identity of Houssaye's skeleton, however fine a cranium it possessed.

It is difficult to assess the contribution of Leonardo to the French renaissance. He certainly supplied plans and sketches for a château at Romorantin, where François wished to establish his mother. The project came to nothing, but it is just possible that out of the suggestions made by Leonardo was born the inspiration of Chambord.

By the time Leonardo da Vinci arrived in France the movement was well on its way. It had received an important impetus from the activities of Charles VIII at Amboise, but with his death the patronage of the Crown diminished and became more old-fashioned. The formative period of the French renaissance, which was to reach its full flowering in such masterpieces as Chenonceau and Azay-le-Rideau, was in the hands of the private builder.

CHAPTER V

Three Great Builders of the Renaissance.
Chaumont, Gaillon, Le Verger, Bury

THE AGE of the renaissance was the age of opportunity. Old families acquired new fortunes; new names attached themselves to old titles; ancient castles were dressed up as renaissance palaces; modern houses were built upon historic foundations. Everywhere there were signs of wealth, and where there was wealth there was building.

There were three main routes to wealth: the Church, the Army and the King's finances. Those who reached the top in these professions were the great builders of the renaissance.

In the Loire valley at the turn of the fifteenth century, three men were reaching the tops of these respective ladders: Georges de Chaumont, Cardinal d'Amboise and Archbishop of Rouen; Pierre de Rohan, Maréchal de Gié and duc de Nemours, and Florimond Robertet, baron d'Alluye and Secretary of Finance. Their three châteaux of Gaillon in Normandy, Le Verger in Anjou and Bury in Blésois, were of capital importance in the development of the French renaissance.

It is interesting to note the similarities between the pattern of French and English history at this time. Both countries began the sixteenth century with a sober, thrifty King upon the throne: Henry VII in England and Louis XII in France. To these succeeded the brilliant, extravagant figures of Henry VIII and François I who made lavish use of the treasures amassed by their more prudent predecessors. In both countries the figure of a great Cardinal Minister dominated the early part of the period: in England Wolsey and in France Georges d'Amboise. Both were Princes of the Church and both were builders; Gaillon was the Hampton Court of France. But whereas Wolsey was 'a butcher's dogge' of humble origins, Georges d'Amboise had issued from a noble house. Behind him were the important châteaux of Chaumont on the Loire and Meillant in Berri.

It was at Chaumont, in 1460, that Georges d'Amboise was born. We cannot tell what the castle was like at that date, for five years later it was slighted and dismantled. Georges' father Pierre had taken arms against the King at Monthléry. His punishment was immediate. 'We have caused to be demolished and thrown down his castle at the said place of Chaumont,' wrote Louis on May 31, 1465.

But it was not long before he was forgiven and reinstated, and when he died in 1476 he was Chamberlain to the King, Governor of Touraine, Provost of Blois and had been Ambassador to Rome; the towers of his ancestral home were already beginning to rise again from the rubble to which his monarch had reduced them.

The Castle of Chaumont, one of the most complete and beautiful of this region, occupies the corner of the high ground that dominates the Loire to the north and a steeply cut re-entrant to the west. On two sides, therefore, it was naturally protected, and on these two sides of the quadrangle the oldest buildings stood. The other two façades overlooked the plateau to the south. This was where, in medieval times, the defences were heaviest, and where, when defence was no longer looked for, the latest additions were made.

Seen from the narrow, cobbled streets of the village below it soars on high—a natural redoubt. This side was dominated by the *donjon*, a great white, windowless drum of masonry with walls nearly twelve feet thick, defended and ornamented by a *chemin de ronde* identical to those of Jean Bourré.

Seen from the plateau it was at that time closely encumbered by the villages of Place and Fradillet and by the Church of St. Nicolas from which the north-east tower takes its name. The gatehouse towers, only completed under Diane de Poitiers, show the typical blend of military forms adapted to more gracious living.

Within the court the architecture naturally assumes a more domestic aspect. Until the middle of the eighteenth century Chaumont was a complete quadrangle, but in about 1745 the whole north range containing the Grande Salle, '*fort spacieuse, qui a vue sur le côté de l'eau*', was taken down, opening up the same view to all the windows of the Court.

We can watch at Chaumont the development of a feature which played an important part in the architecture of the French Château, the Grand Staircase. Until the building of Chenonceau and Azay-le-Rideau, the medieval practice was maintained of building the staircase as a spiral around a central column. But the spiral could be housed in a projecting tower—as at Le Plessis-lès-Tours or Luynes—or it could be recessed *in antis*.

One of the finest examples of a spiral staircase *in antis* is in the Longueville wing at Châteaudun on the Loir. The cage is lit by twin embrasures on each floor. The openings are unglazed, but each is surmounted by a delicately carved canopy and framed between slender buttresses in the late flamboyant style. It can be clearly seen as the prototype of the staircase at Azay-le-Rideau.

The Grand Staircase at Chaumont, approximately contemporary with Châteaudun, is of the other sort. Its cage is housed in a boldly projecting octagonal tower. No attempt has been made to mask the oblique lines of the spiral within, and the windows, where necessary, are undisguisedly rhomboid. If this too were unglazed, it could be seen as a prototype of François I's staircase at Blois. The pilasters and wall-surfaces are richly textured with low relief carvings, giving, at a distance, a brocade-like appearance to the stone, and over the entrance door is represented the coat of arms of the most distinguished member of the family Georges, Cardinal d'Amboise.

It was not, however, on the banks of the Loire, but at his Archiepiscopal residence near Rouen, that Georges d'Amboise was to make his greatest contribution to the French renaissance.

Gaillon has been called a 'château of the Loire in Normandy'. The first phase of the building was carried out by masons from Blésois and Touraine; the second, incorporating strongly Italian influences, had an immediate impact on the architecture of the Loire valley.

The first and least known picture of the house is a fresco in the Chapel of the Castello Gaglianico, near Biella in Piedmont. This house was founded, according to an inscription over its entrance, in 1510 'by Monseigneur de Chaumont, Charles d'Amboise'. A coincidence is at once apparent: the similarity between the names (Gaillon was usually transliterated 'Gaglione' in Italian) and the foundation by the same family. The coincidence is consolidated and confirmed by the two frescoes in which the best portrayals of Gaillon still exist.

It would seem that the painter worked from a detailed drawing similar to one preserved in the Kronstedt collection in Stockholm. He is ill at ease with Gothic ornament and sometimes misrepresents his model. He acts on the understandable principle, 'when in doubt simplify', and when he simplifies he tends to italianize. But he has clearly formed a vivid mental image of the Château before he painted it, and he painted it in the round. Thanks to a worm's-eye perspective the building seems to tower over the spectator; to see it is to stand beneath the walls of Gaillon. By conflating this with the other existing drawings one can build up a picture of the east front which can be brought into precise focus.

Seen from the east, across the flat bed of the river Seine, the Château sits superbly against the wooded hills behind. 'All the roofs,' wrote Jacopo d'Atri, 'are crowned with gilded lead with escutcheons, pinnacles and other ornaments, which, from a distance, produce the most beautiful effect.'

In the centre of the whole impressive composition the Chapel —ornately flamboyant up to the knife-edge cresting of its roof— soars to its climax in a belfry and cupola severely Italian. It sounds the keynote of Gaillon; the superimposition of renaissance ornament upon a structure that remained impregnably French.

To the left, and preserving a medieval independence from the main block are the Kitchens. Their tall, mullioned windows and dignified proportions show that the Kitchens were regarded as an important element in the design—not as menial offices to be tucked away as far as possible out of sight. The dormer windows above emphasize the independence of the kitchen staff from the rest of the household, for here, in close proximity to the scene of their employment, the kitchen servants slept.

Behind and above the Kitchens ride the lofty roof and pencil-pointed turrets of the Great Gatehouse. It betrays, from this angle, no hint of the decorative treatment for which it was to become famous.

To the right of the Chapel, the State Apartments, set back behind a long arcaded terrace, connect the northern transept with the Archbishop's lodging. This was situated in a single tower, the Tour de la Syrène, so called from the brazen figure surmounting its weather-vane. It seems as if, on the very threshold of the renaissance, the art of medieval France has made, in the fantastic superstructure of this tower, a last determined effort. Only the central *donjon* at Lusignan could rival the complexity of its progressive diminutions.

Within the rotund apartments of this tower the Cardinal d'Amboise had fixed his habitation. From its tall windows, or from the terrace walk beyond, he could enjoy the panorama across the wide meanders of the Seine as it made its leisurely way towards the chalk cliffs of Les Andelys and the white ramparts of Château Gaillard.

The Tour de la Syrène, the State Apartments, the Chapel, the Kitchens and the Gatehouse, each clearly articulated in the silhouette, gave to Gaillon the dramatic outline of a medieval château.

But the visitor who approached by the southern Gatehouse and penetrated into the Cour d'Honneur would have been struck by the novelty of the decorations; the two archways through which he had to pass were of an architecture patently borrowed from Italy. Here cornices, pilasters and panels, all richly carved in curling arabesques, encased the flattened arch or framed the mullioned windows.

This gatehouse has been the chief object of antiquarian enthusiasm for Gaillon. In the eighteenth century it was regarded as its only blemish. 'The château could pass as the most beautiful house in France,' wrote Piganiol de la Force, 'if they had only made an entrance worthy of it. You have to go almost right round it to get in—by a small and extremely ugly gateway.' But whatever may be thought of its aesthetic merits, the gateway to Gaillon was the first important renaissance ensemble in France. The medieval outlines were given to it by the first team of builders from the Loire valley. Much of the antique work was done by local masons working from Italian models. The more spectacular features came straight from Italy.

In February of 1508 a complete fountain arrived at Honfleur. It left a trail of expenses in its wake; roads had to be specially repaired, a bridge had to be specially built and the owners of fields specially compensated for the damage to crops caused by the passage of so bulky a parcel. It took two months to piece it together, and the achievement was marked by a special ration of wine to the workmen. It is difficult to say how far the fountain was prefabricated; the accounts show that a considerable amount of the sculpture was done *in situ* after it had been erected.

In 1510 Georges d'Amboise died and his nephew Charles, happily succeeding him in the Archbishopric of Rouen, took over Gaillon as well as his uncle's furniture. In 1517 François I brought his Court here, and to the Court came the Cardinal of Aragon and his secretary Beatis.

There was no room at the Château. The Cardinal and a few of his personal servants managed to get lodgings in the village; Beatis and the rest were boarded out at Tosny.

Georges d'Amboise had now been dead for seven years. He had spent a fortune on the Château and died, Beatis was told, regretting it. 'The money that I spent on Gaillon,' he confessed; 'would to God I had distributed it among the poor!' Beatis, however, was more disposed to praise the accomplishment than to censure the extravagance. 'This palace,' he wrote in his memoirs, 'which is superb, and by reason of its sculptured stones, its ornaments of brass and the style of its roof more beautiful than any I have ever seen, delights the eye both by its interior disposition and by its external elegance.'

A month later Beatis and the Cardinal were in Anjou and took the opportunity to visit Le Verger, which had been built by the great rival of Georges d'Amboise, the Maréchal de Gié.

Born in 1451, Pierre de Rohan was the younger son of one of the greatest families of Brittany. At the age of fifteen he entered the service of Louis XI, who soon recognized his ability and his ambition. '*Grand avaricieux, qui aimait l'argent*', his services were always at a price; but he gave good value for money and Louis XI was not one to grudge a sound deal. '*Il faut le remplir*,' was his caustic comment. '*Bon Français et mauvais*

Breton', Gié's one political objective was the union of Brittany with France—a union which was only finally achieved with the marriage of Louis XII and Anne de Bretagne in 1498. Shortly after their wedding, the royal couple spent three days at Le Verger.

'Although this château did not cost so much as Gaillon,' Beatis observed, 'it is far better planned and the lodgings much more commodious. It has not such a fine view, since it is in the middle of a plain, whereas Gaillon is on a hill. Its park is very fine and enclosed by a high wall.'

Situated in one of the most beautiful corners of Anjou that is almost encircled by a wide meander of the Loir, Le Verger has nothing to protect it but the prodigious excavations of its own moat. Although it was not built for military purposes, most of the components of the fortress were conscripted to make up what must have been one of the most dramatically impressive houses that France has ever seen. It is the more tragic that so much of it should have been demolished.

It was built as the expression of dynastic pride: dynastic pride determined its destruction. In 1770, no longer able to maintain a palace which they no longer used, the family of Rohan-Guémené sold Le Verger to a certain Héard de Boissimon. This man, when being shown the Chapel, was heard to remark that his bones would lie with those of the Rohans. The remark was reported and the report reached the ears of the Cardinal de Rohan at Versailles. He determined that no such profanation of his family vaults should take place, invoked the *droit de retrait lignager*, and by compulsory purchase bought back the Château and pulled it down.

Only the stables, the two towers of the base court and a ruined gateway survive, but thanks to a detailed engraving by Boisseau the whole magnificent lay-out of Le Verger can be imagined in detail. In order that it may be visualized also in proportion it is necessary to visit the site and to gain at first hand an impression of the immense area covered by these buildings. It need only be added that the material of the main block was *régeasse*—a beautiful white stone 'as hard and finely grained as alabaster'—and the historical imagination is fully equipped for the reconstruction of Le Verger.

Four mighty towers, closely resembling those of Pierre de Brézé at Brissac, marked the outward corners of the Cour d'Honneur; four square pavilions, each of which may well have contained a staircase, stood at the inward corners of the court. On three sides of this quadrangle were tall façades crowned with tall roofs and elaborate dormers; the fourth side, towards the east, was closed by a low building of one storey only which supported a level terrace walk between two handsome balustrades. The apartments which surrounded this court had been furnished with the greatest profusion, Gié having obtained the magnificent tapestries belonging to the King of Sicily.

South of the Cour d'Honneur, and separated from it by a further moat, the buildings of the base court were kept low so as not to take the light from the main façade and not to obscure the outlook from its windows.

The entrance front, which thus respected the base court, is one of the finest and most interesting architectural achievements of its age. The façade bears no resemblance to those of Jean Bourré and can only be compared with Colin Biart's work for Louis XII at Blois. Biart is known also to have worked at Le Verger, which was probably completed before he began his constructions at Blois. It is the normal habit with the French to place the 'front door' in one corner of the court and to accord it a relatively unimportant place in the decor. Gié has placed his entrance boldly in the middle of a remarkably symmetrical façade and loaded it with ornament.

Above the door is an equestrian statue of himself, standing in full relief before a backcloth of swagged curtains richly painted in red and white and gold. It is as if the side flaps of one of the gorgeous tents used at the Field of the Cloth of Gold had been looped apart by attendant cherubs, and the Maréchal had pranced out on to his plinth. The horse, with neck arched, mouth lathering and nostrils wide, and the rider '*l'air jeune, la figure pleine et souriante, la tenue droite*', combined to present the very image of military prowess. The whole feeling of the group is neither Gothic nor renaissance, but already baroque.

Gié had an appreciative eye for statuary, and had once particularly admired the David of Donatello in the courtyard of the

Old Palace at Florence. In August of 1502 the Florentine Senate duly took the hint and commissioned from Michelangelo a bronze statue of David which was to be presented to the Maré-chal, and would naturally have had a place of honour in the courts or gardens of Le Verger.

The figure was not ready to be dispatched until November of 1508, by which time there was no longer any advantage to the Florentine Senate in obliging Gié. He was in disgrace.

In 1505, when Louis XII lay dangerously ill at Blois, Anne de Bretagne had tried to convey her most valuable personal belongings by barge to Nantes. Gié interpreted this as a bid to re-establish the independence of Brittany and had the barges intercepted, near Saumur. On the unexpected recovery of the King, Gié was dismissed from the Court. He retired to Le Verger saying that 'the rain had come just at the right time for him to take shelter beneath the beautiful mansion which he had just completed'. The Florentine Senate prudently diverted the statue of David to Florimond Robertet.

In this they showed considerable perception, for two years later Robertet became the leading man in France. *'Depuis que M. le Légat d'Amboise mourut,'* wrote Robert de la Marck, *'c'était l'homme le plus approché de son maître.'* La Marck is super-lative in his praise; he describes him as being 'without any fault, the most intelligent man I think I have ever seen, and the wit-tiest, who has been concerned with the affairs of France, and has born the full weight of them, and been fortunate enough to have acquitted himself marvellously well.'

It was high praise. Robertet was representative of the *noblesse de robe*; in contrast to the coarse brutality of men like Mont-morency, he stood out by virtue of a sensitive and cultivated mind—a man of grave good looks and dignified deportment. He was either the most astute or the most honest of the King's financiers. His motto *'Fors Ungne'* (Except for One) claimed an integrity peculiar to himself, and when he died in 1527, it was neither in disgrace nor on the scaffold. His *oraison funèbre* was preached by the Bishop of Grenoble before François and the Court. The Bishop gives the briefest thumbnail sketch: 'his face was well proportioned but extremely pale, which is the complexion of all great men. His carriage was erect, his way of walking solemn; his hands were the finest you could ever see.'

It was not only Robertet who was eulogized in the oration; the age of the renaissance attracted the Bishop's most rhetorical enthusiasm. '*Que de belles architectures! Que de belles sculptures! Que de belles peintures! Que de ravissantes musiques!*'

Robertet had reached the top of the ladder at the very moment when France was beginning to blossom into a new and glorious artistic epoch. At Le Verger and Gaillon the great families of Rohan and Amboise had already expressed the splendour of their dynasties in stone; in Poitou that of Bourbon-Montpensier had embarked upon the almost unrecorded magnificence that was Champigny. Robertet himself had built, during the first years of the new century, the Hôtel d'Alluye, a building far in advance, in terms of Italianism, of Louis XII's wing at Blois. In 1511, at the full height of his power and wealth, he started on the building of a château at Bury, in which the militant dispositions of Le Verger were combined with some of the classical decoration of Gaillon and Champigny, and a fitting home was provided for the David of Michelangelo.

Some six miles west of Blois, and situated on the steeply wooded slopes of the valley of the Cisse, Bury commanded the old drovers' road along which the cattle passed en route for Paris. It was sited, like Chaumont, on the crest of the high ground. 'From one side,' wrote Elie Brackenhoffer, 'this Château is on a level plain, but on the other side there is a precipitous descent.'

From across the valley, where the straight ride emerges from the forêt de Blois and begins to dip down towards the drovers' road, the first, exciting view of Bury was obtained—a glimpse of white towers and blue roofs rising from the luxuriant foliage of the hanging woods. At the other end of the year, when winter had imbrowned the slopes, the whole of Bury would have been discerned, gleaming between the naked branches.

To the front a high abutted terrace lay between two squat cylindrical towers; perched mid-way between the towers a delicate Chapel—a simpler version of the St. Blaise at Amboise —presented its apse correctly to the east. To the right, a further terrace ended in a further tower, whose lack of chimney-stack and windows identified it as the pigeon house. Above and behind these outposts of architecture the Château proper raised its ordered, elegant façade—a regular rhythm of double and single lighted windows, framed between pilasters and strongly underlined by deep string courses. In the centre of the façade the roof line was broken by a square pavilion, ornate with salamanders, fleurs de lys and Royal cyphers, surmounted by a pyramid of roof. To either side two massive corner towers, whose ample girth suggested those of Chaumont, added both strength and beauty to the scene.

Such was the first and distant prospect from the east. There was still a considerable detour to be made before arrival, for the approach to Bury was from the north-west where the gradients are easier. The drive led down an oak avenue, and, turning abruptly right, brought the visitor along the west front of the house. The façade was blankly uninviting. Across the moat was a blind wall, in the centre of which a gatehouse, turreted and slotted for a drawbridge, seemed to refuse rather than to facilitate admittance.

At either end of this forbidding front were lofty towers, ringed round with cornices and lit by ample windows, but otherwise both military and medieval in their form. The moat, the gatehouse and the towers made the first impression of Bury distinctly feudal.

It was almost a deliberate deception, for once within the precincts of the court the visitor found that he was in a palace and not a fortress. Indeed the curtain wall, the very feature that most resembled a *château fort* upon the outer side, presented towards the quadrangle that most unmilitary element of Italian architecture, a colonnade. Here Robertet contrived a gallery of Roman Emperors, whose marble busts were highly esteemed 'partly', as Brackenhoffer informs us, 'for their artistic merit, and partly for their antiquity'.

In this courtyard, perhaps the most complete and perfect renaissance structure at the time, the David of Michelangelo was finally erected. Its glory was short-lived. In the seventeenth century Bury passed to the family of Rostaign who deserted it for their other château at Onzain. The statue of David disappeared without a trace. By 1872 only a single tower and some crumbling walls remained of Florimond Robertet's masterpiece.

CHAPTER VI

Blois

ABOVE THE city of Blois, and somewhat to the north of west, there rises a little knoll on which there used to stand a solitary tree. The knoll was called the Butte des Capucins; the tree—l'Arbre de Gaston. Here, on September 27, 1785, came the Englishwoman Mrs. Cradock. 'We were rewarded for our labours,' she wrote, 'by a magnificent sight; the view extends so far that one can even distinguish the Château de Chambord.' It was the time of the grape harvest, and the countrymen were in merry mood; *'l'air résonnait de leur chant joyeux'*.

Below them lay the town, its houses closely following the natural contours of the ground—now climbing with its arduous ascents, now cascading with its steeply cut ravines, their terraced lines converging on the point at which the saddle-backed bridge begins its long trajectory across the Loire. To either side of the bridge the great river lay like a polished pewter snake, its lazy curves contrasting with the rigid rectilinear lines of the poplar plantations. 'I could not tire in my admiration of these surrounding landscapes,' she concluded; 'I will not easily forget the scene that spread beneath my gaze.'

In the foreground of this extensive panorama, the Château de Blois, at once a palace and a citadel, presented towards the Butte des Capucins the serene façade of Gaston d'Orléans' wing. A closer inspection revealed the glory and the shame of this historic edifice. 'The staircase is a real masterpiece,' wrote Mrs. Cradock; 'it would be impossible to find any construction at once so elegant in its broad lines and so delicate in every detail.' It was testimony to the excellence of its construction that it was standing at all. 'The walls are all cracked,' she noted, 'but the rest could still defy many centuries, unless it is deliberately destroyed.'

Deliberate destruction was nearer than Mrs. Cradock imagined, for three years later Louis XVI decreed the total demolition of the Château. It was by this time in a pitiable condition. The last Royal occupant, Marie-Casimir Sobieski, a hundred years earlier, had been unable even to glaze the windows, the wooden casements being too rotten. Even in 1641, in the days of Gaston d'Orléans, Elie Brackenhoffer had found the Château shabby and untidy; 'everything', he wrote, 'is abandoned to the forces of nature and invaded by vegetation.' It was his general experience of the French that they were 'prompt and quick to undertake a building, which is then finished slowly if at all'. To this rule Blois was no exception. The Château, 'neither finished nor kept up', was tending irretrievably to ruin.

There are in fact two conditions which represent the opposite poles of danger to a great house; one is to be a favourite seat and the other is to be thought redundant. For a house which is a favourite seat will be continually altered, each generation adapting it to its own needs and each adorning it according to its own fashion; each therefore destroys something, and the loss to posterity is often as great as with a house that is neglected and left to perish.

Blois has been exposed to both these dangers. Charles d'Orléans, Louis XII, François I, Gaston d'Orléans—each loved and each destroyed. They left it a symposium of styles for which posterity had no use. For 150 years it was denied even the most necessary repairs. No château has endured so long a degradation; none came more near to demolition, and none has undergone more copious restoring. It is this that gives its special interest to Blois; if not the most attractive, it is, to the student of architecture, the most instructive of the châteaux of the Loire. Indeed if more remained of the feudal fortress, Blois could claim to present the history of architecture in stone. But the Tour du Foix, in its present form, is a feeble relic for a *château fort*; by contrast, three sides of the courtyard reflect in their perfection three successive styles of French domestic architecture.

There are the homely brick buildings of Louis XII, with pillars and architraves of stone that are rendered dignified but not ornate by finely chiselled ornament. There is the great

white façade of François I with its appliqué Italian decorations
and its open spiral staircase—an audacious, elegant addition.
Finally there is the classic block designed by François Mansart
for Gaston d'Orléans—a gracious, intellectual accomplishment
that reserves its appeal for the connoisseur.

'These three parts,' wrote La Fontaine, 'are, thank God,
without any symmetry, having neither connection nor con-
formity one with another. That which was built by François I,
seen from without, pleased me the best; there is a great number
of little galleries, little windows, little balconies and little ornaments, without regularity and without order; that makes up
something great, which is pleasing enough.'

Blondel, more representative in his opinion than La Fontaine,
was less enthusiastic. Except for Mansart's buildings, the
architecture of Blois had for him 'no real interest apart from its
antiquity'.

Antiquity, however, has an interest entirely its own.
Nathaniel Wraxall must have the credit of being one of the
few eighteenth-century figures to appreciate Blois. Wraxall
was a historian and a romantic; he confessed that he was unable
'to behold the spot where any great achievement has been performed in ages past without the liveliest enthusiasm'. In this
respect Blois had more to offer than any other château of the
Loire. 'I tread with reverence,' he wrote, 'over the ground
render'd in some degree sacred, and view with a solemn delight
the towers once inhabited by Queens and Monarchs, now tending to decay or covered with ivy, which spreads a twilight
through the apartments at noonday. An air of melancholy and
departed greatness is strongly diffused through the whole place,
and increased by the silence which reigns universally.'

Wraxall was well equipped for such experiences; he had in
him the makings of an antiquary—a superstructure of imagination upon a base of scientific knowledge. To both these qualities
the ruined Palace made direct appeal; its history evoked his
erudition, its mournful state inspired his fantasy, and as he
wandered through its empty silences, his receptive mind could
resurrect its pristine form and reconstruct historical events. The
history and the architecture of Blois must not be set asunder.

The succession of Louis XII had transformed Blois from a ducal mansion to a Royal Palace, but as early as 1443 Charles d'Orléans had started the conversion of the feudal Château into a *maison de plaisance* in the simple style later developed at Le Plessis-lès-Tours.

Louis's first act had been to woo the Queen Dowager, Anne de Bretagne. The death of Charles had been a great shock to her; '*ce fut chose impossible à dire et croire,*' wrote d'Argentré, '*combien cette bonne Princesse prit de déplaisir de la mort du Roi.*' It was customary for Royal widows to wear white for mourning; Anne wore black. For two days she would neither eat nor sleep. She was still in this pitiful condition when Louis's little Embassy arrived at Amboise. They found her 'in a corner of the room, lying on the ground, crying incessantly'. Guillaume Briçonnet, who should have been the spokesman, was so overcome with emotion that he could 'scarce say three words, and was obliged to keep silence incontinently'. Jean de la Marck, Bishop of Condom, retained sufficient self-command to persuade the Royal widow to eat.

Whether it was the loss of her husband or the loss of her crown which so distressed Anne is difficult to say; whether it was her person or her Duchy of Britanny which attracted Louis is an equally delicate question. What is certain is that he lost no time in repudiating his first wife, Jeanne de France, and making Anne of Brittany a second time the Queen.

The focus of architectural activity now shifted from Amboise to Blois. Once more it was a question of converting a stronghold into a Palace, but instead of a young Renaissance Prince commanding its construction, there was the staid and sober figure of Louis d'Orléans, '*le Père du Peuple*'.

'The King is of a tall and slender build,' wrote Domenico di Trevisan, Ambassador from Venice; 'abstemious in his diet, he eats little but boiled beef, and is by nature avaricious and reserved.' His buildings were in keeping with his character, and the same simplicity of taste was revealed in his additions to Blois.

For in the first year of his reign he took down the medieval gatehouse and the '*ostel de la porte du Donjon*' and replaced them with his own urbane and undefensible façades. While deliberately harmonizing with the buildings of Charles d'Orléans, Louis XII's wing has a dignity and an originality entirely its own. The two balconied windows that overlook the forecourt, each deeply recessed behind a lace-like canopy of stone, are disposed without regard to symmetry. All the richness is concentrated upon the entrance archway, above which the statue of the King on horseback is housed in Gothic glory; but among the cusps and pinnacles can already be detected an extremely clumsy attempt at Italian arabesque.

Apart from this the effect is built upon the careful equipoise between plain surfaces and finely carved enrichment—fine, that is to say, in execution. The subject matter of some of the *culs de lampe* is obscene and contrasts strangely with the dignified good taste which emanates from the façade as a whole. 'Some of the figures which support the windows,' observed Wraxall, 'are of a nature so very indecent, that in the state of refinement to which modern manners have attained, it excites our surprise how a prince so virtuous as Louis XII, and a Queen so rigid and so reserved in her manner as was Anne de Bretagne, could ever have permitted them to be placed in the most conspicuous part of a Royal Palace. It is a striking proof of the gross and unpolished manners of the sixteenth century.'

By December of 1501 the new building was nearing its completion, for the staircase in the square tower to the north of the colonnade was in use for the ceremonial reception of the Archduke Philip of Austria, the father of Charles V. Darkness had already fallen when his cavalcade began to mount the gentle slope that led from the ravine of the river Arrou to the Porte des Champs—then, as now, the normal access to the Château. The forecourt was illuminated by the flaming torches of a great concourse of people; faces and façades appeared in the unnatural, inverted relief of figures before the footlights.

Arriving at the new entrance arch, Philip was conducted 'from the said gateway to the Great Staircase . . . and from the said staircase to the Great Hall'.

The Great Staircase was one of the finest achievements of Louis' builders. Its decorative scheme forms a mounting crescendo reaching its climax at the topmost landing, where the central newel, encircled by a vast stone coronet, splays out into the deeply ribbed vaulting of the roof. Once again there is the contrast between exalted architecture and crude embellishment. In a conspicuous place, where there is really no need for any sculpture, there is a careful carving of a rather small woman spanking the bare bottom of a rather large boy.

The mixture of coarseness and refinement in the architecture was reflected in the curious compound of luxury and austerity about the Court. The Archduke and his wife were received with the greatest magnificence in the Grande Salle, after which they were served with supper in their own apartments. A whole procession of officers and ladies of the Court brought the Arch-duchess her meal. First came a troop of pages, dressed in yellow damask and crimson velvet, holding the candelabra for the illumination of the rooms; next came a number of noble ladies most of them duchesses, each bearing a golden casket, filled with the napkins, knives and velvet-handled forks for use at table; after these came half a dozen Gentlemen, also laden with golden vessels in which were brought the choicest sweetmeats and preserves. Meanwhile another procession, headed by the Gouverneur du Château, had brought, in a green velvet chest, the minor appointments of the bedroom—mirrors set in frames of silver gilt, sponges, boxes of combs, brushes with velvet handles, and all the linen needed for a lady's toilette.

But Louis did not join in this sumptuous affair. It was a Fast day, and he remained in his own rooms, contenting himself with bread and water.

Louis XII and his Queen occupied the first floor of the new wing at Blois. Later in the reign, Anne de Bretagne moved her rooms to the return of this wing towards the Chapelle St. Calais. From here, her windows overlooked the Loire, whose cities held so many memories for her; her thoughts could go with the stream—down the valley to Amboise; Amboise, where she had first begun her first triumphant reign; Amboise, where her first Dauphin Charles Orlando, young and hopeful Prince, had died; Amboise, where her first husband had cracked his head against the fatal beam . . . downstream to Tours where Charles Orlando and his brother slept prematurely beneath their lovely tomb in the Church of St. Martin; downstream to Langeais, where she and Charles VIII were married, uniting Brittany to France; downstream again to Nantes, and so to Brittany itself.

Brittany was always in her thoughts. Only her daughter Claude survived to carry on the ducal line. On the visit of Archduke Philip she had sought to ally Brittany with the Empire by betrothing Claude to the future Charles V, and in 1505, when Louis lay dangerously ill at Blois, she had tried to convey her jewels and her most costly furnishings and tapestries by barge to Nantes, away from France. But the alliance between Brittany and the Empire was broken and Claude was married to François of Angoulême, heir apparent to the throne. Brittany would now inevitably be swallowed up by France.

On the other side her windows looked down into the courtyard of the Château. Across the court, to the south, were the beautiful buildings of Charles d'Orléans, with their shady loggia opening on to a high terrace. Here, too, was Brittany—for here her personal bodyguard stood massed, waiting to attend upon her, and she could look out on them and exclaim with pride *'voilà mes Bretons!'* For over a century, until Mansart destroyed the whole south range of the Château, this terrace bore the name of *'perche aux Bretons'*.

Louis XII, her husband, was one of the most popular kings to sit upon the throne of France. 'When he rode abroad', wrote Claude Seyssel, 'people came several days' journey to see him, strewing his way with flowers and foliage, and trying to touch even his horse with their handkerchiefs, to treasure afterwards as precious relics.'

Some of the credit for Louis's mild and popular regime must go to his first Minister, Cardinal Georges d'Amboise. On October 25, 1508 the King and Queen paid a visit to him at Gaillon. It was the very year in which the second phase of the construction of this château was begun—the italianization of a hitherto flamboyant building. The master mason Colin Biart, too, was at Gaillon in that year, and between 1508 and 1510 he is known also to have been employed at Blois.

It is tempting on these grounds to link the Royal visit to

Gaillon with the last, and least known, of Louis's additions to
Blois, a building which adjoined the *perche aux Bretons* to the
east, and which is clearly shown in one of the drawings of du
Cerceau. It shows a simple block with three flights of windows,
each framed between flat pilasters. It differs only from François
I's wing in the absence of string courses and in the sobriety of
decoration, especially in the dormers.

On January 1, 1515, François d'Angoulême became the King.
One of the first payments recorded in his accounts was of 800
livres for buildings 'just completed' at Blois—in all probability
a reference to this new renaissance block at the south-east
corner of the Château.

By June of the same year François had embarked upon his own
first building venture, the remodelling of the last remaining
wing of the old feudal fortress. It shows a tentative, groping
method of construction, each phase in the building suggesting
the next, and the conception of the whole only emerging in the
author's mind as the work progresses to its completion. It was
a process not uncommon when the author was a gifted amateur.

Such, for instance, was the method of Charles Cavendish,
first Duke of Devonshire. Mr. Francis Thompson has shown
how Chatsworth was developed on precisely these lines. But
Chatsworth is well documented and Blois is not. If the Château
presents to the spectator the 'history of architecture in stone',
it is from an inspection of the stones themselves that its history
must largely be inferred.

It is surprising how much information a detailed inspection
yields. The visitor should look first at the whole façade which
fronts the court. It does not need a very observant eye to detect
that the right half differs slightly from the left, or western,
half. The tall windows have double, as opposed to single, transoms and there is a greater wealth of decorative carving.

It is tempting, once again, to link the richer treatment of the
northern section with a Royal visit to Gaillon, for François also
inspected this important building in 1517, some two years after
he had embarked upon his reconstructions.

There is enough of the medieval walling left to show that in
the left or western half François retained the original floor

levels and that the eastern half was accommodated to this. The eastern half is therefore the later. But the spiral staircase is clearly an afterthought; it is cut into the façade with little or no regard for the existing framework of pilasters and entablature.

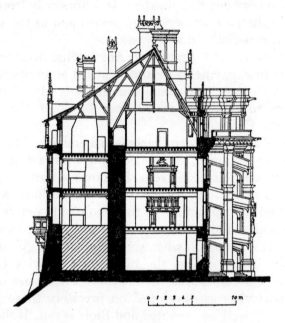

BLOIS: Section of Francis I's wing, showing the later additions to the north (left) of the original outer wall. Drawing by Dr. F. Lesueur.

An ascent into the attics would provide more striking evidence, for here, among the rafters of the roof, the medieval skeleton within the renaissance palace is even more apparent. Above the rooms on the courtyard side is a normal high-pitched tent of timber, looking in section like a capital A. It is clear that this was originally hung with slates on both sides; there are vestiges of dormers on the northern side, towards the town. But this northern half of the capital A is now enclosed beneath an enormous penthouse, by which the roof was later extended to cover and enclose a new range of rooms to the north.

This is a clear indication that the whole range of rooms towards the town formed no part of the original design. The fact that it was added as an afterthought explains the survival of the old outer wall of the feudal fortress, which now became the partition between the north and south ranges of apartments. This sturdy spine—what Balzac called the 'dorsal column' of the Château—shows clearly on the plan. So also does another feature. In the centre of the new, or western range, beneath the Cabinet Neuf of the King's Apartment, is a small, round room, whose openings reveal the same immensely thick walls of the old *courtine*. Here, engulfed in François' additions, is one of the three towers by means of which the former fortress had covered the approaches from the town. There was a hint of Josselin about the old Blois.

In the course of nineteenth-century restorations, parts of the outer surface of this wall were uncovered, and revealed a decoration of pilasters similar to that upon the south front—further proof, if further proof were wanting, that François' original intention was for no more than a single range confined to the foundation of the medieval building.

The Façade des Loges, or north front, which overlooks the town, can also be seen to be the result of two successive phases of construction. The four-centred arches to the right give place to the later, segmental arches to the left.

If the face towards the court was inspired by Gaillon, the Façade des Loges seems to derive direct from the Vatican of Bramante. In 1515, during the campaign of Marignan, François I had had an interview with Pope Leo X at Bologna. They had a common interest in architecture, and it is not improbable that they discussed their building ventures. What is certain is that the ideas of Bramante were most imperfectly understood. The *loges* are in fact only deeply recessed window bays—a translation into classical terms of Louis XII's deep embrasures on the north front. The builders, who were beginning to master Italian decorative themes, were ill at ease with classical construction. Behind the colonnades that screen the ancient Tour de Château-renault, the galleries are roofed with Gothic vaulting.

From the Vatican also comes the last addition to the Façade des Loges, when the dormer windows were replaced by a low gallery. This provided a feature which particularly impressed Elie Brackenhoffer in 1643. 'Beneath the roof of the new wing,'

he wrote, 'are beautiful galleries and walks, provided throughout its length with a balustrade of twisted columns. From here
one commands an interesting view of the town and the country
round about.'

On July 20, 1524, Queen Claude died and the work on Blois
finished abruptly. The *pierres d'attente* on the end of the façade
nearest the Salle des Etats show that François had further intentions for Blois, but there is no record how extensive they
were, nor were the works ever again resumed.

Another Royal Prince, Gaston d'Orléans, was to destroy, a
century later, the remaining fifteenth-century wing of Blois and
make his own additions to the whole. These also remained
unfinished, and, we may add, happily, for had the whole of
Mansart's project been realized, France would have lost one of
her most interesting historic monuments.

She would also have gained one of the most imaginative
works of one of her greatest architects. For the projects of
Mansart for Blois were dramatic in their sculptural forms and
ingenious in the interior arrangements.

Imagine the Luxembourg lifted out of the flat parterres of a
Parisian garden and set upon the rocky outcrop of this once
feudal foundation. From the west the effect may be judged today, for the greater part of this range was built, if not completed.
From the east, in place of Louis XII's demure façade, the new
entrance front must be imagined, rising at the top of a long and
fairly steep ascent; two high pavilions break forward at either
end of this façade, casting ever deeper shadows, as the sun
moves round to the meridian, across the simple architecture of
the connecting wing. From the obscurity of this recessed façade,
the great gatehouse thrust forward to present a frontispiece
almost as elaborate as a baroque Church, its dome and cupola
magnificently framed between two monumental chimney-
stacks.

A triple arch gave access beneath the cavernous rotunda of
this dome, and thence to the Cour d'Honneur. Gone were the
Chapelle St. Calais on the left and the Aile François I on the
right, and in their place ran two symmetrical wings adorned
with niches and coupled columns. At the far end of this classical

perspective the main block stood back behind a balustrade which accentuated a slight but deliberate rise in ground level. As at Versailles, the Prince's Apartment was only to be approached on foot.

The doorway in the centre of this façade opened on to the first floor of the Great Staircase, which, turning left, gave access to a landing which marked the centre of the opposite façade and overlooked the gardens. For the west front, having more space for its development, could be longer than that of the courtyard, and Mansart cleverly disguised the difference of axis by his use of the staircase.

Mansart was one of the subtlest of the French architects of this age, making skilful and even ingenious use of the difference of proportion between the classical orders, and often grouping his masses in a bold and original composition. And yet it cannot be said that his buildings at Blois are entirely satisfying aesthetically. Blondel, a century later, found fault with his roofs as being too heavy. 'The height of a roof,' he stipulated, 'should never exceed a third of the façade.' The height of Mansart's roof at Blois is nearly half that of the façades and contributes neither to use nor beauty. A tall roof only makes sense when it is used to contain an attic storey. If it contains an attic storey it must be lit by dormer windows, and the dormer windows will in turn alleviate the heavy mass of roof. Whoever was the architect to Boughton in Northamptonshire understood perfectly the aesthetics of the Mansart roof.

In 1638 the work at Blois ended abruptly, nor was it ever taken up again. A hundred years later the courtyard was still encumbered with the columns—each of a single shaft of stone— for the decoration of the façade and with the cut masonry for the completion of the building. It was not that Gaston lost interest in Blois, for he continued to live there; it is not that he lacked the means to finish at least the building which he had begun. In 1652 he undertook considerable redecorations in the Chapelle St. Calais. On February 2, 1660 he died in the old Royal Apartments in François I's wing.

Perhaps the reason for the abandoning of Mansart's Grand Design is to be sought in the coincidence of the date with that

of the birth of Louis XIV. Until then Gaston had been heir pre-
sumptive to the throne of France, and the sex life of his brother
would have encouraged him to hope that he would remain such.
Now Gaston could no longer look forward to being King of
France. Apart from one fleeting visit by Louis XIV, Blois was
never again to serve as a Royal Palace.

CHAPTER VII

The Court of France

I T was in 1508 that Count Baldassare Castiglione wrote
his first draft of the *Book of the Courtier*; the book is a discussion on the qualities and virtues to be expected of a
gentleman of the Court; the discussion is set in the context of
the elite group that gathered nightly round the person of the
Duchess of Urbino.

One evening the Count of Canossa, leaving such topics as
white teeth and well turned ankles, advanced the theory that
'the true and principal ornament of the mind in every man are
letters', adding immediately that 'French men know only nobleness of arms . . . and all learned men they do count very ras-
cals'. To this the Lord Magnifico agreed, but with the qualifica-
tion that 'if Monseigneur of Angoulême have so good luck that
he may (as men hope) succeed to the Crown', then letters will
be as much esteemed as arms—'for it is not long since I was in
France and saw this Prince in the Court there, who seemed to
me, beside the handsomeness of his person and beauty of visage
to have in his countenance so great a majesty, accompanied
nevertheless with a certain lovely courtesy, that the realm of
France should ever seem to him a small matter'. The realm of
learning was also at his feet; 'it was told me that he highly
loved and esteemed letters, and had in very great reputation all
learned men, and blamed the Frenchmen themselves that their
minds were so far from this profession'.

In 1515 'Monseigneur of Angoulême' succeeded to the throne
of St. Louis with the title of François Premier, and the predic-
tions of Castiglione were proved to be true. He had not been
unfair in his censure of the French; their philistine attitude is
admitted by Brantôme in his sketch of l'Escun. 'The gentlemen
of those days,' he observed, 'had the greatest abhorrence of
letters;' like the Goths who burnt the books in Athens, they
feared that literacy might beget effeminacy.

It was the special achievement of the renaissance to show that this was not so; that a man could be a scholar and a connoisseur and at the same time a lusty soldier, a mighty hunter and an impressive squire of dames. François I was well fitted to this role; he was well fitted to capture the imagination of his age and to personify its spirit. 'When this Prince came to the throne in the flower of his youth,' wrote Mézéray, 'with the carriage and stature of a hero, with a wonderful skill in all noble exercises of Knighthood—brave, liberal, magnificent; of good manners, good breeding and pleasant conversation—he commanded the adoration of the people and the affection of the aristocracy.'

Brantôme remembered him as a great lover of scholars and of scholarship, adding that 'the King's table was a real school, for all subjects were discussed at it'. The King himself was admirably equipped for such discussion; 'he is a man,' wrote Marino Cavalli, 'of the most solid judgment and of the widest erudition; there is nothing, no branch of learning or of art, on which he cannot discourse most pertinently.' The influence of such a King could not fail to be pervasive, but naturally it took its time to spread.

In 1520 the great scholar Guillaume Budé complained, in a letter to Lascaris, that to be at Court was 'to waste one's time with ignoramusses'. But if Budé did not appreciate the Court, the Court at least appreciated him. His five days there were probably well wasted, for they bore fruit in the foundation of the Collège de France.

Besides the scholars of the age, the great masters of the visual arts received the understanding patronage of the King. One of François's earliest moves was to establish Leonardo da Vinci at Amboise. Some ten years later Benvenuto Cellini was provided with a workshop—contrary to the wishes of the Royal mistress, the duchesse d'Estampes—in the Tour de Nesle adjoining the Louvre. Patron and artist were the necessary complement to one another. 'My friend,' said François to Benvenuto; 'I do not know which of the two pleasures is the greater; that of the Prince who has found a man after his own heart, or that of the artist who has found a Prince who provides him with every facility with which to realize his brilliant inspirations.'

There are, of course, artists who manage very well without a patron: it is hardly possible to imagine an architect without one, and it was as a patron of architecture that François was to play his most distinctive role. In the Loire Valley, at Amboise, Blois and Chambord; in the Ile de France at St. Germains, La Muette, Challuau and Madrid and later at Fontainebleau and Villers Cotterets the King was the promoter, if not the designer, of palaces which hold a position of capital importance in the development of French classical architecture. His example was immediately followed by the aristocracy. A whole galaxy of private châteaux were built, or at least begun, in the course of his reign. Bury and Bonnivet, Champigny and Chenonceau, Oiron, Sarcus and Azay-le-Rideau; Villandry and Valençay, Nantouillet and Fontaine-Henri, Assier, Ecouen and Chantilly were among the most outstanding. 'Thus it is,' wrote Jerome Lippomano, 'that over the whole face of the Kingdom there are buildings which are of a wonderful beauty.'

The interest taken in the art of the architect, the silversmith, the painter and musician, and in the writings of scholars and poets, gave a new, significant dimension to the Court. A country engrossed in war knows only 'nobleness of arms' and is by nature androcentric. The arts of peace confer equality upon the other sex.

'A Court without women is like a garden without flowers.' The words are from Brantôme, but the voice is that of the renaissance. At the turn of the fifteenth century to be 'at Court' meant to be wherever the King's person might happen to be found. In Brantôme's day the gentlemen who accompanied the King on his peregrinations would enquire impatiently: '*quand serons-nous à la Cour?*' The ymeant: 'when can we re-join the ladies?'

Anne de Bretagne had done much, in her two reigns, to prepare the ground for the new outlook. She always had a large number of ladies, both married and single, in attendance on her. François I was far too fond of female society not to surround himself with the prettiest and wittiest in the land. Their advent was not unopposed. The most influential minds of the century were still anti-feminist. 'Woman is always a woman,' Erasmus had written; 'that is, something stupid.' Rabelais, while according them a place of honour at Thelema, said much the same, only in coarser language. Montaigne was hardly more complimentary.

They were, as it happened, quite capable of defending themselves, and it was François' sister, Marguerite of Navarre, who put, in the *Heptameron*, the most convincing case for the ladies. But the arguments which she advances are hardly more significant than the fact that it was a woman who was advancing them.

It was, however, the presence and not the status of women which interested François. They were wanted as ornaments, and he saw to it that they were ornamental. Brantôme remembered with awe the 'chests and wardrobes of some of the ladies of those days, so filled with gowns which the King had given them for various state occasions that they were worth a fortune'.

It was all fantastically expensive. Marino Cavalli, towards the end of the reign, made an estimate of the cost of running such a Court. The grand total for the King, his family, his household and his presents was one and a half million *écus* a year. Of this the Royal Hunt absorbed some 150,000; the *Menus Plaisirs*—balls, banquets, masques and masquerades—50,000 *écus*; clothing, tapestries and gifts to men—another 50,000; gifts to ladies —300,000. François could afford a magnificent setting for his royal person since he was in little or no danger of being outshone. 'His appearance is entirely regal,' wrote Cavalli, 'so much so, that without ever having seen his face or portrait, from merely looking at him you would say at once "That is the King". His every movement is so noble, so majestic that no Prince could equal it.'

Such phrases might have been used to describe Louis XIV, but there was none of his pompous and aloof formality about the Valois. François wore his royalty extremely lightly. In spite of the difficulties of a peripatetic Court he managed to secure for himself an existence at once epicurean and fastidious—'*cette vie délicate et choisie*'; he ate well, he drank well, he slept well; he was particular about his linen, and in the midst of an arduous and in some ways unsuccessful reign *'il ne songe qu'à mener joyeuse vie'*.

Like many whose interests range over a wide field, he was in the most literal sense an amateur. He always creates the impression of sitting lightly to things, and there was a noticeable atmosphere of ease and informality about his Court. He was accessible to all. After dinner (usually at about eleven in the morning) as he passed from his dining-room to his *salon intérieur*, was a good time to catch him. 'Certainly,' wrote Budé, 'so far as he is concerned, the King puts no obstacles in the way of such a liberty; nevertheless I do not like to abuse his tolerance by taking every opportunity which presents itself.'

A highly talented, recklessly generous and easily accessible King could not fail to attract a large and brilliant Court. Large and brilliant it most certainly was, but its largeness dictated a further condition. A cloud of locusts must be nomadic; the Court was almost always on the move.

When Benvenuto Cellini arrived at Fontainebleau in 1540 the Court was about to depart. He was well received by the King and invited to follow in his suite. 'The King travels with upwards of 12,000 horses,' he noted, 'his retinue in time of peace being 18,000.' This is about five times the number of horses used by Queen Elizabeth I for a Progress. As to the retinue, one can imagine the problems caused by the arrival of an extra 18,000 guests. Only Paris was capable of absorbing the influx 'like the sea, which is not increased although it receives all the rivers into its heart'. Provincial towns had to turn away a large number *'qui s'arrange dans les villages environnants'*. Cellini was annoyed to find himself on one occasion lodged three miles from the person of the King, and even more annoyed at having to camp. 'We sometimes danced attendance in places where there were scarcely two houses, were often under the necessity of pitching very inconvenient tents, and lived like gypsies.'

The Royal 'gypsies', however, seem to have looked after themselves uncommonly well. Brantôme, whose brother was a page at the time, devotes several passages to the subject. 'It was easy enough for Lucullus to be extravagant in a large town,' he wrote, 'but bustling about in the fields day after day in villages, wastelands and woodlands, and to carry all the paraphernalia of the Court and to see it on the march . . . that is something unbelievable but to us who saw it.' Always the King's table and those of his chief officers were delicately and abundantly supplied, 'and what was most rare was that in a village or a forest . . . one was served just as if one had been in Paris'.

It was little wonder that the King's personal expenditure should amount to a million and a half *écus* a year. 'If you could see the Court of France,' wrote Marino Cavalli to the Signorie at Venice, 'you would not find such a sum surprising; it normally maintains six, eight or even twelve thousand horses. Its prodigality knows no bounds; its progresses multiply the cost by at least a third, because of the mules, the carts, the litters, the horses and the servants that have to be taken on, and at twice the normal rate.'

This extra expense was embarrassing to the Venetian Ambassadors. 'My mission,' wrote Giustiniano, 'lasted forty-five months; I was almost continually on Progress.' They had been as far south as Marseilles, travelling by way of Auvergne and Languedoc; they had been as far east as Lorraine, passing through Provence and Bourgogne; they had started in the valley of the Loire, they had ended in Paris; 'never, in the whole of my mission, did the Court stay in the same locality for so long as a fortnight'. The Ambassador from Tuscany found it the same; 'this Court is not as others are,' he complains; they had no thoughts but for hunting, feasting and women—and, of course, their continual moves. 'When the Court descends upon a place,' he continues, 'it stays as long as the herons last, and they don't last long, for between the King and the great men in his suite they have more than five hundred falcons.'

For their endless journeys were not allowed to interfere with their passion for falconry. Louis de Brézé, in a letter to Montmorency, tells of an impending move from Chambord to Paris; the King proposes to take his falconers with him and to have some sport en route; the birds will be entered against the kite— '*qui est fort bon*'. The kite, the *Milan Royal*, was the quarry above all quarries, surpassing the heron in its capacity to shake off a gerfalcon, and the huntsman whose bird could take one might be justly proud.

He could be justly proud of his own ingenuity and patience. 'There is a pretty way for the flying at the Kyte,' writes Richard Blome, 'which affords good diversion; it is thus performed; get an Owl, and tye a small Fox tail or some such device to one of her legs, that she may not give you the Go by, and being in the field, the day being warm and clear, you will soon discover a Kyte cooling herself in the air, then let your Owl fly, and the Kyte will not fail to make near to gaze upon her, and when the Kyte is descended pretty near her, then let fly your hawk, and the Kyte, perceiving the surprize, doth endeavour to preserve herself by mounting up and winding the most she can. And here the Combat begins, but oft-times none can see where it ends, both mounting out of sight. But in the end the Hawk becomes Victor and . . . beats down the Kyte, yet not without many turns and wrenches in the air, to the great pleasure of the Spectators.' It need hardly be added that only by the most astute building up of conditioned reflexes could a falcon be got to attack a kite at all.

Hunting with hawk or hound was an extremely skilled profession; it was more of an art than sport, and it often commanded the total allegiance of its devotees. Jacques du Fouilloux is perhaps the most eloquent apologist for hunting, and in a lyrical passage goes a long way to justify his claim that 'hunters live happier than other men'.

The other men, he implies, do not know what it is to be up at the rising of the sun, and out in the clean, cold air; to listen to the song of the birds and the sweet notes of the nightingale; to see the sunlight sparkle on the dew and to hear the sound of the horn, the baying of the hounds and the huntsman's call resounding through the woods. The other men do not know what it is to come home weary and satisfied, *'en gaieté de cœur, ayant l'appétit ouvert pour prendre son repas et son repos à volupté'*. The other men, presumably, succumb to idleness, and idleness is the mother of all the vices. Not so the hunter; 'with such exercises,' du Fouilloux boasts, 'we can escape the seven deadly sins.'

Marguerite de Navarre made the same suggestion in the Prologue to the *Heptameron*, claiming that 'Hunting and Hawking cause us to forget a thousand foolish thoughts'.

But they saw too narrow and they spoke too soon. The sin of the sportsman is not among the deadly seven; it is enshrined none the less in the pitiless game laws, and is expressed in the man-trap and in the spring-gun and in the gallows on the forest wall of Chambord.

Such considerations, however, were hardly likely to trouble the mind of the sixteenth century, nor is it to be supposed that the average huntsman was consciously concerned with the avoidance of sin. He pursued his pleasures as he pursued his stags—intent on getting them.

It was the red deer stag—*la bête rousse*—which formed the principal quarry of the nobleman. If he enjoyed the spice of real danger he might have hunted the wild boar as well, but one did not try to keep other sorts of deer in the same forest, for, Estienne informs us, 'the red deer is a masterful beast, and when the time of his bellowing cometh, he grows fierce and outrageous, so that he will be Lord of the entire field and will kill the fallow deer if they do but cross his walk'.

To hunt the red deer one needed a team of specialists, both men and dogs, and behind their training lay generations of experience.

The hunt began at break of day when the *Quêteurs* went out into the forest to look for signs of a suitable beast. If possible they discovered the *chambre* or *gîte* where the animal had slept, but great care had to be taken not to disturb him or to arouse his suspicions.

Meanwhile the *rendez-vous de chasse* was being prepared by the Palace servants. An idyllic spot having been chosen for the picnic, in the shade of some noble tree beside a spring or brook, the *Sommelier* arrived first on the scene with his barrels, casks and bottles 'which must be full of good wine'. These he set to cool by the water. He then spread the table-cloth upon the grass. Next came the Cook with his burden of hams and smoked tongues, pig's ears and snouts and other cured and grilled meats, which were set upon the table-cloth. The King and his companions

STAG HUNTING: The *Quêteur* or tracker following the footprints of a stag. Woodcut from Jacques la Fouilloux's treatise 'La Vénerie', 1561.

then spread their cloaks on the ground and lay there 'drinking and eating and making good cheer' until the huntsman arrived with their *fumées* and described the stags which they had seen. 'The excrement or dung,' writes Charles Estienne, 'is not alike at all times; if it be large, gross and thick, it is a sign that they are harts of ten years.'

It was not usual to attack a stag of less than ten points. Such a beast often had a companion, known as his *écuyer*, who ran with him, considerably confusing the issue for all but the most experienced huntsmen and all but the most expert dogs. But even if 'it happen that his wiles be found out by the exquisite scent of the dogges and wisdom of the hunters', a further ruse remained to the stag; he would return into his old tracks 'and thereby mock the dogges'. The huntsman had frequently to encourage his pack 'calling unto them in a cheerful and cherishing manner'.

The training of hounds required the same mixture of care and ingenuity as the training of hawks; nevertheless, the most inexpert mistakes were sometimes made. There are records in the Accounts of Charles IX of compensation paid to farmers for cows that had been inadvertently killed by the Royal Hunt.

Once the King had decided which of the stags he would attack, the huntsmen returned to the *gîte* and the dogs were sent in pursuit. The probable line of country to be taken by the stag was judged and 'dogges of easement' were posted to join in at strategic points.

François I was, even in that great dynasty of Nimrods, conspicuous as a mighty hunter. 'You were well used to performing every task that a good huntsman should,' wrote Budé to the King, marvelling at the way he would ride 'at incredible speeds ... through forest and underwood, through thickets, down precipices, with only your arm held before your face and eyes to protect them'.

There used to be a picturesque rivalry between the personnel of the Grand Fauconnier and those of the Grand Veneur. Florange describes how on the day of la Sainte Croy in May, when the falcons had to be interned in their mews, 'the huntsmen came, dressed all in green with the horns and their green *gaulles* and drove the falconers out of Court'. In September the falconers had their revenge '*car les cerfs ne vallent plus rien*', and they in their turn evicted the huntsmen.

François I altered this practice, hunting the stag in winter as well as summer, and preferring *la bête rousse* to any other quarry. It was with an eye to the facilities which it offered for hunting the stag that François embarked upon the most important building of his reign, the Château de Chambord.

CHAPTER VIII

Chambord

TO BE alone amid the great emptiness of Chambord is to see it at its most evocative, for empty it has almost always been. It has perhaps been occupied one week for every year that it has stood empty. Even in the days of its builder it was only intended for occasional house-parties, a Gargantuan hunting lodge to which François could summon his followers with a gay *'allons chez moi!'*—and for a few days there would be tapestries upon the walls and furniture in the apartments, and the offices and ante-rooms crowded with Court officials; for a few days the woods and alleys would resound to the cry of the huntsmen, and the names of the hounds—names like Miraud and Briffaud and Gerbaud—would echo through the stillness of the forest. But they were soon gone, and all their gorgeous trappings with them, leaving Chambord to its silence and its solitude. The stags enjoyed once more the freedom of the forest; the kites bred unmolested in the trees.

Within the empty chambers of the house the echoes of history are few and far between. Once in 1539 the avenue was carpeted with flowers for the coming of Charles V. A century later the great staircase rang to the childish laugh of Gaston d'Orléans, playing hide and seek with his daughter, Mlle de Montpensier. In the early days of Louis XIV the Royal visits were for a time more frequent, bringing the light-hearted music of Lully and the voice of Molière as the 'Bourgeois Gentilhomme'. In the mid-eighteenth century the echoes were revived with the polite society visiting Stanislas Leczinski and the coarse but picturesque soldiery guarding the coarse but picturesque figure of the Maréchal de Saxe.

In the nineteenth century the silence was but rarely broken. Once, when a Royal widow, who could never be Queen, received the Château in the name of her son, who was never to be

King; again when this same son, named after Chambord, refused the throne of France because France refused the white flag of the Bourbons.

With the departure of the comte de Chambord the echoes cease; the emptiness becomes the emptiness of a vast museum with nothing in it—for Chambord's one exhibit is itself. With the hordes of sightseers it has neither its solitude nor its moments of glory; an effort must be made by the visitor to recapture both.

For this reason the approach to Chambord should be taken carefully. It was not the least original feature of the place that it was built miles from anywhere 'in the middle of a solitary park'. The landscape is the overture to the architecture. In place of the new plantations we must see a forest stretching for miles on either side and filled with venerable oaks which no man ever planted. The forest opens upon the watery expanses of the park, with its canals and avenues, and then, suddenly, the first glimpse of buildings—a bewildering medley of white stone and blue slate; towers upon towers, cupolas upon cupolas, chimneys upon chimneys. 'When one first sees it from afar off,' wrote Félibien, 'one is astonished at the number of pavilions, towers and turrets which make up the *donjon.*'

The trees close in once more and shut off the buildings from our sight until the ride crosses an avenue, and there, at a few hundred yards' range, Chambord rises before us—'*un gigantesque bouquet de pierres*'. It is still astonishing, but no longer bewildering. What had appeared to be confusion is seen to be merely profusion; beneath the complexity is discerned an underlying symmetry—a symmetry tempered, upon closer inspection, with strange and numerous irregularities. 'The whole building presents the most singular appearance,' said Félibien, 'for the manner after which it is built is neither Gothic nor modern.' He was perplexed at the marriage of styles, but he admired its issue. '*Quoique ce mélange soit un ouvrage singulier, le tout ensemble a beaucoup de grandeur et de majesté.*'

Reading the history of Chambord, one cannot help being struck by its ability to appeal to men of very different outlook from generation to generation. It was admired by Blondel; it

was admired by Chateaubriand; Englishmen and Italians added
their praises to those of the French. 'I have seen many magnificent buildings in my time,' wrote Jerome Lippomano, 'but
never anything so beautiful or so rich as this.'

The evolution of Chambord from a rather dull italianate
model to a dramatic and dynamically original design, and the
subsequent modification of this design to the more prosaic but
more habitable Château that we know, is a story as involved and
complicated as the building which it produced.

It was in September 1519, four years after his accession, that
François I determined upon the building of 'a beautiful and
sumptuous edifice' at Chambord, and on September 6 he commissioned François de Pontbriant as Superintendent of the
Buildings. Two master masons—Pierre Nepveu (known as
Trinqueau) and Denis Sourdeau—were placed in charge of the
construction.

In October, and again in December, François was on the site,
and it is reasonable to suppose that the exact placing and orien-
tation of the Château were decided. In 1523 he was back, and
traced in person the boundaries of the enormous park. Three
years later, on his return from Madrid, he spent two weeks at
Chambord, and in 1529 he came twice in the spring, distributing
gratuities among the workmen 'that they might be more disposed to work with diligence on the said building'.

It is difficult to guess at what stage the buildings were. A vast
amount was underground. Lippomano was assured that the
rubble alone, needed to bed the massive foundations into the
marshy ground, had cost 300,000 francs. But the structure
which began to emerge amid the forest of scaffolding was not
identical with the Chambord that we see today. Instead of lying
heavily along the uninteresting length of a formal parterre, the
whole building rose steeply from the deep waters of a capacious
moat. The level of the water being considerably lower than that
of the land, enough of the basement was revealed to alter pro-
foundly the proportions of the façades above. The great drums
of the inward towers gained a full storey in height; the blind
arcades which carry the galleries to the corner towers assumed
the lofty elegance of viaducts; most important of all, the whole

composition was doubled by its reflection in the peaceful waters of the moat.

There is internal evidence that these galleries were added in the course of construction by François I. If one can imagine the north front without the galleries, but with the moat, one can see Chambord as it was originally conceived. The dominant impression is now one of powerful vertical movement; the towers stand out in their full rotundity; the tumultuous ornament of the roof is no longer preponderant, and the whole building soars to its climax in the great stone lantern, some hundred and eighty feet above moat level.

The galleries provided the obvious convenience of covered communications between the *donjon* and the two wings, but their addition obscured the vertical accent of the design. It was finally lost sight of in the eighteenth century when the moat was filled in.

Another profound modification to the building may have occurred within the *donjon* itself. The evidence is inconclusive, but it is possible that, as originally planned, the four doors, each placed in the centre of its façade, gave access to a lofty cruciform vestibule, the full height of the building, which divided the *donjon* into four separated blocks of apartments. At the centre of this cross the great staircase, a double spiral contained in an elegant cage of superimposed pilasters, rose from floor to roof, like a gigantic column, piercing the coffered vault and spiralling up into the sky among the rooftops and chimney stacks. To add to the bizarre effect, the windows at each extremity of the cross were unglazed, leaving the vestibules open to the four winds. Even in the mildest breeze the light of the guttering flambeaux could hardly have penetrated their cavernous recesses.

But before the *donjon* was finished this project was abandoned and dramatic effect sacrificed to domestic convenience. Each vestibule was divided by two floors into three storeys, the windows were glazed, fireplaces inserted, and four more enormous chimneys added to the already crowded skyline.

By taking note of these alterations in the structure we can get back to the original design. That design was in itself an alteration of an earlier project represented by a model which Félibien inspected at Blois. It was probably made by Dominique de Cortona, who was paid in 1531 for his works 'during the past fifteen years at Chambord and other places'. Fifteen years takes us back to 1516, three years before the building was actually commissioned; just the time, in fact, when preliminary models would have been under discussion. There is no evidence as to whether Cortona was working from his own designs or not.

The model itself need not detain us. It provides the basic plan of the *donjon*, but without the spiral staircase; every storey is treated as an arcade; every bay has its window; it gives no indication what, if anything, there was above the cornice. It leaves off where Chambord really begins.

Someone—and we may guess it was François—had the elaborate inspiration of the terrace, roofs and chimney-stacks, the impression of an overcrowded chessboard which is the essence of Chambord. To support this enormous superstructure the slender walls of Cortona's model were quite inadequate. The masonry of the towers is so thick that the rooms appear to be excavated, like the troglodyte chambers of Montlouis, out of the solid stone. There is a massive simplicity about the chimney-pieces, a naked strength in the great beams of the ceilings, that gives a rough-hewn grandeur to the apartments in which consists the character of Chambord.

In contrast to this the Cabinet de Travail of François I is a highly finished piece of decoration—a miniature of one of the vestibules at the top of the spiral staircase. Like so much at Chambord (and so much about François I) it has the appearance of being an afterthought. It was built out from the north-east tower and can justly be regarded as a blemish to the front. Within, it is the most beautiful apartment of the Palace—its beauty deriving wholly from its ceiling, a barrel vault which follows the curve of the tower's circumference, deeply coffered and set about with flaming salamanders.

Above this is a balustraded terrace, private to the King's apartment, from which the finest view of Chambord is obtained. Before the building of the gallery between this tower and the *donjon* the view would have been finer still. It is often more logical to live opposite to an impressive building than to live inside it, and François wisely chose to live across the way.

It was a pleasure in which he indulged but seldom. In the next century, Gaston d'Orléans, the somewhat troublesome younger brother of Louis XIII, received the county of Blois in apanage, and with it the Châteaux of Blois and Chambord. His daughter, Mlle de Montpensier, leaves several amusing anecdotes.

'One of the most curious and most remarkable features of the house,' she writes, 'is the staircase, so constructed that one person may mount and another descend without encountering, though they may see, each other. On this staircase Monsieur took a delight in playing games with me; he was at the top when I arrived; he came down as I went up, and laughed aloud to see me run, thinking as I did to catch him.'

At the death of Gaston Chambord reverted to the Crown, and under Louis XIV received, virtually for the first time, the Royal attention which it deserved.

There exists, in the Cabinet des Estampes, a collection of drawings and plans from the papers of Robert de Cotte. Among them is a plan of Chambord, with flaps for each successive floor. Such plans would have been of the greatest use to anyone allotting rooms to members of the Court on the occasion of a visit. It shows that there were, in the Château proper, two hundred and eighteen apartments mostly consisting of two rooms, one large, one small, though the more important apartments had the addition of another small room.

A further hundred and twenty beds, arranged in barrack-like uniformity, occupied the mansardes above the stables. There was certainly sleeping room for some three hundred and fifty in proper beds. The servants would have had a pallet which was unrolled when required and would not have figured on the plan.

The plan provides two other details of domestic interest. Behind the alcove in the bedroom of the King was installed a *poêle*—a porcelain stove in the Alsatian style such as can still be seen in one of the vestibules of Chambord. It was approachable by a narrow passage cut in the thickness of the wall, so that servants could maintain the temperature of the bedroom without intruding upon its privacy: a device employed in later years by Robert de Cotte.

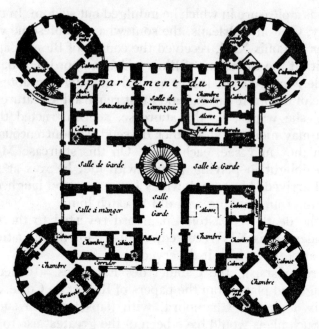

CHAMBORD: Plan of the first floor after Louis XIV's adjustments.

The plan also marks ten kitchens on the ground floor of the Château, the two largest being in the wing adjoining the apartments of François I. We are on the threshold of a new and glorious era for Chambord. Under the Valois it had been the permanent setting for a rather gorgeous camp. Now its naked walls were clothed in panelling and the house was adapted to longer and more luxurious inhabitation.

It was in the autumn that Louis first came with his Court to Chambord, when October had brought the trees to their most resplendent glory and laid its golden carpet along the rides and alleys of the park. The impact was immediate. 'There is no Royal house of a more noble and magnificent design,' wrote Pellisson; 'the park and forest which surround it are full of ancient trees, tall and spreading, which in times past were consulted as oracles.' They were more than commonly fortunate with the weather, and the blue skies and autumn sunshine set off to the greatest advantage the blue and gold uniforms of the Court—for Louis, with his meticulous eye for detail, ordained the colours that were to be worn by his followers on their visits to his various palaces.

This sort of magnificence was something new to the Blésois, new, almost, to Pellisson; 'nothing', he wrote, 'could equal the magnificence of the equipages.' Everywhere they went they brought their own atmosphere with them; it seemed that 'Le Brun, Mansart and Le Nôtre had employed all their talent and all their knowledge on the places passed by the King'. Even the modest château of M. d'Herbaut became as it were the Louvre or the Tuileries as he did the honours to his King—'no one has ever seen a fête prepared in so short a time'.

On October 15, after a fortnight of hunting and improvised entertainment, the Court removed to Blois, and Chambord settled down once more to its routine oblivion. The Governor, M. de la Saussaye, set about repairing the petty destructions caused by so great a concourse of people—balusters broken from the great staircase, stones prised apart on the terraces, cobbles and tiles displaced, and, oddly, 'a great number of locks removed'.

Five more times, and always in the autumn, Louis brought his Court to Chambord, adding Mansart roofs to the forecourt and laying the foundations of two enormous blocks of stables. But despite a considerable expenditure, the Château remained unfinished.

In 1670 the visit was particularly memorable. Mlle de Montpensier, fending off a projected marriage between herself and Louis's brother, was disappointed that there were no organized walks, but of the rest of the programme she was enthusiastic. '*On se divertissait fort à Chambord,*' she writes; '*on avait tous les jours la comédie, on allait à la chasse, on jouait.*' It was the first item on her list which was significant, for here, on October 14, was performed the première of the *Bourgeois Gentilhomme* in which Molière and Lully so happily collaborated. It was a difficult moment for Molière, for Louis gave not the least sign of approval or amusement. But he made up for it after the second performance, explaining that he had 'been conscious of being carried away by the manner in which it was produced', but ending with the fine compliment: '*vous n'avez encore rien fait qui m'ait plus diverti.*'

On September 28, 1685, the Court left Chambord for the last time. There were various possible reasons for the visits being discontinued; Versailles was nearing its completion; Marly was all but ready for habitation. But perhaps more significant still was the fact that there was an observed decline in Louis's zest for riding to hounds. Hunting was no longer his chief amusement, and Chambord was consecrated to the chase.

It was again in the autumn, after some forty years of disuse, that preparation was next made for the reception of Royalty; a multitude of minor repairs was put in hand, tapestries were stretched upon the walls, furniture arranged in the rooms, and Chambord prepared to open its doors to Stanislas Leczinski. A former King of Poland, Stanislas was now, in 1725, father-in-law to Louis XV, and the old hunting lodge of François I was to be his appointed residence. He was at once delighted with the place. 'As for Chambord,' he wrote, 'I am in my element here by reason of its pleasing isolation.'

But as autumn gave place to winter, and winter to summer, Stanislas and his wife Catherine began to find drawbacks in their sumptuous solitude. They were the first people above the rank of concierge to attempt residence throughout the year. In winter it was extremely cold; in summer it was most unhealthy. In July there was a serious outbreak of fever. 'It is attributed to the air here,' wrote Stanislas, 'and to the exhalations from the marshes by which the house is surrounded.' Fifty of his servants (the number suggests an impressive total strength) were down with it, and they were forced to abandon the Château. Menars, one of the most perfectly sited houses in Blésois, became their summer residence.

To remedy this situation it was deemed necessary to fill in the moat. Aesthetically it was a disaster, and the result was hardly more salubrious. In 1746 a further 20,000 livres were spent on drainage, but to little effect. 'Chambord is a hospital,' wrote the Maréchal de Saxe to Le Tournehem; 'I have more than three hundred sick, several dead, and the others have the look of exhumed corpses.'

The new owner of Chambord was a bastard of the House of Saxony and the victor of Fontenoy. Deprived by the bar sinister of the rights of Royalty, he spent his hectic life intriguing for a throne; even Madagascar and Tobago were considered. But in the end he had to be contented with a Marshal's baton and a reputation unsurpassed since Condé. But if he did not succeed in obtaining a Kingdom, at least he became the owner of a Palace. The gift of Chambord not only relieved the King of an expensive white elephant, it gave to one of the most colourful of his subjects a fittingly exotic background.

His arrival was typical. The coachman, Moreau, drove his team full tilt across the courtyard and into the Salle des Gardes. '*Eh bien, où me conduis-tu?*' shouted the Maréchal. '*A vos appartements!*' answered the coachman, and only drew rein when his leaders had their front feet on the staircase.

The new châtelain brought a new life to Chambord. He kept two regiments of Tartars and Uhlans whom he lodged in Louis XIV's stables, and a picturesque bodyguard of black negroes mounted on white horses who paraded regularly in the Place d'Armes before the Château. Besides supervising their manoeuvres and administering savage justice to their defaulters, he made full use of the admirable facilities for hunting which Chambord offered. Given to hospitality, he was continually and lavishly entertaining. As a host we can see him in two roles; either busily organizing concerts on the lake, theatricals in the Salle de Spectacle and dinner parties with up to a hundred and fifty guests, or quietly drawing up an armchair to the bedside of the Marquis de Valfons and reminiscing on his campaigns 'with the charming simplicity which is the special characteristic of the hero'.

His last house party he describes himself. 'Mademoiselle de Sens is spending some of the autumn here,' he wrote, 'with a handful of Court ladies.' They were having a troupe of comedians to entertain them, and they were going to hunt. The hunting was to supply the table of the comedians; 'I am going to make them eat a lot of boar and venison.' The ladies, he hoped, would have a good time. 'I have a fine body of officers,' he adds suggestively; 'all picked men, good looking fellows who have been shut up like monks in the Château de Chambord.'

The old roué did not long survive this entertainment, but died on November 30, 1750. M. J. Raymond has disposed of the theory that he was killed in a duel with the Prince de Conti. 'Life is a dream,' he observed on his deathbed; 'mine is short, but it has been a good one.' He was the last person to inhabit the place who in any way measured up to Chambord.

On the eve of the Revolution the Château was visited by two Englishmen; although they were men of very different outlook, it was typical of Chambord that it made its appeal to both.

Nathaniel Wraxall came in meditative mood. 'I sat down on the bank of the rivulet in front of the Palace to contemplate it at leisure.' The place not only afforded a magnificent panorama; it provided a perfect setting for a picnic. 'I spread my cold provisions on the grass, under the shade of two ancient elms, and after having dined, resigned myself to all that train of reflection naturally excited by the view of so magnificent a structure.'

The huge size of Chambord and its crowded roofscape, 'over which the lapse of two centuries begins to throw an air of decay and waning splendour, produce an effect on the beholder hard to be described'. At a remote view the house was still impressive; 'the architecture of it tho' strictly gothic, is full of beauty and elegance.' But Wraxall had made a closer inspection, and he knew the heavy truth; 'Chambord is fast going to decay . . . its immense magnitude, which makes it require continual repairs, will necessarily hasten its downfall, and motives of economy will probably produce in some future time, its entire demolition.'

Arthur Young came full of prejudice against the French in general and the Valois in particular. 'Great lords,' he grumbled, 'love too much an environ of forest, boars and huntsmen, instead of marking their residences by the accompaniment of neat and well cultivated farms, clean cottages and happy peasants.' The hunting lodge of François I was singularly lacking in any such accessories, but none the less it won his admiration. 'It more than answered my expectation,' he wrote; 'it gives a great idea of the splendour of that Prince. I prefer Chambord infinitely to Versailles.' He spoke in a rare moment of aesthetic appreciation unclouded by historical or agrarian prejudice; the true Arthur Young is discerned in his parting comment: he could not refrain from thinking that Chambord would be a perfect place for the cultivation of turnips.

CHAPTER IX

Chenonceau

THE BEST approach to Chenonceau would be by boat, to come downstream from Moulin Fort in late October and in the early morning, when the sunlight slants across the east façade and throws into dramatic relief the deeply moulded features of the front.

The best moment would be when the sluices had been opened and the waters of the Cher are so low as to be almost static, and yield on their untroubled surface a perfect image of the scene above. Viewed thus Chenonceau looks unreal, like some illumination come to life—an illustration by Pol de Limbourg to a fairy tale.

At first sight it appears to be a Gothic medley of slender towers and soaring pinnacles. A further look reveals its symmetry. Two massive piles united by a bridge form the foundation and impose the limits of the building above. Upon these piles the salient features of the façade are clustered in two similar, but not identical groups. Each group is contained between two narrow turrets crowned with pointed *poivrières*; each pair of turrets frames a triple-faceted projection that breaks forward to the utmost limits of the pile.

Of these the more imposing is the Chapel, a plain but pleasing alternation of ribs and lancets, which provides the highest point of the silhouette with its tall and fragile *flèche*. The inward turrets nestle in the angles of these projections, not reaching high enough to indent the skyline, but breaking up the otherwise oppressive mass of roof. Between these towers, on the façade which spans the bridge, a single flight of windows, disdaining the symmetry of a central position, marks each storey.

It was a plan dictated by the site. Whatever reason led Thomas and Catherine Bohier to build their château on the piles of an old mill imposed upon them the most striking novelty of the design.

They had obviously and understandably set their hearts upon

the place. Bohier owned a house at Tours—'one of the most superb in all the town'—and another at Amboise; he was already Lord of many Manors; but when, in 1494, he purchased the Château des Houdes in the valley of the Cher he was casting covetous eyes upon the debt-encumbered estates of Pierre de Marques adjacent to the village of Chenonceaux. Each time de Marques had to sell off land, Bohier bought it up. At first he did so under a false name. Les Houdes was bought by Semblançay and made over to him. A maddening delay was caused by a relative exercising her *droit de retrait lignager*, and it was not until 1512 that Thomas and Catherine became undoubted owners of the domain.

It was not the Château itself that they had waited eighteen years to possess, for they immediately pulled it down. They must have determined early that the emplacement of the old mill was the site, and the only site, where the château of their dreams could be erected.

It was indeed a *château de rêves* which they built: the inspired response to the demands of an inspiring natural position. Among the many who have recorded their admiration for the site was Mlle de Montpensier; 'wood, water and every commodity of nature that one could well desire, are found here in the happiest possible combination.' We must imagine it without the vast and formal garden to the east, more closely embowered by the trees than it is today; we must imagine it without the bridge and galleries, its façades dipping on three sides directly into the river, and maintaining by the drawbridge of the fourth a tenuous connection with the land. It was not fortified, but it was 'playing hard to get'.

So much attention has been paid to the Italian features in the plan and decorations of Chenonceau that it is easy to forget that the beauty of the building is wholly independent of ultramontane importations. Chenonceau could take its place among the pages of the *Très Riches Heures*. It is but an elaboration of dormer windows against a high-pitched roof; a delicately balanced contrast between smooth stone walls and richly carved embellishment; above all, the dramatic effect of angle towers— of massive blocks off-set by narrow cylinders and pointed cones.

For at Chenonceau, as at Azay, the tower has been reduced to a purely decorative feature—and with the happiest effect. By incorporating these in the main block and by preserving the old *donjon*, the Tour de Marques, Bohier was keeping himself in line with his feudal predecessors. The Tour de Marques was the *chartrier* of Chenonceau. Here were deposited the title deeds which secured the owner in his rights. These, as we have already seen, were usually burnt in the Revolution. By a happy fortune the seigneurial archives of Chenonceau have mostly survived. They provide abundant information about the lay-out of the Château and the economy of its household.

There were two large warrens of coneys, each prudently insulated by a little moat; there were walled vineyards and special plantations of hazel and willow. There was also a large wood called Le Raffou, enclosed by a ditch, 'in the middle of which is the gibbet of the said Châtellenie, with three shafts'.

For Bohier claimed among his seigneurial rights the power to inflict certain rather displeasing mutilations and to execute by hanging, burning, drowning or decapitation. It was in fact an empty formula; the King's Justice or *Cas Royaux*—perhaps more impartial though certainly no less gruesome—had almost entirely supplanted the local courts. The outward forms, however, were tenaciously retained, and most châteaux were equipped with their gallows or *Justice Patibulaire*.

Other feudal rights were still operative, such as the '*banalité du moulin*'—the obligation to grind at the seigneurial mill. Failure to do so rendered Bohier's 'subjects' liable to the confiscation not only of the corn and bread involved, but also of the beast that carried it.

One of the most picturesque and pointless of feudal dues was the *Droit de la Quintaine*. All millers and fishermen had to bring their boats to Moulin Fort on Whitsunday and to erect in midstream a stake bearing the arms of their Lord; they were then rowed full tilt at this shield, and, standing in the bows of their craft, had to break three lances against it. There is perhaps a significant comment on the sport contained in the regulation which obliged those who had already passed the ordeal to be present in their boats '*pour pêcher ceux qui tombent dans la rivière*'.

It was on Whitsunday also that the *droit du seigneur* was exercised over the brides of Chenonceau. It was not the shameful right that forms the basis of the plot of *Figaro*, but the harmless exaction, from the bridegroom, of a new white tennis ball.

By 1517 the Château was probably fit for habitation. The Chapel was consecrated the next year by the Archbishop of Bourges, a relative of Catherine's. The last date on the panelling is 1521. It was in this same year that Bohier left Chenonceau, as it turned out, for the last time. He accompanied Lautrec as Paymaster of the Forces on that disastrous expedition to Italy which saw the death of Bayard, the defection of Bourbon and the most unfortunate financial complications, leading to the execution of Semblançay.

Bohier died before Vigelli in March 1524; Catherine followed him to the grave some two and a half years later. They were laid to rest beside each other in a magnificent Chapel at St. Saturnin de Tours, where their marble effigies kneel beneath the blue and gold ceiling of the vault. They were buried with all the pomp of heraldry and all the paraphernalia of wealth; the château of their dreams had been completed; Chenonceau had passed to their eldest son Antoine.

Nevertheless the family was already ruined. In the general inspection of accounts following the execution of Semblançay the Bohiers were declared to be in debt to the amount of 190,000 livres towards the Crown. Sooner than pay so ruinous a sum, Antoine offered Chenonceau to the King.

It was the first of a whole series of changes of ownership. Each change was marked by a ritual in which the feudal rights of the lordship were conferred upon the new Lord. The archives of the Château preserve an account of this ritual on the occasion of the transfer from Queen Louise to the duc de Vendôme.

On February 20, 1601, César Forget, the Duke's Conseiller Général des Finances, came to take, in the name of his master, formal possession of Chenonceau. First he went to the Court Room, where justice was administered, sat in the seigneurial throne and claimed the right of his master to administer the law. Then he went to the Church, knelt in the seigneurial pew, claimed the right of patronage, had the bells rung and ordered the Curé to pray for the new Lord of the Manor. Finally he went up the avenue to the Château, where the drawbridge was raised. The title deeds were read aloud, the drawbridge lowered, and Jacques Lallemand, Capitaine du Château, offered him the keys. With these he opened all the principal rooms, claiming them in the name of his master. It was a ritual that was performed only too often in the history of Chenonceau.

In June of 1547, three months after his succession, Henri II presented Chenonceau to Diane de Poitiers. It was given, officially, in recognition of 'the great and most commendable services that our late cousin Louis de Brézé. . . . formerly rendered to the late King of happy memory, our most honoured Lord and Father, whom God forgive'. It was the slenderest of pretexts; in the first place Louis de Brézé had died in 1531, and recognition of his services was somewhat overdue. In the second place, his services as Grand Sénéschal of Normandy were not such as to merit so extravagant a gift. It was his widow, the daughter of Jean de Poitiers, who had rendered the services, but they were not such as could be mentioned in a title deed.

Married at fifteen to a devotee of the chase old enough to be her father, Diane had become, at forty-four, the mistress of a King young enough to be her son. She was created duchesse de Valentinois, and her family seat of Anet was magnificently rebuilt by Philibert de l'Orme. She was to dominate the reign.

The secret of her charms is somewhat obscure. According to Brantôme—and he wrote when she had fallen from power— she retained a youthful figure and a perfect complexion till the end of her days. 'I have seen the duchesse de Valentinois at the age of seventy,' he wrote, 'as fresh and lovely as at the age of thirty.' Looking at her portrait, drawn by François Clouet in 1551, it is difficult to agree with Brantôme. It is a face as devoid of beauty as it is destitute of character; narrow, vacant eyes, a mean mouth and a receding jaw, a double chin and far too thick a neck.

Her complexion, it was said, was perfect; perhaps she was possessed of other skin-deep qualities invisible to Clouet. Certainly she knew how to make herself both irresistible and indispensable to Henry. Charm she must have had, but with this charm a cold and calculating tenacity in the pursuit of her own material advantage. Although she was at the receiving end of the King's abundant generosity, she remained a miser and she managed the affairs of her ever-increasing estates with a mean and stringent economy. Her advent to Chenonceau was the occasion of a substantial drop in wages all round and a sustained insistence upon the most rigorous inspection of accounts.

In spite of the precautions taken by Henri II to make his gift of Chenonceau absolute, Diane was not satisfied. There was an edict of François I, dated June 30, 1531, which proclaimed the inalienability of the Crown Domain. In the event of Henri's death, this edict would certainly be invoked against her.

She could only secure the possession of Chenonceau by a further persecution of the unfortunate Antoine Bohier. Imaginary fault was found with the original transaction whereby he had made Chenonceau over to the Crown; this was now declared void and his original debt of 90,000 livres* again demanded. Chenonceau became once more his property in order that it could be confiscated and put on sale. Diane, needless to say, bought it, offering only 50,000 livres. Since she bought it from Bohier and not from the King she could claim that she was not possessed of any of the Crown Domain. It need only be added that the 50,000 livres were never paid.

Throughout this transaction, Henri II had shown himself alarmingly prepared to override any normal tribunal, and Bohier prudently fled to Italy. He took with him the title deeds of Chenonceau. To secure the return of these the King absolved him of his debt towards the Treasury 'in view of the services rendered to the Crown by Thomas and Antoine Bohier'!

It was the most shabby piece of legal pettifoggery, and it availed nothing. Henri had repudiated the transactions of his predecessor; his widow lost no time in repudiating his. Immediately after his death, caused by an accident while jousting, Diane was made to disgorge, but even in disgrace and in retreat she was astute enough to obtain in exchange for Chenonceau the opulent estate of Chaumont.

* 90,000 livres represents the portion of the total 190,000 which was covered by the sale of Chenonceau.

LE MOULIN: gatehouse
and moat

CHAUMONT: in the seventeenth century; drawing by Félibien,
by courtesy of the marquis de Vibraye

CHAUMONT: from the Loire; watercolour by
Prince Jacques de Broglie

GAILLON: the west front; reconstruction by Ian Dunlop

GAILLON: drawing in the Cronstedt collection

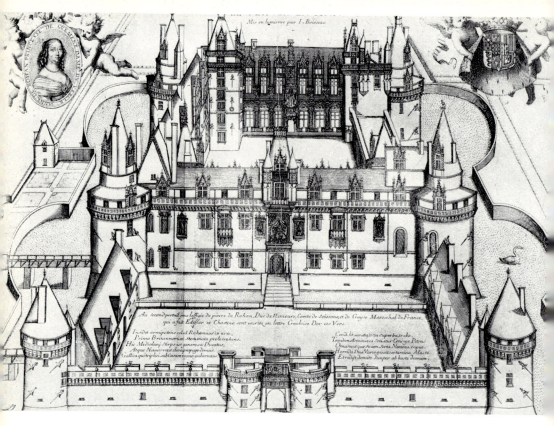

LE VERGER: aerial view; engraving by I. Boisseau

BURY: aerial view; drawing by du Cerceau

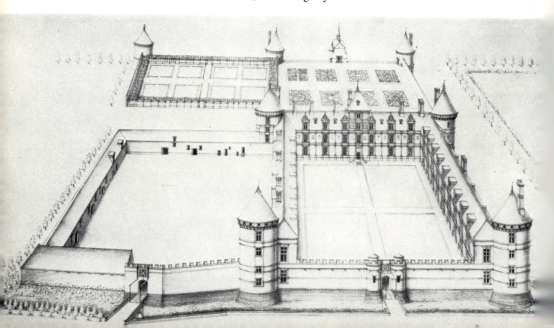

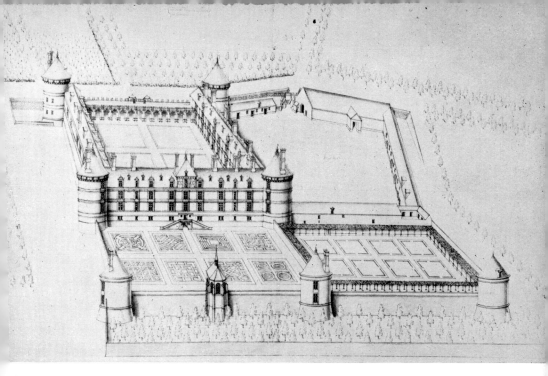

BURY: from the east; drawing by du Cerceau

BLOIS: Louis XII's wing
with the buildings of
Charles d' Orléans, the
'perche aux Bretons'
behind;
drawing by du Cerceau

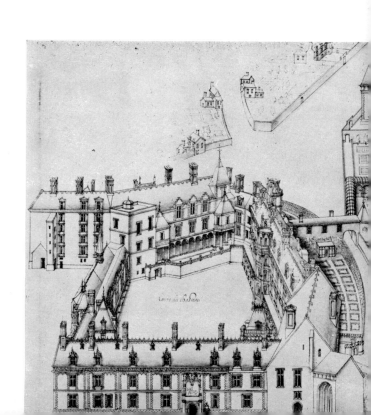

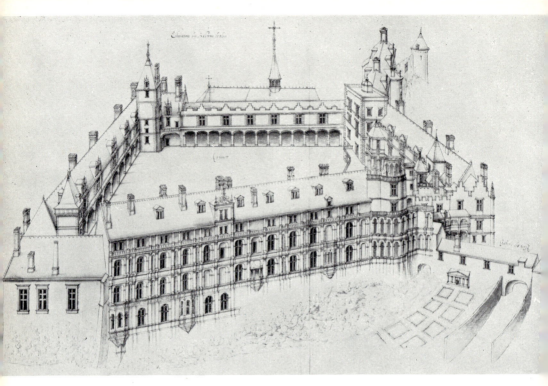

BLOIS: the 'Facade des Loges' with the Tour du Foix top right; drawing by du Cerceau

MANOIR DE BEAUREGARD

VILLANDRY: aerial view today

VILLANDRY: the parterres and the Church

BOUMOIS: interior of the dovecote

CHAMBORD: as it may have been originally planned,
reconstruction by Ian Dunlop

CHAMBORD: the same view today

The assassination of Henri III on August 1, 1589 brought, accidentally, a new and important mistress to Chenonceau. Queen Louise was in residence at Chinon during those troubled times, but she had made an excursion to the valley of the Cher and was at Chenonceau when her husband's letter, bearing the news of the *attentat*, reached her. 'Mamye,' he added in his own hand, 'I have hopes of a good recovery. Pray God for me, and do not move from where you are.' He did not recover from the wound, and Louise took his last instruction literally. It was perhaps fortunate that the letter had reached her at this charming place and did not confine her to a feudal fortress.

In accordance with the mood of its owner, Chenonceau took on a new and sombre decoration. Ceilings and walls were painted in the black of mourning against which the white insignia of death were everywhere depicted. Each room became a gallery of bones and biers and coffins, picks and shovels. There was even a certain luxuriousness about this extravagant display of grief. White widow's girdles and silver tears were delicately embroidered on to the black velvet upholstery; black damask curtains, richly fringed and tasselled, framed the windows and marked the corners of the bed; and black silk hangings masked the decorations of the Chapel.

Against this dark decor the Queen Dowager wore the white weeds of a Royal widow, and is known in history as la Reine Blanche.

Her tenancy of Chenonceau was far from peaceful. In the early days of the new reign she had to complain to Henri IV that the Sieur de Rosny, his lieutenant, had come 'to trouble the peace of my domain and of my blessed house of Chenonceau'. His ravages were causing great distress to her tenants, who, she bids him remember 'are held by me as dearly beloved children'. With the restoring of peace came another threat. Catherine de' Medici had died heavily in debt. Henri III had taken the somewhat autocratic step of declaring that the domain of Chenonceau was free from debt and mortage. Now his decree was reversed and Louise found herself faced with payment, or the alternative of selling Chenonceau.

She did neither. Her revenues were thereupon seized and she

was reduced to the most straitened circumstances, in which, however, she managed to maintain the liberality of her charities.

In 1598 Louise made Chenonceau over to her niece, Françoise de Lorraine, who was betrothed to the duc de Vendôme. During the minority of this extremely juvenile ménage the duchesse de Mercœur administered the Queen Dowager's will.

There had been a large bequest for the foundation of a Capuchin nunnery in Paris. While awaiting their new home, the nuns were lodged in the attic storey of Chenonceau, where there still survives a strange memorial of their sojourn. In order to provide the illusion of being cut off from the world, and perhaps to secure them from unwelcome intrusion from the household below, a little drawbridge was contrived at the entrance to the attic corridor—an elegant *pont à bascule*, supported on Doric columns and operated by a delicately balanced counterpoise. The Capuchin community were the last occupants of any interest for over a hundred years.

In 1733 Chenonceau acquired a mistress who was entirely worthy of the place and was to occupy it with distinction for sixty-six years. Louise-Marie-Madeleine Dupin was one of 'the three Graces'—natural daughters of the wealthy banker, Samuel Bernard—the most beautiful of the three, according to Rousseau, and 'the only one who has never been reproached with the slightest error of conduct'.

Mme Dupin was a woman born to be a hostess; she acted as catalyst to those distinguished by birth and those distinguished by talent. 'One saw at her house nothing but dukes, ambassadors and *cordons bleus*'; the princesse de Rohan, the comtesse de Forcalquier and Lady Hervey were among her friends; Buffon, Voltaire and Rousseau were to be seen at her dinners. Naturally a brilliant society such as this could only meet in the capital, but the taste for country life which Rousseau was to preach and Arthur Young to applaud was already apparent in Mme Dupin. From time to time she would take a select house party off to Touraine for a few weeks of arcadian living at Chenonceau.

In 1747 Rousseau spent the autumn with them there; 'we greatly enjoyed ourselves in this lovely place,' he wrote; 'we ate and drank extremely well; I became as fat as a monk. We had a great deal of music; I composed several trios for voices, full of vigour and harmony.' When he was not composing music he was writing plays. It took him a fortnight to produce *L'Engagement Téméraire*—a piece whose only merit, in its author's eyes, was to have been extremely gay. Nor did these activities prevent him from continuing his scientific studies with M. de Francueil, nor his literary work with Mme Dupin. It was the very purpose for which the Château had been designed—architecture providing a worthy setting for science, music, art and gracious living.

Occasionally a pedant intruded into this arcadia. The Abbé de St. Pierre dedicated two books to Mme Dupin, which showed that he had been her guest, for one was a proposal to reform French spelling—a new system *'que je vous propozai un jour sur les bords du Cher, dans une de nos promenades filosofiques où vous trouviez tant de plézir'*.

In 1782 Mme Dupin, now a widow, retired to Chenonceau and spent a long and peaceful old age dedicated to the welfare of her villagers and tenants. In this she was assisted by the Abbé Lecomte and the Doctor Pierre Bretonneau. A rich lady, a devoted Parish Priest and a rising young physician formed an admirable team, and in their zeal for charity, the upkeep of Chenonceau was forgotten. Visitors from the *beau monde*, who came from Chanteloup to see the show place of the neighbourhood, returned in disappointment. *'Le dénuement était complet,'* sighed Dufort de Cheverny; *'rien n'était entretenu.'* In place of the tidy gravel paths and trim parterres, an air of shabby grandeur began to pervade the scene; Chenonceau assumed the aspect of the Palace of the Sleeping Princess; Château and Châtelaine alike began to savour of a bygone age.

The last visitor to record his impressions was the historian, Touchard Lafosse, who came in 1797 to borrow scenery for a dramatic club in Montrichard. With the old lady leaning on his arm, he was taken round Chenonceau; it was like a conducted tour of pre-revolutionary France. 'She had retained the gift of lively conversation,' he records, 'of vivid memories and odd events. Her wit had not lost any of its past vivacity, nor any of its charm; her talk was like a fascinating book.' Pausing before the door of the room which once was Rousseau's, she turned to her young guest: '*Tenez, jeune homme,*' she said, '*voilà l'antre de l'ours de Genève.*'

The fact that Mme Dupin had survived the Revolution bears impressive testimony to her local reputation for charity. She was in no personal danger during the Terror, and Chenonceau was saved by the revolutionary sympathies of the Abbé Lecomte. He became the President of the local revolutionary committee, and successfully defended the Château against those who would have destroyed it. 'Come now, Citizens,' he remonstrated, 'do you not know that Chenonceau is a bridge? You have only one bridge between Montrichard and Bléré, and you talk of destroying it. You are the enemies of public welfare.'

A further threat came when the Revolutionary government invoked the very argument which Catherine de' Medici had invoked two and a half centuries before, claiming Chenonceau as part of the Royal Domain. By a strange return of fortune the elaborate legal farce, by which Diane de Poitiers had attempted to secure Chenonceau for herself, now saved it for posterity.

CHAPTER X

Four Private Châteaux: Luynes, Le Lude, Serrant, Azay-le-Rideau

THERE ARE two ways in which a building may come into being; it may spring from the single inspiration of a single artist, from one comprehensive design and one uninterrupted programme of building; or it may be the result of centuries of addition and adaptation which cannot properly be called a style, but which often produces an effect of extreme beauty.

The grey, lichenous walls of Luynes seem not to have been built but to have grown, like some ancestral oak, throughout the centuries. Looking at it from the south-east it is difficult sometimes to distinguish between the rocky outcrop which has been built up to form a troglodyte dwelling, and the decaying outworks of defence which have broken down into irregular shapes which might be those of nature.

For a fortress tends to follow and to make use of the natural conformations of the land; its walls borrow the sinuous lines of the contours; its towers are often but the heightening of nature's bastions, its moats the extension of some re-entrant. The works of Art and Nature are so closely allied as to form a perfect harmony. Nothing could look more natural than the way Luynes merges with its escarpment.

Its walls have been built, unbuilt, rebuilt, dismantled and repaired again. Windows have been opened in the walls, then bricked up, then partially re-opened. Here the masonry becomes more regular to frame an arrow slit, now long since filled in; there the projecting remains of a *bretèche* break the cylindrical profile. Built before the days of machicolations, the towers are pierced with holes, to which, in times of siege, hordes could be affixed. In an age of greater comfort, red brick chimneys were inserted, piercing the conical roofs and adding a warmth of

homely colour to the slate and stone. The corner towers are
backed by gables with carved crockets and slender finials, providing a happy contrast of fragile ornament to the rude defences.

Within the court a high containing wall protects the Château
from the north and east. To the west are the lodgings, set
against the distinctive row of towers which dominates the village; to the south the terrace opens towards the Loire. Like most
fortresses, Luynes enjoys an unimpeded view of the landscape.

In the days of Louis XI, town, Château and seigneurial family
bore the name of Maillé, not Luynes. Somewhere in the vast
panorama which they overlooked, across the Loire and east-
wards towards Tours, was another Château belonging to the
family called Montils. In 1463 Montils was purchased by the
King who changed its name to Le Plessis-lès-Tours. It may
have been this propitious sale which enabled Hardouin de Maillé
to rebuild the lodgings of the west range in the same handsome
style of brick and stone employed at Le Plessis. The hexagonal
staircase tower, which gives birth at second floor-level to a
smaller turret in which a narrower stair is carried to serve the
topmost chamber of the tower, was the most distinctive feature
of the style.

In 1619 Maillé also changed hands and simultaneously
changed its name. It was bought by Charles d'Albert, seigneur
de Luynes, who in the same year became a Duke and renamed
Maillé after his Dukedom. The original Luynes was a very
insignificant little place near Aix-en-Provence, which was in no
way qualified 'to support the lustre and magnificence' of ducal
rank.

Charles d'Albert had started his career as page to the comte
du Lude, but had caught the eye of Henri IV who placed him in
the household of the Dauphin. Here he acquired the art of training grey shrikes to fly at sparrows, and this junior form of falconry became the chief amusement of the young Prince. Charles
d'Albert became his favourite companion; from companion he
progressed to confidant and from confidant to confederate. In
April 1617 they planned together the assassination of Concini,
the all-powerful favourite of Marie de' Medici. From then on the
fortune of Albert was made. He became duc de Luynes and

Connétable de France and died in 1621 before his unpopularity could work his downfall.

The Château de Maillé which thus became the Château de Luynes was at that time a pretty little house of the Louis XI style ringed round by the cone-capped towers of the older castle. Its accommodation was not extensive. To remedy this defect the new Duke built a range of apartments right across the south terrace. Only the western portion of this survives today. It is frank juxtaposition of styles, but being built of the same grey stone as the towers it harmonizes better with the medieval *enceinte* than the brick lodgings of Hardouin de Maillé.

In the following reign the house of Luynes united with that of Chevreuse and built the beautiful and magnificent Château de Dampierre within easy reach of Versailles. In 1710, with the marriage of Charles-Philippe, duc de Luynes and Chevreuse, to Louise, comtesse de Dunois, they acquired also the great castle of Châteaudun on the Loir. It was the occasion of a notable act of hospitality on the part of the Duke, for a few years later a disastrous fire destroyed more than a thousand houses in Châteaudun. The castle was thrown open to the homeless refugees and its rooms divided up for their better accommodation. The extra weight of all these new partition walls proved too much for the structure and many of the floors collapsed. By the end of the century Châteaudun was becoming a ruin.

If the historic home of the Dunois was allowed to fall into disrepair, it is not surprising that the same fate should have befallen that of the Maillés. It is to be supposed that the first Duke's additions were pulled down because they were unsound. Their demolition, however, is not to be regretted since it had the happy result of opening up once more the lovely prospect from the terrace.

The practice of converting a fortified castle into a country house had this particular advantage; a fortress, by reason of its military function, almost by definition commands a view. The necessities of defence minister to the attractions of residence. Among the châteaux which have been more or less continually inhabited there are a conspicuous number which illustrate this rule. But Chaumont and Luynes have the inconvenience of

steep or devious approaches; there is a disadvantage in too
much elevation. Perhaps of all the owners who successfully
turned their castles into palaces, none made more happy use of
the dispositions of defence than the Daillons of Le Lude.

Built to protect a bridge, the Château du Lude overlooks in
consequence one of the loveliest reaches of the Loir, and from
its high terraces enjoys the delightful prospect of the Prairies
de Malidor. It is today a dreamy, rural landscape of luscious
meadows and lazy backwaters such as might have inspired the
second movement of Beethoven's Pastoral Symphony.

To the south, the high ground of the park follows the contours traced by the river, sweeping round in a graceful, parabolic
curve to a point where the Loir, doubling back upon its course,
is lost to sight. Tall hanger woods clothe the extremity of the
crescent down to the water's edge, casting their cool, dark
shadows across the sunlit stream. A dry watercourse, crossing
the Prairies de Malidor at some distance from the Château,
gave rise to the tradition that this beautiful reach, *la boucle du
Loir*, was made by man. But M. Paul Candé has shown that the
present bed of the river dates from at least the eleventh century.
If man was ever responsible for the alteration of the watercourse
it was in the interests of defence and not of landscape gardening.
For Le Lude has been a fortress since the days of Foulque
Nerra.

No fabric speaks so clearly of its own history. It begins at the
bottom of the dry moat with the foundations of the thirteenth-
century *château fort*—the great drums on which the towers were
raised and the warren of subterranean passages beneath the outward bastion to the east, known as the Eperon.

Above this is the layer of the renaissance, which only survives
on the north and south façades. The use of military foundations
determined the militant aspect of the façades, but the windows
are large and the decoration abundant.

The seventeenth century removed the Base Court and united
it to the Eperon, making a gay parterre where once had been
an outwork of defence. The eighteenth century demolished the
irregular west wing, opening the courtyard on that side to make
a new entrance from the town, and closing it upon the east with

its tall and elegant façade. It was the last century to have the courage of its artistic convictions and to build boldly in its own style, untroubled by the juxtaposition of old and new.

The nineteenth century preferred pastiche; it saw the rebuilding of the Tour du Diable on the north-west corner, somewhat in the style of Chambord; it saw the provision of new state rooms in the north wing in more or less renaissance style. Each century, in fact, adapted Le Lude to its own requirements, with the result that it is both inhabitable and inhabited. It retains none the less the architectural evidence of every phase of its protracted history.

At the bottom of its precipitous moat one is at the level of the thirteenth-century fortress. Here, beneath the parterres of the Château, are subterranean passages, lengthy and tortuous, whose low-set arrow slits command the approaches from the river. The passages converge on a great vaulted chamber, whose impressive structure has led some to mistake it for a

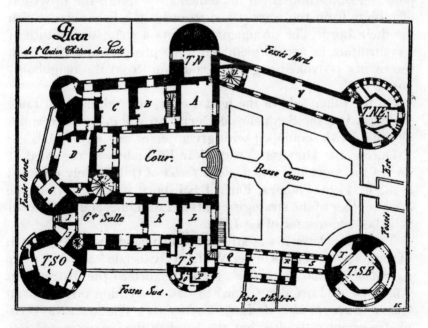

LE LUDE: Ground plan of the Chateau before the destruction of the Basse Cour in the seventeenth century.

Chapel. It was clearly an assembly centre for the defending troops.

The original appearance of Le Lude can only be conjectured from the plan. The main block formed three sides of a quadrangle, opening towards the east by a flight of steps down to the Base Court, which was flanked on either side by a range of buildings each ending in a large tower. The tower at the northeast angle, commanding the bridge, was pierced by a veritable battery of arrow slits which enabled the defenders to concentrate their most devastating fire upon the river crossing. By contrast, the south-east tower was lit by windows and contained the Chapel. This tower was joined to the Château proper by a narrow corridor, in the centre of which was the gatehouse, which in those days provided the only access to the castle.

There is an interesting document of the fourteenth century requiring the bailiff of Le Lude to exercise his rights of *prise* and *ravage* and to provide the Château with tables, chairs, pitchers, pots and other household implements, to secure the provision of rabbits from the warren and to order the fishermen to fish for their Lord. The document suggests a château destitute of any furniture or appointments until the prospect of a visit from the owner provoked a general round-up from the neighbourhood.

On the other side of the feudal scale, the Seigneur du Lude was vassal to the Seigneur de Durtal, to whom he owed annually one hawk 'equipped with green jesses and silver bells'.

During the Hundred Years War Le Lude was regarded as one of the most important *places fortes* of this fiercely disputed area; in 1425 Thomas, Earl of Salisbury was occupying one after another of the strategic points of Le Maine, and on October 9 he became master of Le Lude.

Two years later it was still in English hands, with a garrison of some 1,200 soldiers under William Gladsdale *'qui s'était rendu formidable à toute la contrée'*. He so terrorized the district that Ambroise de Loré determined to risk everything on an assault *'pour emporter la place du Lude de vive force'*. The town was occupied without difficulty, but the English having retreated into the Château, the massive defences which it offered 'put the

French beyond all hope of mastering it'. Breaches, however, were effected by means of the new bombards, and on the fourth day the castle was successfully stormed.

It was the ruins left by these engagements which passed, in 1457, into the hands of Jean de Daillon, the childhood companion of Louis XI. He was on the wrong side at Monthléry and is said to have gone into hiding in a cave in the forest of Maulne which preserved right into the nineteenth century the name of *la Grotte de Daillon*.

In 1468 he was back in favour and lost no opportunity of using his power for his own enrichment. As Philippe de Commines wrote of him, '*il aimait fort son profit particulier*'.

It is perhaps on account of his devotion to his own interests that we owe the repair and renovation of Le Lude. In 1479 Jean Gendrot, *maître d'œuvre* to René d'Anjou, began the task. A special house was built for him near the entrance to the Château, which still survives. In addition, a number of smaller dwellings were put up for his workmen, the memory of which is preserved in the name of the rue de la Gendrottière. Progress, however, was slow, and it was chiefly under Jacques de Daillon and his wife Madeleine d'Illiers that Le Lude began to assume the aspect which it has today.

They borrowed freely from the architectural ideas of the great builders of their day, but chiefly, it would appear, from Florimond Robertet. The towers, with the upright lines of the windows intersected by the horizontal rings of the string courses, are strongly reminiscent of Bury; the decorative use of medallions recalls the Hôtel d'Alluye. But the towers of Le Lude are far more exciting to the eye than those of Bury, for the vertical flights of windows have been cut right into the *chemin de ronde* and rise into elaborate dormers above. Without this device the huge conical roofs would be oppressive. There is even a hint of Chambord about the crowded roofscape of Le Lude.

There is something of Gaillon, too, in the carved enrichments of pilasters and architraves, but the work has not the finesse of its Norman prototype. The execution is coarse and the motifs bizarre—one dormer is encrusted with the scallop shells of the Order of St. Michel; but it must be remembered that these

decorations were intended to be seen from across the great gulf
of the dry moat. A more delicate treatment would not have been
effective at this range. Undoubtedly the whole of the south
front is one of the great successes of the French Renaissance.

If Jacques de Daillon has left us the architecture of the south
façade, his grandson, Guy de Daillon, second comte du Lude,
has bequeathed to posterity an even more remarkable ensemble
—the little cabinet of the south-east tower, wrongly known as
the oratory.

In 1853, when a massive programme of restoration was put in
hand, the presence of this renaissance jewel was unsuspected,
but in that year the architect Delarue had occasion to remove a
portion of what turned out to be a false ceiling. Looking into
the cavity above he found a higher vaulted ceiling entirely
painted in grotesques. This exciting discovery led to a probing
beneath the whitewash of the walls. It immediately revealed
traces of polychroming. All the whitewash was carefully removed and laid bare a complete décor of mural paintings. They
form a series of scenes, some obviously Biblical, which have
long presented a problem to experts. But in 1965 M. Dominique
Bozo produced the answer to the riddle. Four of the scenes are
directly copied from illustrations to the *Triumphs* of Petrarch,
which were done for Jacques de Daillon in 1515. The rest are
based on the engraving of Salomon in *Les Quadrins Historiques
de la Bible* of Claude Paradin. The relevant edition of the
Quadrins only appeared in 1560. It is thus possible to date the
ensemble at approximately 1570.

The question must be asked: why were these paintings so
carefully concealed? It is often assumed that the eighteenth century, with a disdainful disregard for the artistic achievements of
the past, was responsible for this sort of vandalism. The
eighteenth century, however, did not despise the paintings of
the renaissance. The murals of the cabinet at Le Lude were
known to be still visible as late as 1777. M. Paul Candé has
produced evidence, suggestive though not conclusive, that these
were deliberately hidden to protect them. Anything heraldic
incurred the wrath of the revolutionaries, and the Régisseur of
Le Lude, M. Baratte, was precisely warned in July 1790 '*à faire*

couvrir les armoiries de plâtre'. It is at least probable that this exquisite decor was camouflaged by his orders to save it from vandalism.

It was only a few years previously that Le Lude had undergone extensive transformations. In 1787 the first stone was laid of the stately classical façade of the architect Barré which spans the eastern front. An inscription informs us that it was placed there by the *'Haute et Puissante Dame, Madame Butler, marquise de Vieuville'*.

'Madame Butler', as her name suggests, was of Irish descent. Another Irish family to play an important part in the history of this region was that of Walsh. In 1747 they purchased the great estate of Serrant, a few miles west of Angers.

The Walshes were among the most rich and loyal supporters of the house of Stuart. It was a Walsh who had brought James II on board his ship to exile in France. Two generations later Anthony Walsh was ready to reverse the process and to play an important role in the re-establishment of the Stuarts on the throne. 'Walsh knows his business perfectly and is an excellent seaman,' said Prince Charles Edward; 'he has offered to go with me himself, the vessel being his own that I go on board of.' It was thanks to Walsh that the Prince was landed safely in Moidart.

When he returned he found that an even greater honour had been prepared for him. A dispatch, in the archives of the duc de la Trémoïlle, reveals the full intentions of Louis XV. *'Sa Majesté ayant résolu de faire passer un Corps de Troupes en Angleterre, et ayant chargé le Sieur Walsh de diriger les préparatifs . . . elle lui explique quelles sont ses instructions sur les opérations.'* The battle of Culloden postponed indefinitely the proposed assistance of which Louis writes.

Two years later Walsh acquired the Château de Serrant, and a portrait of him with his Royal master still hangs above the mantelpiece in the Gallery.

Like Le Lude, Serrant represents a building started in the renaissance, continued in the seventeenth century and completed in the eighteenth. But here the later additions were made with strict regard to the previous style. The eastern half of the building, including the staircase entrance, dates from 1546, when it was started by Charles de Brie, who ruined himself thereby and left it uncompleted. The western half was added ninety years later by Guillaume Bautru, marquis de Vaubrun. It is almost the exact reflection of the older building. At the same time he raised an attic storey above the balustrade, whose pedimented dormers are the only indications of the later date of these additions.

Vaubrun was killed at Altenheim in 1705. Mme de Sévigné tells the sequel: 'they gave Vaubrun a funeral more magnificent than that of Turenne at St. Denis; she keeps his heart on a little credence table, she gazes at it, she touches it, she has two candles burning before it; she passes her whole life there from dinner to supper, and when they tell her she has been there for seven hours she cannot believe that it was even half an hour.' In token of her grief she commissioned from Coysevox the impressive memorial in the Chapel which is one of the treasures of Serrant. The hero is portrayed lying wounded in the field, still clasping his Marshal's baton in his hand; his wife kneels weeping at his feet, while Victory, descending from the skies, is about to place her wreath of laurels on his brow.

Serrant follows Valençay in roofing its towers with domes in place of the more usual *poivrières*. When the tower is a narrow one, as at Le Gué Péan, the effect can be most ungainly, but here, as at the contemporary Assier, where the towers have an ampler girth, the domes confer considerable dignity upon the façades. It should be noted in this context that the proportions of Serrant are only satisfying when seen from the edge of the moat, from which vantage point the basement storey is revealed. The south façade is magnificent in perpsective, but rather dull in elevation.

An interesting, though not very beautiful, feature is the central staircase pavilion. The landings of a staircase do not correspond with the levels of the main storeys, and the windows thus create an effect of syncopation in the rhythm of the fenestration. The effect is entirely happy at Azay-le-Rideau, and, in a very different architectural context, on the north front of Cheverny. At Serrant it must be confessed that the frontispiece is a mere intrusion which has every appearance of being a later addition. The staircase which it contains, however, is very fine.

Luynes, Le Lude and Serrant illustrate in their several ways the type of building which has grown with time. In contrast to these the Château of Azay-le-Rideau is a delightful example of one that was planned and built *d'un seul jet*.

Once again the traditions of defence have contributed to the attractions of a *demeure de plaisance*, for if a fortress was not placed on high ground from which it could command a wide sweep of country, it was situated on low and level ground and had to protect itself by means of water. At Azay the beauties of its renaissance architecture are doubled by their reflection in the moat.

For Azay too has been a fortress. In the fifteenth century it was known as Azay-le-Brûlé—a name derived from the stern reprisals of Charles VII who had been insulted by Burgundian soldiers here when passing from Chinon to Tours in 1417.

A century later the place was in the possession of Gilles Berthelot, the wealthy Maître des Comptes, and his wife Philippe Lesbahy. Permission to fortify had been sought from Louis XII on account of the continual and unwelcome visits of '*mauvais garçons, larrons publiques et autres gens vaccabuns*', who came, committed outrages, and retreated into the sanctuary of the Forêt de Chinon. On January 8, 1515, there was just such an alarm. News was brought that a large company of 'vagabonds, robbers and pilferers' was advancing on Azay. The citizens were summoned to the Château and issued with arms; watch and ward was established. At three in the morning the alarm was sounded, and Pierre Chaillon, a servant of Berthelot's, brought six loaded *hacquebutes*, which had the desired effect of causing the marauders to withdraw. It is easy to see why the new Château at Azay-le-Rideau retained some of the paraphernalia of defence. For three years later—just after Chenonceau was started and just before Chambord was begun—Gilles and Philippe embarked upon a total reconstruction of the house.

The *comptes des bâtiments*, which only exist for the first two years, reveal a veritable hive of activity—of workmen working day and night, summer and winter, being provided with candles for night work and gloves for the cold. They worked under difficulties, for the foundations were waterlogged and required the attentions of a *pompeur* from Angers; much of the Château had to be built on piles: 120 masons wrought under the supervision of the master mason, Etienne Rousseau. They erected the shell of the masonry, while such specialists as Pierre Maupoint attended to the *culs de lampe* of the turrets. Meanwhile, even more advanced, a Parisian joiner named Thierry was at work on the panelling.

The accounts are annotated in the first place by 'Monsieur de Saint Cyr'—that is to say Guillaume Artault, Curé de St. Cyr; but his signature is appended *'en l'absence de Mademoiselle'*. In addition to his hand is another which occasionally records the payment of a sum to him. It is easy to conclude that this is the writing of 'Mademoiselle', in other words of Philippe Lesbahy to whom tradition has always ascribed the building of Azay-le-Rideau.

Marguerite de Feschal, Catherine Briçonnet and Philippe Lesbahy, the creators of three of the most perfect and beautiful châteaux of the Loire, underline the importance of the feminine role in the buildings of the epoque. Most especially at Azay is this softer touch to be appreciated. The towers here have lost all military significance and are reduced to ornaments; so is the *chemin de ronde*. Each façade presents an ordered symmetry which knows, nevertheless, how to 'break step' for some special feature such as the staircase pavilion.

It must be remembered, however, that two of the towers, those to right and left of the entrance court, are nineteenth-century additions. The tower to the right hand, which is almost detached from the main building, replaces a far older tower, dating perhaps from Hugues Ridel. It was typical, not only of nouveaux riches like Berthelot, but of most of the builders of the renaissance who built upon the site of an historic feudal castle, to preserve, as proofs of ancient title, some tower or *donjon* of the castle which they replaced. Thus we have the Tour de Marques at Chenonceau, the *donjon* at Villandry and the towers of Brézé at Brissac. But whereas the Tour de Marques is an ornament and an asset to Chenonceau, the old tower at

Azay, with its ugly mushroom dome, was a blemish out of all keeping with the refinement of the new buildings. Berthelot paid heavily for his snobbery in retaining it.

The tower to the left of the court, on the north-east corner, is also new. Berthelot left this corner blank, with only a narrow pinnacle to round it off. Without this tower the balance of Azay is seriously upset. The south and west fronts, which are as Berthelot built them, show the most scrupulous regard for rhythm and proportion. The north façade, before its flanking tower was built, presented a wide, blank bay upon the left hand side. It cannot have been intended.

There is but one explanation. It is that Azay was never completed; that Berthelot meant to enclose the courtyard to the east by a wing which reflected that upon the west. It would have put his staircase pavilion central in its façade and made sense of the whole design.

The reason for Azay being left unfinished is not far to seek. On August 12, 1527 there took place in Paris an event which was to shatter for ever the dreams of the Berthelots and to alter completely the destiny of Azay-le-Rideau. Jacques de Beaune Semblançay was led from the Bastille, where he had languished since January, to the gallows at Montfaucon. The old man—he was eighty-two—with his long white beard and sober grey attire, had made a deep impression on the crowd, *'lequel avoit marvileuse pitié et compation dudit seigneur'*; he had behaved with the utmost dignity and composure, even during the interminable delay at the foot of the gibbet while they waited for a reprieve which never came, so that Clément Marot could ask sarcastically, which looked more like the criminal, Semblançay *'ferme vieillard'* or the Lieutenant Maillart who conducted him to execution.

Semblançay was Berthelot's cousin by marriage. He had held the lucrative but vulnerable position of Surintendant des Finances and was accused of failure to pass on vital supplies of money to the army; Louise de Savoie had pursued the matter with an ugly tenacity, and François had acquiesced in the sentence. Berthelot deemed it prudent to quit the country and his beautiful Château was confiscated by the King.

It was perhaps not altogether unreasonable that a house built
with the King's money should be regarded as the King's. An
interesting side-light into the situation is to be obtained from
the story of Galliot de Genouillac and the Château d'Assier.

Genouillac held the important and remunerative posts of
Grand Ecuyer and Grand Maître de l'Artillerie, and in 1524
he caused 'the most superb mansion' to be erected on his seigneurial lands in Lot. Its only blemish was that it was 'most ill-
seated in a most ugly landscape', but in Brantôme's eyes it was
the best furnished house in France, 'both as regards silver
vessels and tapestries and ceilings hung with gold and silver
silk'.

So fine a château so richly appointed could not fail to evoke
jealousy, and enemies of Genouillac managed to suggest to
Royal ears that 'it was not possible he had not robbed the King'.
Summoned to render an account, Galliot boldly confessed. 'Sire,
when I came into your service,' he said, 'I was far from rich;
but by your means and grace I have become so; you have raised
me by the favour which you have shown me . . . you have made
me what I am; you have given me the possessions which I hold.
You gave freely—you are free to take away; I am ready to
return the whole to you.'

He touched the right note. François was not the man to resent
the adornment of his realm with large and lovely buildings. 'I
have no desire to reproach you or to take from you what I gave,'
was his reply; 'you offer it to me—I return it to you with all
my heart. Love me and serve me as you always have, and I
shall always be a good King to you.'

CHAPTER XI

The Manor House and Gardens

T HE LARGE and lovely buildings of Kings and Courtiers must not be allowed to obscure the fact that the sixteenth century was the heyday of the smaller Manor House just as it was called the golden age of the *Gentilhomme Campagnard*. François I took a personal interest in the class, which ranged, Brantôme informs us, from 'knowing most of them and being well able to quote their families and genealogy', to such minor ompliments as never using any oath but *'foi de gentilhomme!'*.

They were a solid, self-supporting class, the Gentlemen of France, whose modest estates provided them with the necessities of life; but the necessities of a Gentleman included a vineyard and facilities for hunting and hawking. Antonio de Beatis noted that when they were not at the Court—a service which they rendered for three months only in the year—'they pass their time in their châteaux or country houses, which are surrounded with woodlands where they hunt, in which they live at very little cost'.

The economy of the *gentilhommière* owed much to the Lady of the Manor. Although mistress of some eighteen to twenty servants she was thrifty and often obliged 'to govern her bread so well as that none be suffered to use it otherwise than temperately'. But economy meant more to her than thrift; it meant stewardship—the husbanding of every resource of nature. She had to be 'skillful in natural Physicke . . . for to have a Physition always is not for the profit of the house'. She had the supervision of all the 'kine, calves, hogges, pigges, pigeons, geese, ducks, peacocks, hennes and all other sorts of beasts'—and had to know and to deal with all their ailments. She was, in fact, the doctor and the vet.

To this end she was also mistress of the Herb Garden and the Physicke Garden, and most expert in the therapeutic properties of both. She had to be ready for every emergency. She could treat a horse for 'hen's dung swallowed by hap'; she would not quail before such gross problems as 'how to loosen an oxe's bellie', nor such nice ones as what to do 'if your nightingale grows melancholicke'. She knew that 'Mugwort hath singular force against the bitings of serpents', whereas the *golden apple* 'provoketh loathing and vomiting'. If her chicken got *the pip*, 'either from want of drink or from drinking troubled or filthie water'—she had the remedy; she knew also that beans roasted on hot ashes were an aphrodisiac for peacocks.

All this, and a thousand other exotic remedies and recipes, she knew because she possessed a little book—or rather a large book—entitled *Agriculture et Maison Rustique* by Charles Estienne. This book of information purported to contain 'everything that can be required to build a country house, to feed and care for animals of all sorts, to maintain vegetables and flower gardens, to look after honey-bees, to plant and cross every sort of fruit tree . . . to create the vineyard, to build the warren, the heronry and the enclosure for game'. It was, together with the *Almanack* of Nostradamus, the text book of the Country Gentleman. It told him how to rule his family, tend his livestock, till his land, and how to build his *gentilhommière*.

He was advised to build upon some gentle rising ground, 'for by this means he shall reap the liberty of the air, and a goodly prospect'. He should site his mansion so that the main windows faced the east, 'that the Sun might enter betimes in the morning', for the Lord and his Lady were hard workers, first up and last to bed. All 'houses for beasts' were to face the south 'and borrowing somewhat of the east' to keep them warm and dry; this placed them inevitably upon the north side of the courtyard. The other outbuildings formed a complementary range upon the south.

Circumscribed by these buildings, Estienne advises his Gentleman to 'draw a great court and wide'. It should cover two acres, contain two ponds, two dunghills and a well. The fourth side of the court was to be enclosed by a high wall, in the centre of which was the main gate, tall enough to admit a cart of hay, but covered to protect the woodwork from the weather. Beside this gate was a smaller residence for the Farmer, the

Lord's lieutenant on the land. He was allowed three upper rooms; one bedroom for himself; another for his family and friends, and somewhat unaccountably a third 'adjoining close unto it, to keep foul linen'.

One of the most charming examples of this sort of house is the Manoir de Beauregard. Some five miles north of St. Aignan, and tucked away in the little valley of the Renne, it has preserved the aspect of a *gentilhommière* by remaining a farm. It is set in an entirely appropriate context of ducks and goats and granaries; there is something suggestive of the hard, unhurried labours of the peasant.

Architecturally it is delightful. Its features are quickly listed —an octagonal staircase tower with a fine flamboyant lintel to the door; a flight of windows crowned by a dormer worthy of Blois, and an interesting machicolated projection immediately overhanging the entrance. This projection, known as a *bretèche*, is exactly what Estienne commended for the defending of the Keeper's house from poachers. Although Beauregard could not, in any military context, be defended, unwelcome guests could receive severe discouragement by means of this device.

But there is at Beauregard an atmosphere of untidiness, dilapidation and abandoned agricultural machines which was not typical of the sixteenth century. Even the humblest outbuildings were kept in a state of scrupulous repair, for it was a principle of the *gentilhommière* that 'there must not anything be let go to decay, be it never so little'. All contemporary drawings show this sort of house in a trim environment of gardens and forecourts. Nor was it usual to make distinction between the useful and the ornamental; the vegetable garden was as beautifully ordered and maintained as the flower garden.

The early morning was the time Estienne commended for the Gentleman to taste the pleasures of his garden—'whiles as yet the clear and pearl-like dew doth perch unto the grass, he giveth himself to hear the melodious music of the Bees, which, busying themselves in gathering of the same, do also fill the air with a most acceptable, sweet and pleasant harmony'.

The aesthetic appeal of the garden was threefold; it appealed to the eye with 'fair and comely proportions, handsome and

pleasant Arbors, and delightful borders of Lavender and Rosemary'; it appealed to the ear, not only by the aforementioned
bees, but by 'the ravishing music of an infinite number of pretty
small birds, which do chatter and chant their proper and natural
branch songs'; it appealed to the nose, for here were Juniper,
Nept and Sweet-Balm, Jasmine, All-Good and Cammomile,
Tansy, Thyme 'and other fragrant herbs'.

The Pleasure Garden, in fact, was divided into two halves,
one 'which may be called the garden of herbs of a good smell',
and one 'which may be called the Nosegay Garden', whose
plants were more selected for the eye. There are only some
twenty species mentioned; Violets, Wallflowers, Daffodils and
Daisies, Mugwort and Marigold and Canterbury Bells, and
among them the more spectacular Amaranthus or Purple Velvet
Flower, the Helitropian, the Crown Imperial and others 'whose
colours being glorious and different, make such a brave and
checkered mixture that it is most wondrous, pleasant and delicate to behold'.

And yet, as the Lady of the Manor cast her eye over their
varied blooms, one feels that she did not enjoy their beauty with
a single eye but could not forbear from making mental note how
Marie Violets 'make good gargarisms for ulcers in the mouth',
that Hyacinths, when gone to seed, could be boiled in wine 'to
stay the flux of the bellie', and Narcissus roots 'brayed in honey'
would take away freckles, whereas the root of the Nénuphar
was 'very singular to procure sleep and to preserve chastity'.

The Pleasure Gardens were divided from the Kitchen Garden
'by the intercourse of a great Alley'. This also, although devoted to vegetables and herbs, was laid out in knots and labyrinths, and the whole plot set about with Arbours or 'turrets of
lattice fashion, covered with Bordeaux vines'. Pleasure and
profit were here, as everywhere, combined, for the vines having
provided shade for the summer, yielded fruit in the autumn 'to
make verjuice for the commoditie of the Household'.

The gardens of the *gentilhommière* differed only in scale from
those of the large châteaux. Both date from the sixteenth century,
for the surrounding of a house by a large area of ornamental
ground was a taste largely borrowed from Italy.

The gardens of the renaissance mostly existed in their own right—often, as at Blois, Gaillon and Chenonceau, being completely detached from the lay-out of the Château. But already the idea was present of the garden forming a delicate and graduated transition from the formality of the buildings to the wildness of the landscape. For whereas the English Garden tried to create a 'natural' landscape which in fact was artificial and idealized, the *Jardin Français* sought to mediate between architecture and a landscape that was truly natural.

This *ordonnance* has been reinstated at Villandry. When, in 1906, the domain was purchased by Dr. Carvallo, both château and gardens were in a lamentable condition. The house itself, 'all windows and balconies and paintings in trompe l'œil' had lost the charm of its renaissance architecture without acquiring the dignity of an eighteenth-century façade.

The gardens were worse. Except for a lawn perforated with little flower beds, reminiscent of the worst sort of municipal park, the whole area was stuffed with vegetation. '*Le Château lui-même*', wrote Dr. Carvallo, '*disparaissait au milieu d'arbres et de verdure.*' Nevertheless he saw the capabilities of the place, and set about the restoration of the Château and the reconstruction of the gardens. The plans of du Cerceau furnished him with abundant models.

The gardens are disposed in three terraces, each level corresponding with one storey of the house. Dr. Carvallo insists on the function of these levels. 'The Base Court is low,' he reasoned; 'the forecourt is higher, and the Court of Honour higher still. The owner, the passer-by and the animal are each in their place, each in relation to one another, but without possible confusion.' As at Versailles, so at Villandry the gradation of the courts had been replaced with a single, gently sloping ramp, 'so that by an imperceptible declivity Man gravitates toward the stable, and Beasts, without the slightest effort, can come right up to the Salon.'

All this at once was changed. The nuances of class distinction were restored, and reason reigned once more in the courts and policies of Villandry.

Level with the Base Court is the Kitchen Garden. It is disposed in nine squares intersected by four gravel paths. At each

of the four cross-roads there is a fountain, and at the four corners
of each fountain stands an arbour of roses. Within the sub-
divisions of these squares the vegetables are planted with an
equal eye to use and beauty. One is reminded of a remark of
Cardinal Georges d'Amboise, the builder of Gaillon; 'I saw
cabbages,' he wrote from Rome, 'almost as *beautiful* as those in
the Kitchen Garden of my Château.' It is in this *Jardin Potager*
that Villandry reproduces most exactly the formal gardens of
the renaissance.

The second level is that of the reception rooms—an open-air
extension to the Salon. These are the parterres, each a labyrinth
of square-cut box—trim, symmetrical and complex as a Persian
rug. But this is not geometry for geometry's sake. The designs
are symbolic and represent the theme *'Cœur d'Amour Epris'*.
For just as human hearts had throbbed beneath the starched and
corseted correctness of the age, so now the rigid rectilinear
designs depict the motions of the human heart; fluttering fan
and piercing sword are clipped and disciplined in box.

The third level is that of the upper storeys of the house. The
whole area is marked out by lime trees. By following the contours of the re-entrant or borrowing the gentle gradient of the
cross-section of the valley, these avenues, though strictly
regimented, begin to yield to Nature's forms. Encompassed by
these double rows of lime is the Pièce d'Eau, the next stage in
the transition from Art to Nature; for here, where the landscape
is first permitted to be informal, it is reflected in a formal frame.

The use of reflection to assimilate the background with the
foreground suggests another purpose to the clipped parterres.
From the upper terrace, at the point at which it crosses the canal,
the village of Villandry forms the view. Seen from this angle
the Parish Church looks like a demonstration set for a lesson in
solid geometry—an ordered pile of cubes and pyramids and
cones, turned by perspective to triangles and diamonds and
parallelograms. Whether by chance effect or by deliberate contrivance, these shapes are to an astonishing extent answered
and reflected by the patterns of the box parterre.

The last outpost of the garden is the latest addition, the apple
orchard planted by M. François Carvallo on the highest ground

that overtops the gardens—the *couronne fruitière renaissance* which gives the final touch to the design.

This was an old tradition highly praised by Charles Estienne and not to be neglected by his Gentleman even in a humble lay-out 'where we are more to regard profit, joined with a mean and moderate beauty, than any unnecessary sumptuousness'. Having made his Kitchen Garden and his Flower Garden, the Gentleman is now urged 'to trim up a green plot for fruit trees'.

The siting of this plot was matter for great care and attention, but one thing is axiomatic: 'the situation of the orchard should be upon some hill top, or some small hill', for thus it avoided the process of mutual overshadowing to which the trees of a level orchard were subject, for 'such as stand in plains do annoy one another with their shade'. More important still, the hill-top orchard would be 'more pleasant and delightsome for contentment of contemplation and view'. To this end it should be to the north of the house, where it could be seen in full sun, for on the south side 'it would not stand so fair for prospect'.

Beyond the orchard lay the pastures and meadows of the farm, and beyond these lay the park. This also came within the economy of the household, for whereas great Lords might hunt the stag and fly at kites and herons with great expense and very little profit, the Gentleman, with modest stables, modest kennels and modest mews, could combine his own diversion with the provisioning of his household. His outlay was small, and the game he took went either to the larder or the market.

Happy was the man whose paternal lands embraced both hill and dale and afforded within their ample confines a rich variety of ground, 'part high wood, part grass or champion, part coppice or underwood'. The high places Estienne would like to see clothed in ancient trees, 'goodly high woods of tall timber, as well for the beauty and gracefulnesse of the Parke, as also for the echo and sound that rebound from the same'. For the park was the hunting field, and the trees would echo back the calls and clamours of the chase 'doubling the music and making it ten times more delightful'.

The Lord himself must spend much time and patience on the training of his dogs, which he would follow in the field with hawk or arquebus, walking up his hares and partridges. 'The way to train him to his knowledge,' wrote Estienne, 'is by all loving means, or else awful where love taketh not effect.' To this he adds a plea for limited vocabulary; 'by no means use many words or change of words, for that breeds a confusion in the dogge's brain.' Finally he must be taken out into the field, and when he is hot upon the scent—'which you shall know by the business of his tail and by a kind of secret whining'—he must be made to lie still 'until such time as your hawk be at her pitch . . . and the game being taken, you shall not forget to reward your dogge'.

The most detailed account of the life of a *gentilhommière* comes not from the valley of the Loire, but from Normandy, from Gilles de Gouberville, Lord of the Château du Mesnil-au-Val. The outstanding features of his memoirs are the direct care which he took of his lands and the expert knowledge which he possessed of agriculture. He was nearly always on the spot; the commonest phrase in the book is *'je ne bougé de céans'*. Although a person of considerable local importance, he was his own foreman; he was not one who could 'commit himself to the mercy and discretion of a farmer'. Because of this he lived at close quarters with his household of eighteen servants. Socially he touched both extremes; he was well received at Court, and when at Blois, he danced with a daughter of the great Montmorency. But when at home and without guests, he was careful to eat the same bread as his servants. He marks his recovery from an indisposition with the significant phrase: *'redescendu à la cuisine'*.

The kitchen, in fact, seems to have been to the French what the great hall was to the English—the common room of the household. It was here that the lord ate in company with his domestics; it was here, on rainy days, that he would spend the evenings reading aloud to them 'in Amadis des Gaulles, how that he conquered Durdan'.

No one would have approved more warmly of this than the great Montmorency. According to Olivier de Serres, he poured scorn on the way 'a gentleman, having attained an income of 500 *livres*, no longer knows what it is to make good cheer, for, wishing to cut an imposing figure, he eats in his dining-room at the whim of his cook', whereas formerly, eating in the kitchen, *'il se faisait servir à sa fantaisie'*.

Part of the economy of the château or *gentilhommière* which expressed itself architecturally was the *fuie* or dovecote. The birds were bred for the table, and were most profitable since 'they got their own livings . . . and lay, six or seven times a year, two eggs apiece'. They 'got their livings', naturally enough, at the expense of the local farmers, and perhaps because of this, the right to possess a dovecote, the *Droit de Colombage*, was restricted to 'such as be Lords in fee simple'. One pair of pigeons was allowed per hectare of land. The size of the estate could therefore be inferred from the capacity of the dovecote, which thus became a status symbol, and for this reason figured conspicuously in the architectural ensemble. When Fouchaux, near Villandry, was sacked in 1791, the demolition of the dovecote was demanded by the revolutionaries *'comme signe de féodalité'*.

One of the finest surviving dovecotes stands in the forecourt of the Château de Boumois, mid-way between Angers and Saumur. The building itself, a single drum of masonry, was crowned with an elegant stone louvre; but whereas a real louvre was designed to let out smoke, this cupola was to permit the comings and goings of 1,200 pigeons.

In order that the birds might easily be taken, a simple but ingenious mechanism was devised. A central mast rotated on its axis. From this mast extended a beam or gibbet that formed the radius to the circle. To this beam was attached a ladder, which, by the rotation of the mast, could be brought alongside any portion of the wall, providing easy access to the niches.

A deep and cunning knowledge of the pigeon was brought to bear upon the productivity of the dovecote. The insertion of young house doves to accompany lone males of the flock could lead to extra broods provided it was done 'so as the dams do not perceive it'. Brown, black and ash-coloured birds were best for breeding, but rough-footed ones or those 'of a colour like unto a snail's bellie' were to be rejected as 'too mournful'. The white ones were both sturdy and prolific, but 'most subject to the kite and other ravenous birds, because they are very easily perceived'.

The dovecote was as carefully sited as the château, having its window to the south, 'because this bird doth greatly delight in the sun'. It was to be kept not only clean but sweet; 'perfume oftentimes your Dovehouse,' Estienne advises, 'with Juniper, Rosemary and sometimes with a little frankincense; for that doth mightily retain and keep them, and causeth them to love their own house more than any other.'

Two more magnificent examples of the dovecote can be seen today at Talcy and at Villesavin, a château hardly larger than a *gentilhommière*.

Situated in the valley of the Beuvron, mid-way between Chambord and Cheverny, this delightful little château was built in 1537 by Jean le Breton, the builder also of Villandry. Jean le Breton was at that time in charge of the works of Chambord, but already by then the style of Chambord was archaic. It was at Fontainebleau, Madrid and Villers Cotterets that François I developed the style from which French Classicism was to grow, and it was Jean le Breton who imported this style into the valley of the Loire.

Although Villesavin derives its inspiration from such princely houses as Ecouen and Chantilly, there is something essentially homely about its low façades and lofty roofs. The service court to the west of the Cour d'Honneur is full of rustic charm; so is the spacious kitchen which overlooks the court. In such a room we can picture Gilles de Gouberville, *'redescendu à la cuisine'*, reading aloud to his family and domestics, of the exploits of Amadis des Gaulles.

Villandry and Villesavin are among the last of the Châteaux of the Loire in the generic sense of the term. Already the region was ceasing to be the centre of influence; it no longer had a style to call its own. The new architecture, which radiated from the Ile de France, marked a further stage in the de-fortification of the château. Of all the paraphernalia of defence, the moat alone was now retained.

The move was premature, for France was on the brink of a long period of Civil War. The local history of the second half of the sixteenth century was to centre on the citadels of Amboise and Blois.

CHAPTER XII

The Time of Troubles

WHEN, IN 1784, Arthur Young went round the
Château de Blois he was treated by the guide to
many gruesome anecdotes, all related 'in the same
tone, from having told them so often, in which the fellow in
Westminster Abbey gives his monotonous history of the tombs'.
But if Young was bored by the delivery, he was no less repelled
by the subject matter; 'the character of the period,' he reflected,
'and that of the men that figured in it, were alike disgusting.
Bigotry and ambition, equally dark, insidious and bloody, allow
no feelings of regret. The parties could hardly have been employed than in cutting one another's throats.'

There is an obvious and superficial truth about his comment,
but Young was no profound historian; the duc de Lévis-Mire-
poix is a better guide to the period. 'The country now enters,'
he writes, 'upon a drama that is to run for a third of the century.
It will have its horror and its grandeur. Men of noble qualities
will not be lacking; but they will not be disciplined either by a
man or by an ideal. Public-spiritedness will be cancelled out by
the spirit of faction.'

With the death of Henri II the great days of the Valois were
over. The throne passed to his son François II, a sickly boy with
a pale and puffy face and a pustular infection of the ear. The
power passed to the House of Lorraine.

Of the twelve children of Henri de Lorraine, first duc de
Guise, three only concern us. François, the second Duke;
Charles, the Cardinal of Lorraine, and Marie, the Queen of
Scotland, whose more famous daughter Mary Stuart was now
the Queen of France. Her husband was King, but uncles ruled
the land.

The two men could hardly have been more different. The
Duke was a man of war with a military figure and a militant

125

approach to life. Tall, imposing, supremely self-assured, and with an air of sinister distinction enhanced by a deep and honourable scar, he was a man made to command and to command affection. 'There was not a soldier in the army,' claimed Montluc, 'who would not willingly have risked any hazard on his orders, so completely had he won their hearts.' Among the officers of the realm he stood out, as Brantôme puts it, 'like a great and sturdy oak has pride of place in the plantation'.

When such a man espoused a cause that cause at once became personified in him—and with this came a danger; for a cause that is identified with a single dominant personality can receive a mortal blow by his removal. The pre-eminence of Guise in the Catholic ranks did disservice to their cause. But this strength of personality gave him also his own safeguard against the assassin. His very presence was so annihilating as to disarm attack. Captain Mazères, one of his would-be assassins, explaining under interrogation why he had had no short-sword on him, admitted 'when I considered your furious presence, I straightway lost the courage to attack you at close quarters'.

His brother Charles was in almost every way his opposite. Thanks to a corrupt and senseless system of preferment he had been an Archbishop since the age of fourteen. Crafty and oblique by nature, he was an avaricious but astute financier, a persistent intriguer and an implacable enemy. He began his nephew's reign by re-opening hostilities against those who wavered in their catholicism. One of the last acts of Henri II had been the condemnation for heresy of the Councillor Anne du Bourg. Du Bourg had been tactless enough to suggest in the Parlement de Paris that the high principles of a heretic compared favourably with the low morals of an adulterer. Henri and Diane de Poitiers came well within the meaning of that word, and the King had vowed to see du Bourg burnt with his own eyes. He did not live to do so. But in December 1559 the Cardinal of Lorraine resumed the proceedings, and du Bourg was hanged and his body burnt in the Place de Grève. Du Bourg died with exemplary courage; 'his one speech,' wrote Florimond Raemond, 'did more harm to the Catholic cause than a hundred Ministers could have done.'

This renewal of persecution led, not unnaturally, to a reaction from the Protestant Party. Their leaders were the King of Navarre, his brother the Prince de Condé, and two members of the Châtillon family, the Admiral de Coligny and his brother d'Andelot.

It was not, however, in such high circles that the movement of reaction started, but with the *petite noblesse*, men of the sturdy breed that was nurtured in a hundred *gentilhommières* in every province. When it came to the touch, these were the ones who paid the forfeit with their blood.

Typical of this class was Godefroy de Barry, Seigneur de la Rénaudie—'*homme de grand esprit et de diligence presqu'incroyable*', he was reputed by Belleforest to be one of the most eloquent men in France, though one of the least learned. Apart from his religion he had a personal grudge against the House of Lorraine, for his brother-in-law, the Sieur de Buy, had been imprisoned at Vincennes by order of Guise, and had died under torture. In the early months of 1560 la Rénaudie began to assemble supporters for an attack upon Guise.

The King had been moved by his physicians from Fontaine-bleau to the Valley of the Loire for the sake of the air—'*le meilleur et plus gracieux air de tout le Royaume*'. It is ironic that one of nature's most innocent endowments to this region should have made it the scene of the atrocious events that were to follow.

Towards the end of February, la Rénaudie established his headquarters in the Faubourg St. Germains at the house of a Huguenot called des Avenelles. Des Avenelles was not a party to the conspiracy but it was not possible to conceal from him what was afoot, and being at last informed, he took fright and gave information to Lallemand de Vouzé, an agent of the Guises.

The first move on their part was to transfer the King to the greater security of Amboise. Here François summoned Coligny and d'Andelot, and here, on March 8, was issued the Edict of Amboise, granting amnesty to Protestants.

In spite of this amnesty, the conspirators went ahead with their design. The plan was to infiltrate sixty men into the town and thirty into the Château; their zero hour was to be 'dinner time' on March 17, when Condé—*le Capitaine Muet*—was to give the signal, and the troops, massed in the neighbourhood, were to assault the castle. It was a plan whose success must in any circumstances have been doubtful, but now a second time it was betrayed.

At this point the narrative is taken up by two men who watched eagerly from positions of privilege within the Château —the English Ambassador, Sir Nicholas Throckmorton, and the Spanish Ambassador, de Chantonnay. Throckmorton gives the clearest sequence of events in a letter to Cecil dated at Amboise, March 21.

'On the 14th of this present,' he writes, 'there came to Tours a Captain called Castelnovo, a Baron of Gascoigne . . . with five other Captains, all of them esteemed men of very good skill in the wars.' After a scuffle with the comte de Sancerre and his men, they moved to Noizay, a small château 'three English miles from Amboise' on the road to Vouvray. It was at this point that Captain Lignières, anxious for the safety of Condé, informed the Queen Mother of the rendez-vous.

The result was immediate panic. The two Ambassadors reported in haste to their masters. 'This night,' wrote Throckmorton, 'a new hot alarm is offered, and our town doth begin again to be guarded. It is a marvel to see how they be daunted, that have not at other times been afeared of great armies of horsemen, footmen and the fury shot of artillery.' 'The terror was so great,' wrote Chantonnay, 'there might have been an army at the gates of the Château.' The duc de Guise and his brother wore coats of mail; 'they know not whom to mistrust, nor to trust,' continues Throckmorton; 'this day they license some to depart; tomorrow they revoke them.'

Meanwhile, across the river at Noizay the plans were going quietly forward as if nothing were amiss. Lulled by a sense of security for which it is difficult to account, they did not even take the elementary precaution of posting sentries. On the morning of the 15th, two of the conspirators, Raunay and Mazères, were strolling together in the grounds, when the duc de Nemours, sent on a preliminary reconnaissance, seized them

CHENONCEAU: entrance front as altered by Catherine de'
Medici; engraving by Clarey Martineau

CHENONCEAU: the same, as restored to its original appearance
by Madame Pelouze

LUYNES: the north-west towers

LUYNES: interior of courtyard

LUYNES: from the south; engraving by Delpech

LE LUDE: south front from the moat

LE LUDE: entrance front

SERRANT: painting of
Anthony Walsh landing
Prince Charles Edward in
Moidart

SERRANT: south front from the moat

AZAY-LE-RIDEAU: before the nineteenth-century additions;
engraving by Clarey Martineau

AZAY-LE-RIDEAU: with two towers added in the
nineteenth century

AZAY-LE-RIDEAU: as it may have been originally planned;
reconstruction by Ian Dunlop

SULLY-SUR-LOIRE: from the south

BRISSAC: the salle des Gardes

BRISSAC: Staircase Pavilion
and tower

and carried them off to Amboise. The same night he returned to Noizay with a troop of five hundred horse. His principal weapon, however, was deception. Castelnau and his men were persuaded to come to a parley by the offer of a safe conduct. Once within the Château they were arrested and imprisoned.

On the morning of the 16th it looked as if the conspiracy had faded out, and the Court felt it could be lenient. Of fifty prisoners, 'mostly artificers', all but four were released, the King even presenting to each a crown, 'and to one who was hurt in the head five crowns'.

The majority of the conspirators, however, including la Rénaudie, were still at large. These now began to behave with the greatest stupidity.

'On the 17th,' continues Throckmorton, 'a company of a hundred and fifty horsemen well appointed approached the Court gates and shot off their pistols at the Church of the Bonhommes.' This seemingly pointless gesture caused a serious change in the attitude of the Court. The alarm was sounded, 'the drum was stricken', and the Guises began on their reprisals. 'This heat caused upon a sudden a sharp determination to administer justice. Eleven men were hanged, divers were drowned in sacks and some appointed to die on the wheel.'

On the 20th la Rénaudie was shot in the course of a skirmish and his body was hanged on a gibbet before the Château. But still the damp squib of the conspiracy continued to splutter. Pitifully small forces made unco-ordinated attacks which were immediately repulsed. 'It seems as if God has turned their minds,' wrote Chantonnay; 'they allow themselves to be captured like children.'

There is no reliable tally of the executions, but they can certainly be reckoned in hundreds. Hanging, drowning and decapitation were daily spectacles, and according to tradition some of the victims were hanged 'on long cords' from the balcony above the Grande Salle, so that the close-up of their agony could be witnessed from the windows. '*La vengeance est un plat qui se mange froid.*'

There were tales of heroism and of revulsion. Villemongey,

going to the block, dipped his hands in the blood of his companions and raised them in prayer. 'Heavenly Father,' he cried; 'behold the blood of thy children. Thou wilt repay.' The duchesse de Guise, according to one account, withdrew from the balcony. 'Such scenes revolt me,' she told Catherine de' Medici; 'never has a mother had more cause to feel afflicted. How great a storm of hatred and revenge is gathered over the heads of my unhappy sons.' Her premonition was not at fault. Her husband and two of her sons were to die by the hands of an assassin.

On Sunday, March 31, the Court left Amboise and its stinking corpses for the valley of the Cher, where the Queen Mother was to be their hostess at Chenonceau. Spring had already begun to touch the woods and hedgerows with the delicate enrichment of colour which precedes the foliage, but the new châtelaine was not content with Nature's annual renaissance; every device of Italian art had been employed to adorn and beautify the domain of the Bohiers, and the whole population of the village had been conscripted for the pageant.

As the Royal cavalcade turned down the long straight drive to the Château, the women and children of Chenonceaux, in large and multicoloured rustic headgear, lined the avenue and scattered flowers on the way. The men, mustered in military escort, deployed behind them.

At the entrance to the gardens a vast triumphal arch, of Tuscan columns wreathed with ivy swags, stood athwart the drive. It bore the inscription: 'To Francis the Divine, son of Henry the Divine and Grandson of Francis the Divine, the Best and Happiest of Princes.' This apotheosis of the House of Valois had been devised, it seems appropriately, by Elie de Hodeau, Seigneur de Paradis; but his title derived from a merely terrestrial estate within the domain of Chanteloup. For the architectural features he had enlisted the services of 'Le Seigneur de St. Martin'. Behind this title hides the well-known name of Primaticcio, for it was the habit of the Valois to provide for their architects by means of ecclesiastical livings, and Primaticcio was Abbot of St. Martin-de-Troye. The practice was later derided by Ronsard in his poem 'La Croix et la Truelle'.

As the Royal party passed beneath this first triumphal arch, the whole forecourt and garden of Chenonceau was seen to be set about with colonnades and porticoes and statues, and looped and flounced around with floral garlands. Trees, as they reached them, burst into cascades of fireworks; fountains gushed with wine; everywhere were tablets on which verses were inscribed —verses that were littered with extravagant and far-fetched compliments.

On their left, in the new walled and moated gardens of Diane de Poitiers, was raised an antique altar in the heavy pall of mourning—a delicate allusion to the widowhood of Catherine which was repeated in the white and black banners of the village guard. It was piquant hypocrisy in this place, since only by the death of her husband had she been able to displace her rival and attain the political power which she now enjoyed and the ownership of Chenonceau where she now entertained her family and Court.

In the evening the façades and forecourts of the Château were illuminated with a brilliance which penetrated '*presque dans le profond de la grande allée*'. But in spite of all the effects of artifice, it is doubtful whether much could have added to the beauties of Chenonceau. The Seigneur du Plessis, to whom we owe our information on the Fête, wrote significantly: 'It is by nature enriched with every single beauty that one could well desire in an estate to crown it with every gaiety and delight.'

His views do not seem to have been shared by Catherine. She did her best to spoil Chenonceau. Her taste was for the florid and the grotesque; she masked the main façade with a heavy screen of Caryatides, added the gallery to Philibert de l'Orme's bridge and commissioned a plan, perhaps from Bullant, for two enormous courtyards in front of the entrance. Her additions, if built, would have been imposing and original, but they would have overwhelmed the little Château of the Bohiers. It is fortunate for Chenonceau that they were never built.

Catherine needed the extra accommodation, of course, for her entertainments of the Court. The later Fêtes de Chenonceau were of a more licentious nature. In May of 1573 the whole Court took part in a frankly transvestite debauch. Women were dressed as men; Henri III and his *mignons* were gorgeously attired as females;

> 'Nobody rightly knew which they had seen,
>   A woman as King or a man who was Queen.'

They were waited on by the ladies of the Court 'half naked, with their hair down as if they were brides'. Pierre l'Estoile, who describes the scene, does so without any hint of censure. Indeed, such were the moral standards of the Court that it was accepted as *'un beau banquet, tout y était en bel ordre'*.

By the end of 1587 the situation in France was as bad as ever. For three years, since the death of the duc d'Anjou, the heir to the throne had been the Protestant King of Navarre. Against his succession was consolidated the formidable coalition of the *Ligue*. Once again the Catholic party centred upon a Duke and a Cardinal of the House of Guise—the sons of the Duke François, murdered in 1563.

In September 1588, for the second time in the reign, the States General met in the Grande Salle at Blois. Seated on a throne of lilac velvet between the central pillars of the room, the King made wordy protestations of his devotion to the country. They availed him nothing. He was made immediately and unmistakeably aware of his waning popularity and power. The comte de Brissac had been blatantly outspoken; the people, he said, were strangely colder—*'merveilleusement refroidi'*—in the love they used to feel towards the throne.

But if the power of Henri de Valois had visibly diminished, that of Henri de Guise had correspondingly increased. Like most of his race he was of the stuff that Kings are made of; magnificent in physique, magnanimous in mind, he had distinguished himself by his most careful courtesy to men of humble rank. 'These Lorraines had such an air of distinction,' claimed the Maréchale de Retz, 'that alongside them the other Princes looked plebeian.'

His pre-eminence wrought its own nemesis. 'The too great authority of the duc de Guise,' wrote Beauvais-Nangis, 'began to annoy not only the King, but all who loved the welfare, peace and quiet of the Realm.'

On November 30 the Maréchale de Retz expressed her un-easiness at the risk which Guise was running, but he brushed it aside; 'I have nothing to fear from that man,' he told her; 'I know him well; he is too much of a coward.' But the Maréchale was the more astute psychologist; 'that is exactly what makes me distrust him,' she replied.

On December 18 the King, discussing the haughty preten-sions of the Guises with his own familiars, heard the idea of a judicial murder openly advocated. One of the deputies, Lamezan by name, reminded him that he was the Premier Judge of the Realm; that the duc de Guise and his brother were guilty of lèse Majesté of the first degree; 'Say that they are to be put to death,' he concluded, 'and they will be put to death.' Henri demurred—but Henri was an adept at dissimulation. In the next few days he laid the plans that were to lead to the famous murder; he laid them with a body of adventurers known to his-tory and to fiction as Les Quarante-Cinq. The day was fixed for Friday, December 23 in the early morning.

On December 22, as Guise sat down to dinner, a paper fell out of his napkin. On it was written *'prenez garde à vous, on est sur le point de vous jouer un mauvais tour'*. With the greatest coolness Guise appended the words *'on n'oserait'* and tossed the paper back on to the table. To his friend Schomberg he had justified his attitude. 'I know of no man on earth,' he said, 'who, in single conflict with me would not have a half share of the fear'; as for a concerted attack, he did not think it could succeed since he never went abroad without a personal bodyguard who always accompanied him *'jusqu'à la porte de la chambre du Roi'*.

'Right up to the door of the King's Bedroom.' In these words the duc de Guise laid down succinctly the conditions for his own assassination. Right up to the door: but beyond that door?

Looking back on the events with the perspective of history, the outstanding fact is that every move had been foreseen and every person forewarned. 'The one real danger to which he is exposed,' wrote the Spanish Ambassador, Mendoza, 'could only be in the Cabinet du Roi, where one is only admitted on one's own, and where this Prince would have every facility to have him attacked and killed.'

It is at this point that we must form the clearest picture of the rooms which formed the King's Apartment at Blois, for the curious, piecemeal manner in which François I had gone about his reconstructions played a vital role in the drama that was to ensue.

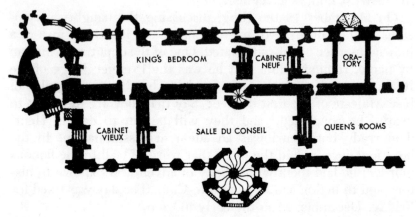

BLOIS: Plan of the second floor of Francis I's wing as it was at the time of the murder of the duc de Guise.

On the second storey of this wing, the landing of the Great Spiral Staircase gave access to two doors; on the left that of the King's rooms; on the right, that of the Queen's. The left-hand door opened into the Salle du Conseil whose windows overlooked the courtyard. Thus far were the attendants of the duc de Guise allowed. Opposite this door was another, leading into the King's Bedroom, whose windows overlooked the town. From the far end of this room, nearest the Tour de Château-renault, another door led on to the Cabinet Vieux.* This room overlooked the courtyard, and was in fact next door to the Salle du Conseil, but in those days there was no direct communication. If a person were summoned from the Salle du Conseil to see the King in the Cabinet Vieux, he would have to pass through the Bedroom.

Owing to the piecemeal way in which this wing had been

* The room was destroyed between 1635 and 1638 to make way for the reconstructions of Gaston d'Orléans.

built, the partition wall between these rooms and the Bedroom was the outer *courtine* of a feudal castle. It was immensely thick and the doors formed a narrow tunnel through the fortress wall. A thick wall and a narrow passage were essential to the King's design. His orders were that Guise should be attacked as he entered the second 'tunnel' leading to the Cabinet Vieux.

The duc de Guise was at that time Lieutenant-General of the realm, and as such received the keys of the Château after the doors had been locked for the night. In order to remove the keys from him without arousing suspicion, the King announced that he was going on a pilgrimage to Notre Dame de Cléry. His coaches were ordered for four in the morning of Friday, December 23. So that the King's Guards could be thronging the great spiral staircase it was arranged with their captain, Larchant, that they should present a petition to the Council.

As for the Quarante-Cinq, they had orders to enter through the gardens and were to wait in the attics in a series of rooms which the King was at the time fitting up for the use of his Capucin monks. It was typical of the age that a building should serve simultaneously the requirements of piety and murder.

By seven o'clock in the cold grey of a December morning the trap was fully set and sprung.

Three months later, at the request of the duchesse de Guise, certain men who had been at close quarters to the assassination made formal depositions before the Court of Parliament concerning what had happened. Among them were Jean Péricard, secretary to the Duke; Olphan de Gast, one of the Quarante-Cinq; Estienne Dourguin, Chaplain to the King; Michel Marteau, Prévôt des Marchants for the city of Blois, and Pierre d'Espinac, Archbishop of Lyon. From their accounts the murder may be reconstructed.

At four in the morning Pierre du Halde, Valet de Chambre in ordinary to the King, had gone to the Queen's apartment to arouse his master; he had found him already awake. One can imagine that sleep would have been difficult under the circumstances. He dressed and went to his Cabinet Vieux.

It was not until now, records de Gast, that the Quarante-Cinq were fully initiated into the nature of the plot. Some four or five of them were armed with poignards and stationed in the King's Bedroom; others disposed about the suite, de Gast himself at the entry to the Cabinet Neuf and its little spiral staircase.

About the same time two priests, Estienne Dourguin and Claude de Bulles, were taken to the oratory beyond the Cabinet Neuf and ordered to pray for the success of a certain enterprise which the King 'desired to undertake for the repose of his realm'.

*

On the other side of the Courtyard, in the wing formerly occupied by Louis XII, the duc de Guise had passed his last night on earth in connubial infidelity; he remained with Charlotte de Beaune-Semblançay, *'une des plus belles dames de la Cour'*, until three in the morning when he returned to his room. There were several warning notes awaiting him. He ignored them.

He had scarcely been asleep one hour when his valet, alarmed by the disturbance caused by the arrival of the King's coaches, decided to rouse him; but Guise would not listen to his apprehensions and went to sleep again. At six o'clock he was again awakened, according to his routine, and dressed himself in a suit of light grey. It was cold and still dark, and raining as it had never rained before. *'C'était le temps le plus obscur, ténébreux et pluvieux qui fût jamais vu.'*

At about eight o'clock the Duke, accompanied by Péricard, crossed the courtyard and mounted the Great Staircase to the King's Apartments. Larchant, whose troops were thronging the steps, presented his petition, and Guise promised to see him satisfied. He entered the Salle du Conseil, where Rambouillet, Maintenon and one or two others were already waiting.

The Duke was cold and he was hungry. He sent Péricard back to his rooms to fetch his *drageoir*—a silver box in the form of a scallop shell in which he kept preserved fruits which were his only breakfast. In the crisis which was to ensue this *drageoir* was to be his only weapon.

Péricard was not allowed to return by the troops, who still blocked the Staircase, and the Duke, growing impatient, asked the King's Secretary to find him something to eat. He was brought some Prunes de Brignolles. Soon afterwards his brother, whose lodgings were at the Hôtel d'Alluye, joined him in the Salle du Conseil.

*

In the room next door, the King was becoming the prey to the acutest nervous anxiety. '*Il allait; il venait,*' wrote Miron, his Physician; '*il ne pouvait durer en place.*' Now he was at the door of his Bedroom; now he was back in his Cabinet. He was afraid that his plans would miscarry; he was afraid that Guise might get to grips with him. 'He is big and strong,' he was heard to mutter; 'I should have cause to regret it.'

At the last the news arrived. The Duke and the Cardinal were both in the Council Chamber; the door of the trap was down. The King dispatched Revol, a Secretary of State, to summon Guise. In half a minute Revol was back in the Cabinet, white and shaken; he was a nervous person and unsuited to his mission. The doorkeeper, Philippe de Nambu, had been told to open to no one; he would not open for Revol, who had to return for the King's assistance. 'My God, Revol,' exclaimed the King on seeing him; 'what is the matter with you, man? You look so pale —you'll ruin everything. Rub your cheeks, Revol, rub your cheeks.'

The King sent hasty word to Nambu, and Revol returned the second time to the Council Chamber door. This time he was admitted. He approached Guise. '*Monsieur,*' he said in a low voice; '*le Roi vous demande; il est en son Vieux Cabinet.*'

*

Meanwhile Péricard, finding the staircase blocked, and all access to the King's rooms forbidden, had jumped immediately to the right conclusion. He had managed to reach the apartment of the duchesse de Nemours, and begged her to intercede with the Queen before it was too late. She was prevented by the Guards. But although access to the Council Chamber was rigorously barred, those inside were still able to communicate with those without. A message reached Péricard that Guise was demanding a handkerchief. Once more he tried to effect an entry. It nearly cost him his life, but by jumping down some seven or eight steps of the Great Staircase, he managed to dodge into the Queen Mother's apartment on the first floor. Her rooms were directly below those of the King.

Here Péricard found Schomberg and Lansac. He implored their assistance. Schomberg assured him there was no mischief intended; Lansac offered to go up and see the King in person. Péricard waited. Suddenly, from overhead, came sounds—*'le battement des pieds et la rumeur de la chambre de dessus'*—a rush of feet that meant his master's murder.

*

In the Oratory, two rooms away from the fatal Bedroom, the priests, Dourguin and de Bulles, had been at their dubious devotions. They had been told to keep praying for the King's 'enterprise', but Dourguin had peeped from behind the arras into the Cabinet Neuf. There he saw a strange sight—two of the Quarante-Cinq, Laugnac and de Gast, holding naked daggers, were dancing together. He listened to their conversation. From it he gathered that when 'he' came into the room they would fall upon him and stab him to death. Correctly assuming that 'he' must be the duc de Guise, Dourguin changed the tenor of his prayers, begging that God might 'preserve this good Prince'. But his prayer was cut short by 'a very great noise in the King's Bedroom' and someone repeatedly crying in a loud voice 'Ah! Ah!'

*

In the Council Chamber, Pierre d'Espinac, Archbishop of Lyon, had observed the arrival of the Duke and the Cardinal. The Duke seemed ill at ease. He had had a nose-bleed, and had sent for a handkerchief. He had complained of cold, and had had the fire built up. A matter of finance was under discussion, and d'Espinac was about to address the Council, when Revol had entered and summoned Guise to the Royal presence.

'As soon as he had entered the King's Bedroom, the door was closed, and immediately afterwards there was a great noise as of a rushing of feet.' D'Espinac ran to the door and listened. Above the hubbub he could hear the voice of Guise: '*Ha! Messieurs!*

... *O quelle trahison!* ... *Mon Dieu, Miséricorde!'* And at the last words, the sound of a heavy fall.

Turning back into the Council Chamber, he found the room crowded with soldiers armed with arquebuses and halberds. The Cardinal de Guise had been arrested, and in the next instant he too shared the same fate. They were conducted by a dark and winding stair and by narrow passages to a little cell, having three oval windows, heavily barred and no fireplace.

At four in the afternoon they were transferred to another room. It was smaller and had no direct access to light or air, but it had a fire. At six they were offered fish and bread and wine, of which they partook sparingly and with apprehension. They asked that their breviaries, nightgowns and a light might be brought them, and the request was granted. They spent a sleepless night in repeating their Offices and hearing each other's confessions.

At eight in the morning the door opened and a valet de chambre entered, carrying a flambeau. Behind him came de Gast. With a low obeisance towards Cardinal de Guise, he pronounced the fatal formula: *'Monsieur, le Roi vous demande.'*

*

Michel Marteau was attending a meeting of the Tiers Etat on the morning of the Duke's assassination. Their debate was disturbed by ugly rumours from the Château. While they were trying to discover what was afoot, the Sieur de Richelieu appeared at the door. *'Que personne ne bouge!'* he cried; *'on a voulu tuer le Roi.'* To his astonishment, Marteau was arrested, along with some half a dozen others, for complicity in the alleged *attentat*.

They were led over to the Château and up the Great Staircase into the Chambre du Roi, where they were told to wait. Near the door of the Cabinet Vieux were 'two great pools of blood, still smoking'. A servant came and mopped them up. They heard that Guise had been killed. They heard Nambu receiving instructions to have a gallows and a scaffold erected, and they did not doubt that the gibbet was intended for themselves.

One of the Corps of Archers, called Hamilton, was given

custody of them and they were taken to a small room at the top of the Great Staircase in the Louis XII wing, near to the Grande Salle. One day, on returning to this room by means of the staircase, they noticed that the central newel was heavily stained with blood. There was also 'a great stench as of burnt flesh'. Here, they were told, the bodies of the Guise brothers had been burnt, and they were regaled with the details of how the Cardinal, immediately after receiving his summons from the King, had been stabbed to death by the soldiers.

Unfortunately this double murder has become the most prominent historical association with Blois; it has provided abundant scope for the talent and imagination of generations of guides, certainly as far back as the eighteenth century. To Mrs. Cradock it was tedious beyond belief: 'our conductor, who repeated his lesson by heart, was of a verbosity which was the despair of foreigners.' To the duc de La Rochefoucauld it was entrancing. '*Ce qu'il y a de charmant dans ce château,*' he wrote, '*c'est le suisse.*'* With unflagging zeal he led his visitors from room to room, describing and enacting the events which had taken place in each. '*Passons plus loin,*' he would say, if any lagged behind; '*je vais vous faire une jolie interprétation de l'histoire.*'

* The nearest English equivalent to '*suisse*' is 'usher'.

CHAPTER XIII

The Seventeenth Century

WHEN, in 1602, Maximilien de Béthune, Marquis de Rosny, acquired the fortress of Sully-sur-Loire, he took on a heavy task of reconstruction. In the whole vast ensemble of what had been the home of the La Trémoïlles *'il ne se trouvait plus rien de logeable'*. The Château was in ruins, the town was in ruins; and in this respect Sully-sur-Loire reflected in little the condition of the country; France was in ruins.

The Wars of Religion had left a sorry scene of desolation. 'It was not France,' wrote Etienne Pasquier, 'that emerged from the forty years of conflict, but the carcase of France.' To the proud monarchy of the early Valois had succeeded a King 'with his shirt in tatters and his doublet out at the elbows'. Throughout the country public works had been suspended. 'The roads are severed by morasses; the bridges are tottering or fallen in; the banks and dykes of the rivers are melting away.' Buildings had suffered badly, both from direct destruction and from want of upkeep. The number of houses destroyed has been estimated at 184,000; the number of châteaux at 6,000. In Paris there were hundreds of inhabitants sleeping in the church-yards from lack of housing. Béthune was made Superintendant of Buildings and the work of reconstruction was put vigorously in hand. 'If you don't return to Paris in two years time,' wrote Malherbe to a friend in 1605, 'you will no longer be able to recognize it.'

For Maximilien de Béthune was a prodigious worker. 'Though he holdeth great offices,' wrote Sir George Carew, 'yet it seemeth the worth of his own person hath rather made his places great than they have exalted him.' On one occasion Henri IV, finding his faithful Minister hard at work in the early hours of the morning, turned to his followers; 'how many of you would like to lead a life like that?' he asked. The Sire de Roquelaure answered for all—'No one, Sire, not for all the riches in your treasury.'

In February of 1606 Béthune received the rank proportionate to his position; he chose Sully for his Dukedom and celebrated the occasion by inviting some sixty guests to dinner with him at the Arsénal. He arrived to find the King already seated at his table.

'Monsieur le Grand Maître,' said the King, 'I have come to your party without so much as inviting myself. Shall I have a poor dinner?'

'You may well, Sire,' came the answer, 'for I was not expect-so great an honour.'

'I can assure you I won't,' continued the King; 'while I was waiting for you I inspected your kitchens, where I saw the finest fish you could possibly imagine, *et force ragoûts à la mode.*' He had already sampled some of the oysters and had tasted Sully's vin d'Arbois—'*le meilleur que j'aie jamais bu*'.

Sully worked hard for the King; it was natural that the King should do what he could for Sully. 'I ask you to accept 6,000 écus for the embellishment of your own houses,' the King urged him; 'I want, as your good master, to have a share in them.' So Maximilien de Béthune was called upon to be the restorer both of France and of Sully-sur-Loire. His destiny and that of his country were closely allied; her fortune was his. He had the happy task of being able 'to build up with the same hand the glory of his family and the glory of his country'. From the moment that he became the owner of Sully, he set about the work of renovation.

There were practically no floors. He immediately ordered a large consignment of *sapins de France*—and their great boles, forty feet long and nearly three in diameter, came floating down the Loire. In the margins of his accounts he noted proudly: '*mes planchers de Sully.*'

For everything was done with the same minute attention to detail and the same strict adherence to contract that marked his administration in the affairs of State. There is a foretaste of Colbert's meticulous accounting for Versailles.

There were practically no windows. He ordered the gaping apertures to be reglazed 'lozengewise with glass from Nivernais, jointed with lead'. The workmen were to be exempted from their contract in the case of 'thunderbolts, tempests, lightnings or great hailstones breaking the glass'.

The work of restoration tended in two directions; to making a princely residence out of a fortress and to increasing its efficacy as a fortress.

The west tower, which covered the approaches from the town, was built deliberately low for the use of cannons. Gunpowder had wrought various changes in the appearance of castles; we noticed it first in the austere strength of Langeais as compared with the fragile superstructures of Saumur or Mehunsur-Yèvre. At the beginning of the sixteenth century some of the châteaux lost the distinctive conical roofs to their towers in favour of a flat platform from which artillery could play. But artillery fired from such an altitude was found to cause 'more alarm than damage', and by the end of the century the low artillery tower had been evolved. Béthune was building in the latest fashion in thus equipping Sully.

Here the great Minister was to live in retirement, maintaining a large household and working almost as hard as he had worked for the King on the maintenance of his estates and on the editing and printing of his copious memoirs.

We must imagine the Grande Salle, *'qui, après Montargis, est la plus grande qui soit en France,'* in all its glory, panelled on all sides, and painted in *cartouches*, each with its emblem and its motto recalling some exploit or achievement of the King and his Minister. Over the mantelpiece, which was of a size proportionate to the room, Béthune placed a picture of the King, bravely mounted upon a chestnut horse—*'de toutes les figures de ce Monarque,'* wrote the Abbé de l'Ecluse, *'la plus parfaite et la plus ressemblante.'*

At dinner he kept two tables, one for his own age group and one, presided over by his Captain of the Guards, for the younger generation. 'You are too young for us to eat together,' he would explain; 'we would bore one another.' After dinner a great bell sounded and the whole household formed a double rank down which the family, preceded and followed by Swiss Guards, would walk out into gardens.

The gardens, which occupied an island east of the Château, were laid out in squares and the squares planted, for the most part, with fruit trees. At the height of spring the Château de Sully could be seen rising from a cloud of blossom—restored, renewed and re-inhabited. There could not be a fitter monument to the life work of its new proprietor.

Even more vividly than Sully, the Château de Brissac presents the picture of its age: the new France rising from the ruins of the old. The site is equally adaptable to war and peace; it offers a natural stronghold, a beautiful park and a particularly delicious wine.

Unlike most buildings of the seventeenth century, the façades of Jacques Corbineau are of almost vertiginous height—that of the west pavilion attaining to seven storeys. But if the west front is the loftiest, it is the east, or entrance, front which is architecturally the most interesting. The two towers of Pierre de Brézé, built in the middle of the fifteenth century, have been permitted to survive, but the right hand, or north, tower is nearly half demolished. Corbineau's tall and elegant pavilion seems to have edged its way behind the jagged profiles of the older masonry, preparatory to pushing it right out of the façade, as a young cuckoo might jostle with a smaller fledgling before evicting it from the nest. But—no doubt on account of the death of the first Duke in 1621—the final push was never given; the ill-assorted pair remain locked in their original embrace.

The high pavilion—known as the *donjon*, but containing the staircase—is a tour de force of mannerist architecture: a triumphal arch upon a triumphal arch upon a triumphal arch. Its five storeys represent the five orders. The vertical movement is subtly enhanced by the use of broken pediments which open like double doors from storey to storey, enabling the eye to travel quickly from ground level to the imperial dome, 120 feet above. To complete the picture, the historical imagination should supply a cupola on top of this, which was removed at the time of the Revolution.

The towering façades of Brissac may be compared with the soaring ambition of its builder. Charles de Cossé was a man cast in a classical mould; he was a fine soldier and an impressive orator. He was the elected spokesman of the Nobility who harangued Henri III at the States General at Blois; he was the Governor of Paris who opened the City gates to Henri IV in 1594. With Monarchy restored, he attained the highest honours to which a subject can aspire—the marshal's baton and the ducal coronet—but in the troubled days of the League he had dreamed of other peaks. He might have been First Consul in France's first Republic. Instead he built Brissac.

It was an undertaking of the greatest audacity: a palace poised upon the platform of masonry which once had supported a fortress. Looking at Brissac from the south, from across the park, one's first impression is of the size and number of the windows. Corbineau seems to have disliked the naked wall: he has left as little of it exposed as possible. The narrow interstices between the windows are so encroached upon by the stone quoins as to produce, over all the façade, the scintillating, many-faceted appearance of a cut-class decanter.

Within doors the effect of this ample fenestration is at once apparent. The huge windows are divided by a mullion and three transoms into eight squares; each square has its separate shutter, and each shutter folds back against the plain side wall of the deep window recess, exhibiting a complex, polychrome design. The perspective of these window recesses makes the Salle des Gardes one of the most striking and impressive decors in French architecture.

As in the older châteaux, the beams and joists of the ceiling are left exposed, but their entire surface is covered with paintings—for the most part landscapes set about with *cartouches* and arabesque designs. This painting is often on a very small scale and contrasts its minute intricacy with the vast proportions of the rooms.

The richness and warmth of colour with which all this gilding and painting endows the apartments is again in contrast with the monolithic simplicity of the Staircase and the bare masonry of the Entrance Hall. The great doorways, their pediments charged with elaborate heraldic achievements, savour of exterior architecture rather than of interior decoration.

The immense size of Brissac and the number of its apartments forces the question upon us 'what was it all built *for*?' Undoubtedly there was a connection between the size of a house and the rank of its owner. When, in 1675, Le Lude was erected into a dukedom, the title deed quotes, as one of the qualifying circumstances, that the estate was *'une des plus capables de soutenir l'éclat et la splendeur de cette dignité'*. A ducal mansion had to house a considerable household. It was also required, on occasion, to house a still itinerant Court.

In August 1620, before the Château was even finished, the Court descended upon Brissac. It was the occasion of the reconciliation between Louis XIII and his mother, Marie de' Medici. She had been made Governor of Anjou and was using her position there as a fulcrum from which to apply leverage on the King. He arrived with an army at Ponts-de-Cé, just south of Angers, and defeated his mother's supporters.

Peace terms were proposed, and, as ever, a suitably neutral ground was sought for the armistice. The duc de Brissac was on the King's side, but he had already on several occasions entertained the Queen Mother at the Château. Brissac thus became the obvious place for the reconciliation.

On Wednesday, August 12 the King arrived, and the next day Marie was summoned. She was met as she left Ponts-de-Cé by the Maréchal de Praslin *'avec force noblesse'*, who accompanied her cortège to the village of Homois, just short of Brissac, where Louis was awaiting her. On seeing him she precipitated herself out of her litter and hastened to meet him; *'avec toute la peine du monde leurs Majestés se purent joindre,'* wrote Barthélemy Roger, *'vue la foule de noblesse qui était spectatrice de cette tant désirée entrevue.'* The King then remounted his horse, the Queen returned to her litter and the whole cavalcade proceeded to the Château.

One of the go-betweens in this act of reconciliation had been Armand du Plessis, Bishop of Luçon, later to be famous as Cardinal de Richelieu. Five years later he was to start on the rebuilding of his ancestral home, the Château de Richelieu, some twenty kilometres south of Chinon in the undistinguished valley of the Mable.

If one were looking for a bad place on which to site a palace and a town, it would be difficult to find a poorer one than Richelieu. It was not an area endowed by Nature; it had no beauty to attract a builder, and no commodity to compensate the lack of beauty. It was low-lying and undrained, a place of sodden earth and sleeping waters. To this unpromising emplacement the proximity of a dense wood ensured a minimum of ventilation, keeping the air heavy, humid and unhealthy. The marshy ground impeded agriculture; the lack of waterways discouraged trade. Even the local wines were disappointing; the Château was perforce without a cellar 'because one cannot dig by reason of the water and the marsh'. Deprived of cool cellars *'fraîches et profondes'* the wines did not arrive at their perfection.

Of all these disadvantages the Cardinal was well aware, yet Pride caused him to build where every counsel of Reason forbad. The great Minister's intention, Elie Brackenhoffer was informed, 'was to raise to the rank of a Duchy the home and cradle of his family . . . where he himself was born and bred;* and this was to perpetuate eternally the glory of his name'. It perpetuated also the foibles from which the greatest men are not exempt. 'Consider the weakness of this man,' wrote Tallement des Réaux, 'who could have made the most obscure corner of France the most illustrious, in thinking that a great building appended to his paternal home, could add anything to his glory, without considering that the place was neither beautiful nor healthy.'

On this flat and uninspiring situation Lemercier began, in 1631, to raise his heavy, uninspired façades. The lay-out of the Château proper was wholly conventional. Four high pavilions marked the corners of the square; a fifth, the centre of the entrance front. The lodgings occupied three sides of the quadrangle; the fourth was closed by a stone screen in the centre of which rose an elaborate, domed gatehouse. It was the formula of Monceaux and Coulommiers.

The diversity of domes and roofs, the multiplicity of statues and the sheer size of Richelieu made it an imposing coup d'œil, but in detail it was not remarkable. *'Du côté du jardin,'* wrote des

* He was, in fact, born in Paris.

Réaux,' *la face du logis est ridicule.*' La Fontaine devoted more attention to the statues than to the architecture. Of outstanding importance were two figures of slaves by Michelangelo, ensconced in niches above the main entrance. These figures were transferred from Ecouen, and symbolize the fall of Montmorency and the rise of Richelieu.

As at Ecouen, so at Richelieu, the Château was set in a moat which, following the trend in contemporary fortification, was elongated into spear heads at the angles. Brackenhoffer found the water full of mare's-tails and putrid—a condition which was not improved by the presence of four latrines, one at each corner of the moat, '*qui se déchargent dans le fossé*'. It was the commonest objection to the place. In 1675, John Locke complained that 'the standing waters . . . stank horridly'. Evidently the defect was remedied from time to time, for La Fontaine found the waters clean and clear.

House and moat were set at the end of a deep perspective of offices and stables—a symmetrical progression of ever wider courts and ever smaller buildings. It was an architectural device derived, perhaps, from Charleval, a grandiose and largely unrealized project by du Cerceau for Charles IX.

The magnificence of Richelieu and the fame of its builder made it a place of pilgrimage; travellers turned aside from the main route to see for themselves its almost legendary riches. They needed time on their hands to see it all; it did not lend itself to quick inspection.

'Judged by the standard of truth,' wrote La Fontaine, 'the avenue may have measured half a league; but judged by my impatience it seemed a full league at the very least.' His eager haste defeated memory; when writing to his wife he could not recall the details of the approach—'nor can I remember what the Base Court, the Fore Court or the Back Courts consisted of, nor the number of pavilions and wings to the Château, and even less how they were built. It is enough,' he concluded, 'that the whole has a beauty, a magnificence and a grandeur worthy of its builder.'

It was just impossible to see so vast a château in so short a time. They passed rapidly from room to room, pausing occasionally before a Titian, a Poussin or a Dürer, until they came to a little cabinet *'tapissé de portraits'*. Here were Kings and Queens and Richelieus, great Lords and greater Personalities; 'I make the distinction between great Lords and great Personalities,' remarked La Fontaine in parenthesis, 'knowing that it is well in all matters to avoid confusion.' Not only the Kings but those who had conquered them (in the amorous rather than the military sense of the word) were represented; *'enfin, c'est l'histoire de notre nation que ce cabinet'*.

His inspection of this cabinet was the only breathing space allowed them. 'We left this place and passed through I don't know how many rooms—magnificent and all of the finest decoration—of which I shall say nothing.' What time had he for gilding and panelling with all these Old Masters and Antiques to claim his attention? Brackenhoffer supplies some of the details which La Fontaine omits. 'All these rooms,' he writes, 'have the richest decoration in the world; all carved and gilded; all hung around with costly silken tapestry of the finest workmanship. In most of the rooms the windows are inlaid with solid, pure silver, the footpace is paved with *marbre jaspé* . . . the shutters are richly painted and gilded so that it is not only within the Château, but from without that one is dazzled by the brilliance of gold.'

Brackenhoffer was bourgeois enough to be excited by mere opulence; La Fontaine was more blasé. 'There was so much gold,' he stated, 'that in the end I became bored with it. Just think,' he added in philosophic mood, 'what great Lords can do, and what poverty it is to be rich. One would have to invent rooms of plain plaster where magnificence disguised itself beneath a semblance of simplicity.'

In all this sumptuous ensemble, one room stood out beyond the rest for the extravagance of its ostentation—the Grande Galerie. It stands in architectural history mid-way between the gallery of François I at Fontainebleau and that of Louis XIV at Versailles.

From either end of this imposing piece, Louis XIII and his Minister, life-sized and bravely mounted, looked down from their tall gilt frames upon the achievements of their reign. 'The

whole length of the room,' writes Brackenhoffer, 'on both sides
are large paintings representing the exploits of the King and
Cardinal, and over each a Roman exploit or Labour of Hercules
by way of comparison. In all these exploits the Cardinal is
depicted on a white charger, whose mane and tail reach even
to the ground.' The Gallery, and indeed the whole Château, was
an apotheosis of the Cardinal's career.

In a sense every great house is a monument to a family; this
was a monument to one man. Neither the Château nor the town
were primarily designed for habitation, and they were never
really inhabited. During his lifetime Richelieu had tried to lure
people into his town by offering them free building sites and
exemption from the *taille*. If anyone so much as nibbled at the
bait the great Cardinal was running after them at once. '*Le
jeune Bouthillier s'est offert de bâtir une maison dans la ville de
Richelieu*,' he writes; '*dites à Desroches qu'il en fasse souvenir de la
faire promptement*.' But the response was poor. 'It is useless to
expect anything from the local inhabitants,' complained his
agent; 'they are so beggarly they have not the means to build
a pigeon house.'

The tragedy of it all was that Richelieu never saw his Château. He died in 1642, and the town died with him. The over-
doors destined to receive the escutcheons of the occupants
remained blank; the stables intended for the horses were used
for pigs; the schools were closed for want of any scholars.
Brackenhoffer was afflicted by the oppressive emptiness of the
place. '*On ne voit ni commerce ni population*,' he sighed; '*il semble
que tout soit mort*.'

In order to achieve the local supremacy of these ill-advised
constructions, Richelieu determined upon the demolition of
what must have been one of the finest of the châteaux of the
Loire—Champigny-sur-Veude.

Looking at the site today one has two impressions. The first
is of the vast scale of the lay-out, suggested by the far-flung
offices and gatehouse and the great bastion which contains the
Sainte-Chapelle. The second is of the purity of the architecture
—a clean-cut classicism, more advanced than that of Chambord
or Blois, more comparable with Ancy-le-Franc. The only known

description of Champigny confirms this impression. It comes from the Manuscript of Dubuisson-Aubenay, preserved in the Bibliothèque Mazarine. It is dated 1634.

The Château, he tells us, was in the form of a square, surrounded by a moat. Only one range of buildings, that which fronted the town, had been completed. This he describes as being 'of a very beautiful white stone, of three storeys, each marked by pilasters of the Doric order, which is thus triplicated'. The level of the courtyard was higher than that of the town, for on the inner side of this range were only two storeys, this time distinguished by two superimposed Corinthian orders. Of the interior he mentions only the Grande Salle 'panelled all round and of about the same size as that of the Louvre in Paris'.

The Chapel, which stood opposite the centre of this façade, happily survives with all its stained glass, though unfortunately none of its furniture. Begun in about 1507 under Louis I de Bourbon, it was still being built in 1543—a date appears on one of the gargoyles. Louis I died in 1520, leaving a son aged seven to succeed him. It is possible that building operations were discontinued during his minority. This would explain the evolution of style apparent in the contrast between the Chapel itself and its entrance portico.

The construction is entirely Gothic—an elegant lierne and tierceron vaulting that owes nothing to the renaissance. The conception is entirely Gothic—an alternation of windows and buttresses with an exquisite little cloister running round the base. But the decoration, especially of the pinnacles, has lost the lightness of the late flamboyant age and partakes of the sculptural solidity of the renaissance. The portico, added as late as 1570, is richly classical. It provided an appropriately magnificent means of access from the Château.

For this was, of course, a private Chapel. Honours are evenly distributed between the Almighty and the family of Bourbon-Montpensier. The bosses over the Nave bear the arms and insignia of the family; those over the Choir are devoted, as a delicate concession to the Clergy, to Angels displaying the instruments of the Passion. The side Chapels, in each of which the presence of a comfortable fire-place betokens the family pew, were not dedicated to Saints but described as the *'chapelle de Madame'* and the *'chapelle de Monsieur'*—for the sexes worshipped in those days on opposite sides of the Church.

But it is the stained glass which is the true glory of Champigny. The eleven windows, divided either into three or into four lights by slender mullions, their broad but pointed arches filled with a simple lozenge tracery, contain a complete and perfect set of renaissance glasswork. The scenes are vividly pictorial—the colour being clearly secondary in the artist's mind. Three themes run horizontally throughout the series. The life of Christ—confined to the lozenges; the life of St. Louis—which occupies upper and larger portion of the tall lights; and the Bourbon-Montpensier family—whose portraits claim the lower but more conspicuous portion of the windows.

The first of these family portraits is of their two most distinguished Churchmen Claude, Cardinal de Givry and Louis, Cardinal de Bourbon. The first named of these presented the windows to the Chapel, which can thus be dated after 1538, when his niece Jacquette de Longvy married Louis II de Bourbon, and which were nearly completed at his death in 1561. Some of the family figures are of a later date than this, and must be subsequent insertions.

To this shrine of her maternal ancestors La Grande Mademoiselle made her first pilgrimage in 1637 while staying with the duchesse d'Aiguillon at Richelieu. The duchesse d'Aiguillon was the Cardinal's niece, and found the whole visit acutely embarrassing. She did not relish the presence of a social superior; 'she was so accustomed to receiving the respect of everyone,' wrote Mademoiselle, 'that it was painful to her to find herself with someone to whom she owed respect.' A more particular embarrassment arose through the visit to Champigny, which had only just been pulled down. Mademoiselle went straight to the Sainte-Chapelle and prayed for the eternal repose of her ancestors. 'I don't think my piety in that place was very acceptable to Mme d'Aiguillon,' she observed; 'what was even more painful to her was that the inhabitants of Champigny . . . felt, on seeing me, a revival of that tender affection which the memory of the benefactions and bounties of M. de Montpensier had engraved upon their hearts; they showed by their tears and by every possible demonstration of affection, their sorrow at their loss.'

Mlle de Montpensier, whose father's official residences were Blois and Chambord, leaves in her writings some vivid details of the châteaux of the Loire and of their owners. In particular she was the devoted friend and admirer of Cécile Elizabeth, marquise de Montglat, châtelaine of Cheverny.

The marquise is described in the *Portraits* under the name of Delphinia by Mademoiselle herself: 'a beautiful and fresh complexion, the finest teeth you could possibly see, a slightly turned up nose, dark eyes, brown hair but of the finest quality in the world . . . admirable hands and the loveliest elbow I have ever seen.'

Cheverny had been built by her father, Henri Hurault, the son of the more famous Philippe Hurault who was Chancellor of France during the last years of the sixteenth century. Henri had nearly ended his career in a melodrama with his first wife, Françoise Chabot. In 1602 he was engaged in military service at Court and she was in rustication at Cheverny. One evening the King, wishing to amuse his followers, made the sign of a cuckold behind the head of the young Count. A small mirror unfortunately revealed the gesture to his victim. Without a word he left the Court and rode straight to Cheverny, arriving at five in the morning. The Countess's page had just time to jump, Cherubino-like, from the window, but broke his leg in the process and was finished off by the outraged husband. The Parish records of St. Martin de Blois complete the story. 'On Saturday, January 26, the comtesse de Cheverny was poisoned, as the common rumour goes, for her adultery' and on the same day the page 'suspected of the deed, was killed at the said Château de Cheverny'.

It may have been the distasteful memory of this double murder which caused Henri to abandon the magnificent castle built a hundred years previously by Raoul Hurault. The enforced leisure which his exile to his estates imposed upon him certainly gave him the opportunity to rebuild. It was, however, some twenty years before the work began. The first firm date is 1629, when the window frames are known to have been in process of construction. It suggests a fairly advanced state of the building. The decorations of the staircase were completed in 1634. The woodworker Hammerber was still in residence—and therefore presumably still at work—at Cheverny in 1640.

The Château, which was the design of Jacques Bougier of Blois, is a perfect example of the pure *style Louis XIII*. No older buildings were incorporated; the plan was not conditioned by any site restriction imposed by a previous foundation; the façades are dictated by the plan.

The main fronts, facing north and south, are divided up in what John Evelyn called 'the French pavilion way'. Two massive end pavilions, each crowned with an imperial dome and cupola; a narrow staircase in the centre, surmounted by a pyramidal roof and belfry and two symmetrical *corps de logis* uniting the pavilions, each with its separate high-pitched roof. The variety of the roofline is one of the great successes of the style.

The north and south fronts are perforce identical in silhouette. But whereas the emphasis on the south front is on the horizontal lines obtained by the string courses and by the continuous rustication of the masonry, the north front has been given a vertical accent by the striking use of stone quoins to each flight of windows and to every corner of the pavilions. This effect is enhanced by the four storeys of smaller windows to the central staircase well and by the fact that the end pavilions have two, and not three, flights of windows. The north front is thus the more elegant of the two.

One of the first visitors to record his impressions of the new Cheverny was Elie Brackenhoffer. 'The park,' he wrote, 'is composed of five or six avenues which converge at a point just in front of the house and radiate out like the beams of a star. It is a great pleasure to stand at the centre point and to see the perspective of all these alleys at once.' The façades he does not trouble to describe. 'The house is neither vast nor large, but it has none the less good and beautiful apartments adorned with fine tapestries, good pictures and valuable furniture. In particular there is a gallery in which are to be seen full-length portraits, life-sized, of the most illustrious of our Kings and notables; they are very well painted.'

For the interior of Cheverny glows with a warmth of colour and a richness of gilding that is in no way suggested by the austere façades. The panelling, painted by Jean Monier in brown and gold and blue, with brightly coloured insets of flowers or scenes from mythology; the ceilings, brilliant and elaborate as those of Brissac; the tapestries, including a complete and magnificent set of the Labours of Hercules after Vouet; the pictures, mostly framed in the panelling and forming thus an integral part of the whole decor, and the monumental fireplaces with their gilded statues and grotesque caryatids, all combine to produce an overwhelming impression of sumptuousness that has hardly any rival in the land.

'You were born in an enchanted Palace,' wrote Mlle de Montpensier to the marquise de Montglat; 'for nothing could be more beautiful than Cheverny.' The countryside, the house, the gardens with its *parterres* and its *pièces d'eau*, were worthy of Alcine or the Palace of Apolidon.

But it was the mistress of Cheverny rather than her house that was the subject of the eulogy. She had all the gifts that a hostess requires to make her home a centre of gracious and accomplished living. She was well read, which lent substance to her conversation; she was musical and maintained an excellent orchestra as well as a troop of comedians; she was a connoisseur of architecture and of art. All these gifts were employed and integrated in an infectious capacity for enjoying life. *'Vous aimez les plaisirs au dernier point,'* her Royal friend informed her; *'vous aimez fort la bonne chère et on la fait grande chez vous et avec beaucoup de politesse.'* It must have been a most enjoyable experience to have stayed at Cheverny or to have been the guest at one of her receptions. As Fénelon was to observe—*'une femme iudicieuse est l'âme de toute une grande maison.'*

The marquise de Montglat was one of a long line of châtelaines who played a dominant role in the development and life of the French château. In the late middle ages it had been the absence of the Lord on military service which had left the Lady in charge of the construction; in the renaissance it was also his absence at Court. Thus we have seen Marguerite de Feschal conducting operations at Le Plessis-Bourré, Catherine

Briçonnet and Philippe Lesbahy at Chenonceau and Azay-le-Rideau. Even with the strong centralization of the Court under Louis XIV there were still ladies such as the duchesse de Liancourt or the duchesse de Lude who preferred to maintain their own households in their own châteaux while their husbands were lodged at Versailles or St. Germains in the most inadequate apartments.

The château of the feudal age had been a private fortress; it now became a private Court. It is as courtiers and 'familiars' and not merely as servants that we should consider the huge number of domestics which the new, unfortified châteaux were built to contain.

For a great château was a microcosm; the whole social spectrum was reflected in little in the structure of the household—the nobility in the Pages; the professional classes in the Aumônier or Chaplain, the Intendant or Steward, the Ecuyer or Master of the Horse, the Maître d'Hôtel and Secretary, all of whom had a personal valet; finally there were the under servants who formed the Tiers Etat or Troisième Table.

The Pages were boys of illustrious house 'who were placed there to learn the art of living and to do their exercises'. Since these exercises included a high standard of horsemanship, they were under the discipline of the Ecuyer. Undoubtedly the most responsible position was that of the Intendant who had oversight of the entire material resources of the domain. He could make or ruin a family. At his table were entertained men of education whose birth did not qualify them to eat with the Lord. In some households, such as that of the duc de Penthièvre, they were admitted to coffee with him. Next to the Intendant came the Maître d'Hôtel who was paymaster and caterer to the household, the Secretary 'who must be incorruptible, discreet and prudent', and the Officier de l'Office or Sommelier. He was the equivalent of the English butler. He had the keys of the cellar, he supervised the laying of the tables, he washed the glasses and he devoted such spare time as he had to the confectioning of marzipans, syrups and liqueurs.

Intermediary between the Office and the Troisième Table was the Valet de Chambre whose lower salary was compensated by his extensive influence. For he was the closest of all to the master of the house. Discretion was his highest virtue. His position overlapped on the one hand with that of the Secretary; it descended on the other to such menial tasks as shaving his master and dressing his wigs. Unless the household was so lavish as to include a Valet de Garderobe, he had to undertake himself *'la grosse besogne qui concerne la chambre et la garderobe'*. Sanitation in those days was always primitive and sometimes portable.

By no means to be confused with the Valet was the Laquais— who might have been anything from errand-boy to flambeau-bearer, or even regarded as wholly ornamental. It was not unknown for an applicant for the post to claim *'une physionomie très intéressante'*.

With them were classed the whole host of Garçons de l'Office, Garçons de Cuisine, Servantes de Cuisine, Garçons de Carosse, the postillions, the grooms and the valets who waited on the higher servants.

Some of the hierarchy had their opposite numbers on the female side. The Damoiselle Suivante was largely ornamental. It was therefore expedient that she should be addicted to embroidery 'for indolence is the route to every imaginable defect'. The Femme de Chambre was the equivalent to the Valet. Their twin roles are admirably illustrated in some of the plays and operas of the time.

The problems of running a large household were many and various, but the châtelaine of the seventeenth century was expected to grapple with them in person. There were a number of Livres de Raison or Household Books to assist her. *La Maison Réglée et l'Art de diriger la Maison d'un Grand Seigneur*, written by a former Maître d'Hôtel named Audiger, is one of the most informative.

'If masters and mistresses wish to have good servants,' he advises, 'they must themselves be good to them, and not regard them as slaves but as their adopted children of whom they have a duty to take care.'

In the eighteenth century Audiger's advice seems to have been neglected. The world of the Servants' Hall and the Office was becoming more remote from the world of the State Apartments. Mme Roland gives us a fascinating glimpse below stairs. When invited to dine with Mme Penault at her château she was astonished to find herself set at table *'non pas avec elle, mais à l'Office'*. She took the rebuff philosophically and soon found her experience entertaining enough. Here was the *beau monde* of the dining-room at second hand. The Femmes de Chambre, in the recently discarded finery of their mistresses, were overdressed; so likewise were the Valets. Dickens was not at fault in equipping a valet of the marquis de St. Evrémonde with two gold watches. Their efforts at conversation only betrayed their want of education; it was reduced to a pretentious name-dropping. *'La conversation fut tout remplie de* marquis, *de* comtes *et de* financiers.' The food came, largely untouched, from the dining-room, and was passed on, with further depredations, to the Troisième Table.

'I perceived a new world,' wrote Mme Roland, 'in which I saw the reflection of the prejudices, the vices and the stupidities of a world which was hardly of greater value.' It was the epitaph of a degenerate society.

In the eighteenth century the classes grew further apart. Underground passages to the kitchens, as at Menars; *tables volantes* which rose up through the floor, as at Choisy and Trianon, kept the servants out of sight and out of mind. The privileges of rank were becoming dangerously divorced from its responsibilities.

CHAPTER XIV

The Eighteenth Century

THE EIGHTEENTH century found the valley of the Loire as much to its taste as previous generations had done; English, French and German visitors united in its praise. 'No language,' claimed Nathaniel Wraxall, 'can describe the beauty of the Loire or the fertility of the country through which it flows.' '*Je ne puis toujours répéter le plaisir que me fait la route de la Loire*,' wrote François de La Rochefoucauld; '*il est impossible de rien voir de plus beau et de plus varié.*' '*Welch ein herrliches Stuck von Gottes Erde habe ich gesehen!*' exclaimed Sophia la Roche; '*alles ist wie ein blühender, fruchtbarer Garten.*'*

There was, as ever, one dissentient voice. Arthur Young found the countryside between Tours and Amboise 'more uninteresting than I would have thought it possible for the vicinity of so great a river'. But Young saw through the single eye of an agricultural reformer; he was not susceptible to the charms of unproductive land. Joseph Jekyll was more appreciative; 'the prospects on the banks of the Loire from Amboise to Tours,' he wrote, 'are highly picturesque. Immense rocks on each side, excavated into dwelling houses . . . tapestried with vines, and here and there an old feudal castle, in ruins, hangs over the summit. We enjoyed this scene heightened by the sublimity of a dark thunderstorm. It was a subject for the pencil of Salvator Rosa.' In his appreciation of rugged Nature and ruined Castles, Jekyll was more typical of his age than Young.

The age was marked by a 'back to Nature' movement heralded by Rousseau, and it became once more the fashion to make visits to the country. This practice was made the easier by excellent communications. 'The roads are incredibly fine,' wrote Jekyll; 'causeways as lofty as the Roman ones, nicely

---

* 'What a splendid piece of God's earth I have seen! Everything is like a flowering, fruitful garden.'

paved in the centre, of a vast breadth, straight as an arrow for leagues together, and usually planted with trees on either side.' Posting from Paris the journey to Amboise took little more than thirteen hours, and the Loire valley became once more the centre of a *vie de château* which only an age of opulent security could have produced.

'All the younger set,' notes Dufort de Cheverny, 'made frequent visits to the Maréchal de Saxe at Chambord, of which he had made a second Versailles.' Chambord had been the gift of a grateful country to the victor of Fontenoy. It was not the only château of the Loire to rob Versailles of its supremacy. Chenonceau, purchased by Mme Dupin, Cheverny by Jean Dufort, Menars, enlarged for Marigny, Montgeoffroy, rebuilt for Contades, and Chanteloup, bought, enlarged and magnificently maintained by the duc de Choiseul, gave to Anjou, Blésois and Touraine a brilliance and a distinction which they had not known since the renaissance.

The seventeenth century had seen more in the way of demolition than construction. The Royal Palaces were in their glory, the private ones deserted or destroyed. But now the grip of Louis XIV had been relaxed and the nobility began once more to look to their estates. Already in 1710 the building of Chanteloup had marked a turn in the tide. By the middle of the century that tide was in full flood. Private châteaux come to life once more; the Royal houses steadily decline.

The traveller Louis Dutens does not trouble to mention Versailles or the capital; 'I pass over the little time that I spent in Paris,' he writes, 'that I may mention Chanteloup.' Here he stayed for several weeks, enjoying the open hospitality of its owners. 'The Duke de Choiseul,' he states, 'has given the French nation the first and best example of the happy effects of the nobility paying proper attention to their estates. Everything around him wears a new face, and Chanteloup is a delightful residence, where the establishment is more complete and magnificent than that of any other Lord which I have seen in Europe.'

Everything was done in the grand style. 'There was one feature which shows the Duke had some merit,' admitted Arthur Young; 'he built a noble cow house.' 'The Dairy, the Cow

House and even the Dog Kennel are elegant to a proverb,' wrote Joseph Jekyll.

In addition to a hundred horses and seventy cows, there were fifty pigs, housed in ducal splendour in one of the base courts, and daily visited by Choiseul and his guests. Dufort noted with amusement how the polite tone and courtly manners of Versailles had penetrated even the outbuildings of Chanteloup. The Duke, whose habit was to converse freely with everyone, enquired one morning after his pigs. The *gardien* advanced towards them, hat in hand: '*Monseigneur leur fait bien de l'honneur,*' he replied: '*ils se portent tous à merveille.*'

Choiseul on this occasion found it difficult to conceal his laughter, for with all their grandeur and with all their wealth, he and his wife were the most straightforward and unaffected people. There was, Dufort assures us, 'no touch of haughtiness or ostentation'; a visit to Chanteloup was an extremely enjoyable experience.

The drive led from Amboise, following the banks of the Loire and shaded by magnificent plane trees. For most of the way the Château could be seen on the left 'at the end of a long avenue which cuts across immense vineyards'.

Unlike most houses of its type, Chanteloup presented a straight façade towards the entrance approach and an open courtyard to its gardens. This meant that the first impression which a visitor received was one of prodigious length. The house itself was 174 feet long, but this was more than doubled by the extension of a colonnade on either side ending in a terminal pavilion. Façade, colonnades and pavilions offered a united frontage of 350 feet; at one extremity was the Chapel and at the other the Pavillon des Bains. Cleanliness and Godliness could hardly have been set farther apart, but architecturally they received identical expression.

Even before Choiseul's additions, Chanteloup was regarded as something out of the ordinary. '*Il y a peu de maisons de Prince qui en approchent,*' wrote the traveller La Valette; '*un Roi pourrait y loger.*' The gardens were laid out like those of Versailles, and as at Versailles, great trouble and expense had been incurred to furnish water for the fountains. 'The interior,' continues La Valette, 'is charming and very well thought out; there is no commodity that has not been contrived.'

This is just what would be expected of the architect, Robert de Cotte. In place of the traditional suite, in which one room could often only be reached by passing through all the others, Cotte arranged for groups of rooms and private means of access, and by a system of backstairs and corridors, catered for the activities of the domestic staff. Not the least attraction of a mansion by Cotte was the atmosphere of unobtrusive service. It lent itself to the sort of informality that is bred of a self-assurance so perfect that it can dispense with being formal.

Informal they most certainly were. 'We have no rules for anything,' wrote the Duchess to Mme du Deffand; 'only dinner and supper are fixed.' Dinner was at twelve o'clock and supper was at nine. Their amusements were few and simple; tric-trac, dice and shuttlecock; riding, walking and music—'a poor clavicord at which the Abbé pounds, and to crown all, my little falsetto voice—those are all our pastimes. Always contented with the present moment, we make no plans for the next.' The Abbé Barthélemy completes her record of the soirée: '*le souper; minuit. Bonsoir, Madame la duchesse! Bonsoir, toute la compagnie! Et chacun s'en va coucher tout seul.*'

A small menagerie added to their distractions. Its range was unambitious. A few sheep, some lemurs and a monkey—who was usually dressed as a grenadier—were its only inmates. The sheep were allowed to graze on the lawn before the Château and even enticed into the Salon with handfuls of bread. The Monarch of their diminutive realm was an enormous ram called *Cathédrale*. He was a creature of a great natural dignity—'*il se promène gravement*'—but on one occasion he disgraced himself in the Salon in front of the Archbishop of Tours. The incident set the dogs barking and *Cathédrale* stampeded, causing considerable damage to the waxed parquets.

In 1770, with the exile of the duc de Choiseul, who had omitted to genuflect sufficiently before the altar of Mme du Barry, Chanteloup ceased to be an idyllic backwater and became the fashionable centre of France. 'He immediately received the homage,' wrote Dufort, 'of every honest man and every malcontent.' For several years Chanteloup was the scene of continual house parties, and entertainments, of which Dufort has left the liveliest descriptions.

'Arriving after dark,' he wrote, 'one would have imagined oneself to be arriving at Versailles.' Brilliantly lit from within and from without, the complexity of Chanteloup enhanced the impression of its size. The dark bulk of Mansart roofs against the diffused glow of an illuminated court behind; façades and colonnades on either hand receding into the darkness of the night; ghostly pavilions and cupolas floating in the background suggested an unexplored dimension, *'une suite prodigieuse de bâtiments'*.

Doubtless Dufort was exaggerating when he compared the sensation with that evoked by arrival at Versailles, and when he states that it took him twenty minutes to go from his own rooms to those of the Abbé Barthélemy, he cannot be taken seriously. Nevertheless, judged by country house standards, Chanteloup was large—a Petworth in the valley of the Loire.

In 1775 Choiseul added a Pagoda to the already elaborate ensemble. Apart from its general proportions it gave no hint of Chinese style to justify its name, but resembled, if anything, the spire of one of Sir Christopher Wren's London churches.

The most impressive view of Chanteloup was undoubtedly from the top of this Pagoda. Here, from an altitude of well over a hundred feet, one could survey the whole magnificent layout and be conscious of the ground plan as well as of the elevations.

One could look down into the sunny courtyard enclosed between the two projecting wings. Since the main entrance was from the other side, this court was not required for the circulation of coaches and could be used as a sun-trap and an orangery.

Seen thus from the south, Chanteloup had a dignity conferred by its size and a charm derived from its simplicity. Tall casement windows that opened on the court; a Doric colonnade against the main façade repeated in the porch on each pavilion— this was the only architectural contrivance. But where Cotte has chiefly shown his skill is in his treatment of the roof. Its lines were broken by a central frontispiece and by a maximum array of dormer windows; its mass was divided into pavilions of varying height; these, together with the double gradient of the Mansart roof, confronted the eye with a complex, many-faceted construction which was the reverse of boring.

The Pagoda was erected in memory of the great number of people who visited Choiseul during his exile from Versailles. But although the company was as distinguished as it was numerous, the air of easy informality was still predominant. The guests did as they pleased and wore what they liked. But when, at eight o'clock, they all assembled in the Salon 'one had to be in Court dress; all the ladies *en grand panier*, superb in costume and coiffure'. Instead of the Abbé pounding a clavicord there was a small orchestra playing 'whatever was best and newest'. The guests indulged in cards and conversation, not omitting to inspect the Duke's remarkable collection of engravings. As Louis Dutens noted with approval, 'that polished ease and freedom derived from good humour among the well educated, were here to be seen in perfection'.

At midnight the company retired, but the Duke and the Duchess with a small circle of their closer friends continued to talk until two or three in the morning. It was these morning watches—'*les charmantes veillées de Chanteloup*'—that provided Dufort with the highlights of his visits. 'I have never heard more interesting conversation.'

Of the interior of Chanteloup Joseph Jekyll and Mrs. Cradock leave the most evocative descriptions. 'The library, the theatre and the concert room are exquisite,' wrote Jekyll, 'but the little cabinet of Madame is a work of witchcraft. It is about ten feet long, totally inlaid with ivory, ebony and every elegance in miniature. The Duchess herself is the prettiest fairy imaginable, and the chairs and tables in the cabinet are so adapted to four foot five that I had some doubt whether I was in France or in Lilliput.'

Adjoining this was the Duchess's library: 'narrow small and lit from overhead', it was the room which most appealed to Mrs. Cradock. 'Once the door is shut,' she noted, 'one cannot discover any entrance, nor guess by what means one might have access to the gallery above. On touching a spring, a door which has the appearance of being part of the bookshelves, opens on a small spiral staircase by which one reaches the gallery.' In this room the Duchess carried on her famous correspondence with Mme du Deffand, Horace Walpole and other *littérateurs* of their age.

Chanteloup, in fact, was the epitome of all that a château had ever sought to be. Here was the patronage of literature and art preached by Rabelais in his Abbey of Thelema; here was an agricultural estate promoted and enriched by a residing landlord, the ideal of Sully. But in one respect Sully's hopes had not been realized; the peasant was rare who managed to put his chicken in the pot on Sundays. Nor could this be explained by the price of poultry. 'A fat goose,' calculated Joseph Jekyll, 'was fifteen pence English, and a fat fowl fourpence; yet in spite of fat geese and fat fowls, the poor live on bread and water from Monday to Sunday.'

Bread and water was a *façon de parler*. Sophia la Roche has left a more detailed menu. She cross-questioned a poor woman at Châtellerault about her economy. The family diet consisted of soup and bread four times a day—meat being beyond their means. The soup was made of mangel wurzel, cabbage or onions, with a limited admixture of oil. Their daily drink was water, but on Mondays the father drank wine with the other men at the local inn—'a thing that every woman has to tolerate'. Her bodice was old and shabby, but she revealed beneath it a clean and undarned vest. 'It pleased us,' wrote Sophia, 'to see the pride they took and comfort they derived from the cleanliness and smartness of their linen.'

In such a social structure, the place of almsgiving was all important. At least the wealth of Chanteloup found its way into the pockets of the peasants, for Choiseul was as lavish in his charity as in all things. 'His death,' wrote Mrs. Cradock, 'was an occasion of mourning for the whole countryside throughout which he had so abundantly distributed his bounty—especially among the poor, to whom he brought his generous relief.' One of these poor, the gateman to the bridge at Amboise, added his testimony: 'if they could have restored the Duke to life by making the cobbles cry,' he said, 'they would have squeezed tears out of them.'

Another nobleman of the Loire valley whose devotion to charity earned him the affection of the people was Louis-Georges-Erasme, Maréchal de Contades. During the Revolution he wrote to his daughter-in-law at Montgeoffroy urging her not to diminish the extent of their almsgiving. Although reduced, through loss of his charges at Court, to very straitened circumstances, '*il trouve que de faire vivre les pauvres est une trop bonne action pour ne pas le continuer le plus qu'il pourra*'. Nothing therefore was to be changed; he would rather suffer from financial difficulties than suspend his relief to those 'who have more need of it than ever'. The grand old man died in 1795 at the age of ninety.

It was just twenty years since he had finished the rebuilding of Montgeoffroy. In 1775, three years after work had started, the inventory had been drawn up to mark the completion of the Château. It is possible to go round Montgeoffroy today and see each piece of furniture in the same room. Here is the perfect example of the eighteenth-century château perfectly preserved.

Montgeoffroy is a lesson in the beauty of simplicity. It is set in a context of outbuildings which end, typically, in twin towers, ringed with machicolations and roofed with *poivrières*—the carefully preserved insignia of the feudal domain. At the far end of the Cour d'Honneur stands the Château proper, serene and white against the massed plantations to the north. The main front, eleven windows long, is framed between two boldly advancing pavilions whose steep, detached roofs reflect the triangular lines of the *poivrières* in front.

The façade itself is divided equally into thirds, the central portion breaking slightly forwards and supporting a triangular pediment. To avoid the monotony of this triple row of eleven windows, the architect has introduced a subtle variation in the ratio of window to wall-space. The frontispiece has three windows to each storey; the façades to either side have four; the pavilions have only one, and here the full contrast may be enjoyed between the smooth stonework and the close pattern of glass and glazing bars of the tall French windows.

A further note of variety is introduced at ground-floor level by the use of the rounded arch, and at first-floor level by the addition of a shallow pediment, to the windows of the frontispiece and pavilions. It is by such attention to detail that simplicity is removed from dullness.

Montgeoffroy follows the fashion, common enough in France, of siting the main entrance to one side of the building. This gives the place of honour in the centre of the façade to the Grand Salon, whose windows thus command the main axis of the park.

The Grand Salon is the most beautiful room in the house. It is a perfect example of the style inaugurated some ten years earlier by Gabriel at the Petit Trianon.

Although it is a large room it is utterly devoid of ostentation; an atmosphere of reserve and charm pervades the whole. Once again it is a question of simplicity enlivened by a subtle variety —a combination of the static beauty of proportion and the gentle movement of rhythm. The rhythm is built on an alternation of tall, rectangular panels and smooth round arches. A minimum of judicious ornament, in which the crossed batons of the Field Marshal provide a recurrent motif, accentuates the proportions of the panelling and emphasizes the movement of the arcading. The interplay of crisply carved decoration and plain surfaces is delicately enhanced by the use of seven different shades of grey in the painting.

It is noticeable that the ornament is confined to the upper portions of the wall space, so that if the room were empty it would appear top-heavy. The furniture provides the counterpoise. For it is the furniture, specially purchased in Paris, which is the real ornament of the Salon. It provides a rich but subdued variety of forms and colours; the straight, clean lines of the gaming tables, the graceful curves of the little work tables, the almost architectural structure of the consoles—all are here. So are the three most obvious varieties of the armchair—the stately, almost throne-like *fauteuil à la reine*, the lighter, more portable *chaise à la cabriolet*, and the wide and comfortable *bergère*, suggesting in its ample accommodation the broad paniers of contemporary ladies' fashion.

The reminder of the human element is timely, for our picture of the Grand Salon must be matched with an appropriate

scene painted from life; the room was not built to offer a perfect example of the *style Louis XVI* to the scrutiny of the connoisseur. It was the Grand Salon *de Compagnie*—the assembly
room of the polite society which centred on Montgeoffroy.

'*Ce que la Société développe dans l'homme,*' wrote Taine, '*c'est la
finesse.*' Only the portraits now introduce this note of human
warmth and vivid colour to the scene. We must visualize the
Grand Salon as the setting to a conversation piece.

'One talks in a low voice in a Salon,' continues Taine; 'sudden
outbursts of voice are forbidden here, as also any too brusque
movement. A man must control and check himself; he must
moderate his gestures and soften his expressions. The plane of
decorum has passed over originality and has removed its pro-
trusions; everything is easy and flowing. Everyone avoids causing offence, nearly everyone seeks to please. Animosities dis-
appear behind salutations, contradictions are tempered with
smiles. Politeness, mutual and select, seems to have set aside
the danger and the violence of real life, as the carpets and candle-
light have banished the rudeness and unevenness of the natural
climate.' It was as a context for such refinement of social intercourse that the eighteenth-century château was designed.

On the other side of the house from the Salon, the dining-
room, curving into a graceful apse at either end, derives its
beauty from the same subtle gradations of grey and the simple
rectilinear proportions of the panelling. Three tall windows,
with curtains of white linen, occupy the outer wall and overlook
the gardens to the north. Opposite to these a large niche, where
one would expect a fireplace, harbours a magnificent *faïence*
stove in the unusual form of a white palm tree. The Maréchal
de Contades was Governor of Strasbourg, where his cook
evolved the recipe for *pâté de foie gras*, and he brought with him
to Anjou this typical and effective form of heating common in
Alsace. Round the room stand the twelve chairs *en cabriole* as
listed in the inventory.

This inventory, which would appear at first sight to be of
merely academic interest, yields, upon closer scrutiny, some
informative sidelights on the way of living of the age. It shows
the distinction, for instance, between the status of the valet de

chambre, who was accorded a decent room with a comfortable canopy bed hung and upholstered in blue and white striped *siamoise*, and that of the plain manservant, who slept—presumably on a palliasse, for no bed is mentioned—in the gentleman's *garderobe* whose furniture consisted entirely of articles of toilet and 'one old white curtain at the small window'.

The guest rooms were on the first floor, and each was accompanied by a valet's room and *garderobe*. The single rooms are designated 'man's room' or 'woman's bedroom'. In what the distinction resided is far from clear. 'Hooks for a man's watch' as opposed to 'watch hooks with cushion' provide the only discoverable discrepancy in their respective appointments, while in the *garderobe* an equally nice distinction may be detected. The gentleman was provided with two chamber-pots *tout court*, but the lady with two chamber-pots *à la Bourdaloue*.

The remarkable state of preservation in which we can see Montgeoffroy today makes it all the more to be regretted that Menars has only survived as an empty shell, for undoubtedly Menars would have equalled if not surpassed its rival in Anjou.

'It would take a book,' wrote Grignan Vandebergh, 'to describe to you the varied riches of this enchanted dwelling. All that Art and all that Nature could provide is found united in this delightful spot. We devoted four hours to going round the apartments only.' Perhaps the highest compliment that could have been paid to the valley of the Loire at this time was the decision by Mme de Pompadour to retire here to Menars. She never lived to accomplish her design, and the estate passed to her brother, the marquis de Marigny. In 1780, when he considered selling the place in order to purchase Sceaux, he spoke of it in terms of the most extravagant praise:

'Menars is one of the most beautiful properties in the Kingdom, and certainly the most charming in Europe by its position and embellishments. Menars is furnished with an elegance and recherche to which no Royal or Princely dwelling approaches. Menars is in its prime; all the plantations made in the last twenty years have been completely successful.'

This was clearly no unbiased view. Menars was largely Marigny's creation, but behind his boasting there was a just pride. He liked to praise the place and hear it praised. His *régisseur* Lefèvre reported to him the comments of distinguished visitors whom he had shown over the house. '*M. le duc de Noailles a paru enchanté de la distribution de votre château,*' he recorded, '*et il louait dans chaque appartement la beauté et la propreté des meubles.*'

These interested opinions, however, can be matched by those of visitors who were under no obligation to record their praise. It is clear that the site was one of almost universal appeal. 'The situation, which is on a high range of hills overhanging the Loire,' wrote Wraxall, 'is of unparalleled beauty, and the eye is continually entertained on every side with a prospect the most extensive, delicious and cultivated.' Fat pastures vied with expensive buildings to create an impression of opulence as well as beauty; 'towns and palaces and castles, intermixed with forests, hamlets, abbeys and vineyards, are spread below, while a noble river pouring through the plain, diffuses plenty and fertility in its progress.' Menars does not occupy the proud height suggested by this passage. It does not overlook the valley as from some eagle's eyrie, but from a decent elevation commands a view as beautiful as it is extensive.

Another Englishman to record his admiration for Menars was Joseph Jekyll. He came in 1775 at the age of nineteen to spend a year at Blois in order to improve his French. He was not naturally disposed to admire the architecture of France, particularly its classical style; 'the châteaux of the gentlemen are in a vile, stiff taste,' he wrote to his father, 'with regular vistas of trees leading to them.' But when he visited Marigny he found reason to change his opinion. 'The Palace of Menars,' he wrote, 'is one of the first in point of splendour in this Kingdom.' Mme de Pompadour not only possessed the means, she had 'that constitutional love of beauty which produces taste and order'. His views doubtless reflected those of the society in which he was living; he could hardly have had first hand knowledge of Pompadour's taste.

Owing to some recent pilfering, Menars was not at that time open to the public, but Jekyll boldly sent word to Marigny that there were some English gentlemen from Blois who begged to kiss his hand. They were admitted, and found him 'in the gout and a nightgown, the latter sparkling with the cross of the Holy Ghost'.

Despite his gout, Marigny showed them round, drawing attention to certain objects which had come from England. 'Here is an edition of Terence,' he remarked when they reached the library, 'printed and given me by Walpole of Strawberry Hill.' His command of English was perhaps more fluent than idiomatic; he drew their attention to some chairs which had been made this side of the Channel. 'How beautiful,' he said, 'is your manufacture of horsehair for the bottoms.'

While they waited for the Marchioness to vacate her rooms, they inspected the gardens. The figure of Phaeton being turned into a poplar particularly impressed Jekyll; 'the statue is colossal and of the finest marble,' he noted; 'the feet are rooted, and the left side already enclosed in the bark, and the whole frame agonizing. I was more touched at it than by the famous Daphne of Antiquity.'

Wraxall was 'detained for some minutes' by the same group but accorded his most enthusiastic admiration for the answering figure of Atlas, 'than which nothing can be more perfect'. Just as Phaeton was being turned into a tree, so Atlas was becoming a rock. 'The artist has found means to give a sort of suction to the stone, which makes it appear to draw in the limbs of Atlas, and in some parts to have taken possession of them. It is a masterly production of sculpture.'

The gardens and groves of Menars had occupied Wraxall for a whole afternoon. He had lingered on the terrace, which did not yield, in his opinion, to that of Windsor or of St. Germains; he had wandered through the plantations; 'the woods,' he wrote, 'through which winds a murmuring rivulet, are of the most secluded solitude.' Finally he found his way back to Blois. 'I am fatigued,' runs his last entry for the day, 'but it is the fatigue of pleasure.'

Wraxall was writing as a tourist, and saw, perforce, from the outside. Joseph Jekyll had become a resident; he was received into the polite society of Blois and was invited to their country seats. 'I passed four or five very agreeable days last week,' he

writes, 'at the Château of Monsieur La Vallière.' The house was
overfull, and 'as Mlle Chartier, a very pretty girl of seventeen,
was to sleep in the room we supped in, and as *Messieurs* liked
their Burgundy too well to leave it very early, she very fairly
retired to the other end of the apartment, undressed, went to
bed and after having sung us two or three songs in her nightcap,
fell asleep with all the politeness possible'—a touching if
slightly unexpected episode.

''Tis in these domesticated visits,' he claimed, 'one frenchifies
most.' Soon he was so 'reconciled to *soupe* and *bouilli*, such a
convert to frogs and so naturalized to the wine (which is excellent here, and never disagreed with me) that I reflect upon tea,
porter and cold boiled beef without a sigh.'

On at least one occasion Jekyll stayed in really distinguished
company, at Saumery, a château at the gates of Chambord. The
marquis de Saumery was Governor of Chambord and of an old
family; he lived in great style. Unfortunately the protocol of a
noble house was too much for Jekyll's pen. 'I will not enter into
the details of etiquette observed in a French family of rank in
this ceremonious country,' he wrote; 'suffice it to say that
Monsieur [himself] had a suite of five apartments allotted him,
and was always preceded to table by an officer of the household.'

But if Jekyll does not describe the ceremonial, at least he
gives in outline the *emploi du temps*. 'The morning is usually
passed separately in the respective apartments. At one o'clock
the young men assist at the toilette of Madame la Marquise;
at two dinner is served; at five cards commence; at nine we
supped, and after supper we usually had the Comédie Bour-
geoise or Allemande till midnight.'

Jekyll had the good fortune to coincide at Saumery with the
now almost legendary figure of Choiseul. 'He appears to be the
most agreeable of Frenchmen,' he noted, 'and that is to say a
good deal.'

When Choiseul died in 1785 he left his residuary estate to his
sister the duchesse de Gramont. To his wife, whose money was
her own, he bequeathed three items: the contents of the library
at Chanteloup; a ring representing two hearts, the one a ruby
and the other a yellow diamond; they were bound together by a

ribbon set with white garnets, and one, perhaps significantly, was broken. To these was added the gift of a little snuff box 'on which are painted various views of Chanteloup'.

The box has survived. It was made by Pierre-François Delafons of Paris, and in 1767 the six miniatures in gouache by van Blarenberghe were set beneath crystal panels in each of the facets. It measures 3⅛ by 2¼ by 1⅜ inches. In this tiny, exquisite production the whole of Chanteloup has been depicted. It would be difficult to say which is more typical of the age, the vast extravagance of the lay-out or the minute precision of its depiction. Sacheverel Sitwell has deftly summed it up: 'a microcosm of a world of luxury.' There could be no better epitaph for eighteenth-century France.

CHAPTER XV

Revolution

THE PICTURE of a brilliant society thus elegantly cultivating the art of living must be set against the background of its age. It was a background dark with poverty.

There were some Frenchmen detached enough to see the defects of their country and their age. François de La Rochefoucauld, although a member of an aristocratic house, was a remarkable humanitarian. At Nantes he had been disgusted with the slave trade; 'the manner in which those poor negroes are treated,' he wrote, 'is a real blot on our humanity.' The peasants of Brittany moved him no less to pity and compassion. 'They really are slaves,' he stated; 'their poverty is excessive. They eat a sort of porridge made of buckwheat; it is more like glue than food.'

La Rochefoucauld found the harshness of Brittany softened by its contact with the Loire—'*la barbarie se relâche un peu sur les frontières*'—and once he had left Brittany behind him, he forgot all else in his rapture at the countryside of Touraine.

To Nathaniel Wraxall it was the very contrast between the loveliness of the land and the sordid condition of its inhabitants which chiefly moved him. 'The extreme poverty and misery of the peasants in the midst of a delicious paradise—producing in abundance all the necessaries and elegancies of life—impresses me with pity, wonder and indignation. I see much magnificence, but still more distress; one princely château surrounded by a thousand wretched hamlets; the most studied and enervate luxury among the higher orders of society contrasted with the beggary and nakedness of the people.' There is no poverty so distressing as poverty in the midst of plenty.

Joseph Jekyll, also writing from Blois, a year earlier than Wraxall, expressed the same opinion. 'The peasants in this part

174

of France,' he wrote, 'are miserably poor.' In spite of this they managed to be merry. 'I was much pleased,' he continues, after a fête at Blois, 'with the gaiety of the peasants, who danced *cotillons* with more natural ease than M. de Villeneuve's scholars.'

He witnessed, too, the harshness of the age. At Orléans a criminal was broken on the wheel beneath the windows of his hotel; at Blois he saw 'three hundred wretches, chained by the neck like dogs . . . on their way to the galleys at Brest . . . some of them had undergone the torture and could scarce support themselves on crutches. They were fed on the ground in the market place.'

During the Revolution another convoy, no less wretched, passed in the opposite direction through Blois under the charge of the infamous Lepetit. Four peasants and five priests were arbitrarily executed on the quay to demonstrate to the Blésois what Liberty, Equality and Fraternity really meant.

The Revolution was recorded by the owner of one of the châteaux of the Loire, Jean Dufort; thanks to his memoirs we can watch its progress through the windows of Cheverny.

Dufort was one of those memorialists who write for their own amusement. His record is a lively mixture of vivid scenes and chronological confusion; but the confusion of his tumultuous account so answers to the chaos which he depicts that it only serves to increase his artistry.

In the summer of 1789 Dufort had been to Paris and had recorded the first tremors of the earthquake; '*c'était un désordre inexprimable; la police, les lois étaient sans force.*'

In July he was back at Cheverny, and on the 16th the blow fell. 'We were quietly at dinner,' he writes, 'when the letters and papers reached us from Paris, we learnt of the deaths of Foulon, Berthier and Flesselles . . . my wife felt quite ill and dinner was disrupted. The private letters contained the most appalling details.'

At the news of the fall of the Bastille the emigration started. Neighbours of the Duforts, the Martainvilles, left at once for Switzerland; the Polignacs fled and Chambord was deserted. Dufort decided to remain. 'We feel that our duty is to stick to our country,' he writes; 'to do what we can, according to our feeble means, to re-establish order. We feel that our presence among the people with whom we have lived now for thirty years, to whom we have always been good, would provide us with a peace and a security which we would not find in a country where we had no acquaintance.'

So far as the local inhabitants were concerned, his confidence was not misplaced. Blésois was recognized as one of the most moderate regions. Professional agitators largely failed to excite the people to revolutionary fervour.

The first shock to reach the province came in August 1789, when a wave of madness swept the countryside. Everywhere the tocsin sounded; refugees, their chattels stacked on carts, poured from the villages and towns, thronging the narrow roads and driving their bewildered livestock in front of them. Men who neither knew what they were running from nor where they were running to, fled, and as they fled they cried: 'The Enemy! The English!'

The Duforts, who had a house party of eighteen at Cheverny, were—once again—seated quietly at dinner. From the dining-room windows they saw a man ride full tilt up the avenue and burst in on them shouting: 'The Enemy! The Enemy! They are coming up the drive!' Even as he spoke the tocsin rang and hordes of villagers began to throng the policies and courtyards of the house. Dufort addressed them: 'Messieurs!' he cried, 'will you nominate a leader.' And they all clamoured: 'You! You!' He took immediate charge. A small patrol was despatched to ascertain the nature and the whereabouts of this enemy, while the remaining men were armed with anything that came to hand.

In less than half an hour his patrols were back. There was no enemy. The people were in the thrall of panic: they fled from an imaginary foe. But thanks to a firm and timely leadership, the villages of Cour and Cheverny could settle into an uneasy peace.

It is interesting to see how the traditional leaders of the countryside, the gentry and the clergy, where they stuck to their posts of danger and responsibility, were sometimes able to retain the respect of the people. 'I had to give a civic dinner,' writes Dufort; 'I had chosen my orangery for it—a huge place.

It went off very well ... Everyone was so pleased that, in defiance of the agitators, they came to thank me, throwing their hats in the air and making the loudest acclamations in my honour.'

The clergy, too—a class that had some knowledge of administration—found that they had a natural contribution to make towards the running of the new democracy. 'The Parish Priests of Cour and of Cheverny were men of ability, the latter having a reputation for virtue. It was not long before their influence in the Parishes caused them to be elected Mayors, and we worked together to try and preserve a little calm in our part of the country.' It was a task they were to find by no means easy.

There lived at that time, in the little Château de Clénord situated in the valley of the Beuvron, mid-way between Cheverny and Blois, an English widow named Mrs. Dayrell. Large, wealthy, good-looking and under thirty, she had attracted a second husband, M. Courtin. It was an odd time to choose to establish oneself in France, but she had ambitious plans for Clénord, for which the fall of the Bastille provided an unlooked-for opportunity. '*Les Polignac étaient en fuite,*' wrote Dufort, '*et le superbe mobilier de Chambord fut mis en vente.*' Mme Courtin bought it for a hundred thousand livres. While Clénord was being rebuilt to house more worthily this sumptuous collection, they lived in a small house in the vineyard opposite. Such houses, known as *closeries*, were usually only occupied for the harvest.

Being rich and being English made Mme Courtin doubly odious to the revolutionaries, but she was brave and resourceful and proved herself more than a match for them.

One day three soldiers turned up on her doorstep, announcing that they were going to cut her throat. Apparently unmoved by this suggestion, she proposed that such a proceeding should be prefaced by a drink. They interpreted her invitation in such liberal terms that in half an hour she was able to bundle them out of the house contented with a very modest tip.

Some months later a more serious attempt was made. It was more deftly foiled.

A party of some eighty sans-culottes, taking advantage of the absence of their Commandant, helped themselves to firearms

and set off from Cheverny, vowing that they were going to sack
Clénord and kill the English woman. Loyal villagers roused
Dufort at seven in the morning, and warned him of this attempt.
He summoned a few young officers, and having no saddle horses,
set off in a calèche as fast as he could go. '*Les chevaux vont à
toutes jambes; il n'y avait pas de temps à perdre.*' From Cheverny
to Clénord is three short miles.

Meanwhile Mme Courtin had been warned by a cabinet-
maker from Cour of the coming assault. She sent her daughter
at once to the *closerie*, packed off her husband, and, hurriedly
dressed as a man, galloped down through the woods to join her
daughter. The rabble, who, fortunately for her, had been brows-
ing like stray horses in the vineyards, reached the bridge over
the Beuvron at the precise moment that she was crossing it. She
had a very narrow escape. 'There was a strong wind,' relates
Dufort, 'which caught her large plumed hat and laid it on the
ground. The lady, in man's clothing, dismounted nimbly, re-
covered her hat from underneath their noses, was complimented
on her lightness, and continued on her way.'

The leading men were beginning to attack the door with axes
and crowbars when Dufort and the officers arrived. One of the
officers was beaten to within an inch of his life, but the next day
discipline was re-established and the offenders sent to prison in
Blois.

The leadership which Dufort retained in his own part of the
country had to be tempered with a democratic spirit. The cry
'*Vive la République!*' was almost a password, requiring the same
answer, and wherever he went he was accosted with it. Petty
annoyances alternated with serious losses, and almost humorous
encounters masked the real danger to which the Duforts were
continually exposed.

On one occasion they had to entertain an *enragé* to dinner.
The man, whose name was Velu, had been sent to inspect the
Muniment Room at Cheverny. He stopped first for a drink at
the Inn, and while he was drinking, the Inn-keeper managed to
get word to Dufort of the impending visitation. As Velu could
scarcely read and was too proud to admit the fact, he was somewhat easily handled.

His attitude towards Cheverny was not unmixed. The republican in him was on the look out for offence. His eye fell on a coat of arms which ornamented the proscenium in the private theatre; he registered immediate disgust—'a cat drinking vinegar could not have made a more ugly grimace'. Yet there was something in him which was pleased and proud to be dining with a count and in a château.

There were several embarrassing moments. Seeing a particularly beautiful femme de chambre, Velu turned to Dufort's son. 'If you're a good republican,' he said, 'you'd go to bed with her and marry her.' At dinner he took the footman by the hand and suggested changing places with him. 'I beg you, brother,' he said ostentatiously, 'you have my place and let me take a turn at serving you.'

This gesture was made because the Duforts had not adopted the new fashion of master and servants eating together at one table. Indeed, their servants were of the 'old retainer' school who would have been horrified at the idea. All except two were over sixty; none had been with them for less than ten years. As the result of the Revolution Dufort had been obliged to reduce their wages—an occasion which had discovered the depth of their devotion, for Quéru, the cook, who had been receiving 600 livres a year, offered to stay on free of charge, an offer which was naturally refused, '*mais qui nous tira des larmes des yeux*'.

Their servants, like their friends, shared with them their trials and privations. At one time they all had to live for nearly a fortnight on black bread.

During the Terror the Duforts continued to exist in precarious isolation at Cheverny. They had no communication with their friends. 'During the long winter evenings,' Dufort writes, 'we were all huddled together in one small room, the Parish Priest, his cousin, my wife, my son and myself . . . Not a single day passed without our hearing of some new calamity.'

Looking back after the worst of the storm had passed, it seemed that in five years he had not known one day free from anguish. 'A man who lives in a time of Revolution lives more than a hundred years in five. Mental sufferings bring on an unremitting harassment which ends by causing a stupor, a disenchantment with life which I cannot convey. One is caught up in a fearful course of events, and one lives in a continued state of torment.'

Each morning their faithful servant Jumeau went on foot to Blois, returning with the dreaded *Moniteur* and its daily list of victims—'*la nécrologie de la guillotine*'. Dufort would not have the paper read before dinner, but one day his son got hold of it and began to read. The name of their old friend the marquis de Romé, who had walked straight from the Tribunal to the tumbril to cut out the suspense of waiting, struck them speechless; the dinner was left uneaten—'*nous sortons de table le cœur navré.*'

Another day it was his brother-in-law, M. de Salaberry, whose noble character could not outweigh his noble birth; a man so upright that he had refused an opportunity to escape, knowing that the gendarmes would be held responsible and made to suffer for him. 'What, you want me to compromise these two honest men?' he had asked, 'I could not do it.'

Another day, April 20, 1794, two cousins of Dufort's were guillotined together. 'They made a magnificent end,' he wrote with pride, 'going to execution as if they had been going to some religious ceremony. Their faith and their sense of dignity upheld them to the last.'

Another day it was the duchesse de Gramont, the sister of Choiseul. How bitter now were the memories of the old days and of those delightful carefree visits—*les charmantes veillées de Chanteloup*!

The duchesse de Choiseul survived the Revolution. She had been ruined, imprisoned, released and washed up by the tide to die in poverty and oblivion in 1802. But her poverty was mitigated by one of the most touching acts of human gratitude recorded in the annals of Touraine.

While building had been in progress on the enlargements of Chanteloup, one of the workmen had attracted the attention of the Choiseuls by the zest with which he worked. His name was Léonard Perrault, but they called him Petit-Pierre.

'How much do you earn a day?' the Duke had asked him.

'Ah, Monseigneur,' said Petit-Pierre, evading the question; 'my fortune would be made if I had the means to buy a donkey.'

'And how much does a donkey cost?'

'Two *louis*, Monseigneur.'

The Duke produced two *louis d'or*. '*Tiens, les voilà,*' he said; '*fais ta fortune avec ton âne.*'

Towards the end of the Revolution, when the Duchess was living more or less in hiding at the Couvent des Recollets, the duc de Pasquier came to visit her; he found her in a state of high emotion. 'Just imagine,' she told him; 'a moment ago a man was shown in who came from Chanteloup.' She had not recognized him. 'Do you not remember, your Grace,' the man had asked, 'Petit-Pierre who used to gather stones along the road to Chanteloup, and to whom you showed so much kindness?' He had then reminded her of the long-forgotten gift of the donkey. That gift had indeed been the foundation of his fortune. 'I am rich now,' he concluded, 'but you know, your Grace, it all belongs to you. I heard that you were in difficulties, and I have come to give you what is yours.' So saying he took out a purse containing two hundred golden pieces, placed it on the table and disappeared as suddenly as he had come.

While most of France was interpreting equality in terms of inhumanity and injustice, these two persons, a former Duchess and a former carrier of stones, between whom birth could not have placed a greater gulf, had found the one equality that matters—equality of human kindness.

The story goes further. When Choiseul's mausoleum was being dismantled by the *enragés*, Petit-Pierre bought the marbles and at a safer time, and at his own expense, he had them re-erected. When the Duchess died he had her coffin surreptitiously transferred and laid beside her husband's in the tomb. Finally, in his own will, 'not wishing to be separated, but to be protected in death as he had been in life' by his ducal benefactors, he directed that his own memorial should be raised in the same place that Choiseul had chosen in a corner of the cemetery, 'beneath a single cypress, looking towards Chanteloup'.

Dufort also experienced the loyalty of those he had befriended, but all the time the danger of being a *ci-devant* count and living in a noble mansion grew more acute.

Emancipated but embittered minds scrutinized his bearing

and behaviour, eager to note an un-egalitarian remark. '*Tu ne me tutoies pas,*' complained one *enragé*, '*tu n'es pas dans le sens de la Révolution.*' He was not. 'We never sported any of the accoutrements of the Citizen,' admitted Dufort; 'we went dressed and powdered as under the Ancien Régime, showing kindness to all and familiarity to none.'

Covetous and malevolent eyes scanned the façades and the policies of the house for possible causes of offence. The drive was lined with wooden posts and iron chains that formed a white and black festoon on either side. '*Voilà encore des marques de despotisme et féodalité,*' cried the sans-culottes, and Dufort had the offending posts removed.

Exception was taken to the twin cupolas that crown the two imperial domes of Cheverny, their lead was valuable and should be offered to the Nation. On this occasion Dufort stood firm. 'I will not listen to talk of demolishing a monument that is in the best of taste.'

Suspicion fell upon the marble busts of Roman Emperors which occupied the roundels on the front. 'I assured them they were of Greek Sans-culotte Philosophers,' declared Dufort, and the busts remained.

Unfortunately his audience contained one educated man, Duliepvre, that most dangerous of revolutionaries, a priest turned Jacobin. 'Duliepvre remembered that in the muddy depths of his heart, to make use of it when occasion served him.' This man was Dufort's most tenacious enemy. He was always trying to incite the loyal inhabitants of Cour and Cheverny against their former Lord. 'My friends,' he would say, though he was friend to none, 'you will never be happy so long as you let this Château stand, and all those aristocrats inside it.'

At one point Dufort considered going into hiding, but he at once rejected the idea; 'the life of a proscript living in concealment is worse than death.' They literally lived from day to day; his morning greeting to his wife was: '*encore un jour de passé.*'

It was almost a relief when the end came. It came in the form of an unpleasant little man called Hézine, Procureur to the District, who stopped one day to take refreshment at the Inn of Cheverny. Across the road, before his outraged eyes, there rose, white and majestic, the beautiful mansion built 160 years earlier by the son of President Hurault. He saw it, not as a work of art, but as an affront to his republicanism. 'There's a fine great Château,' he was heard to remark; 'I shan't be happy until that becomes the property of the Nation.'

Six days later Dufort was arrested by the triumphant Duliepvre. By the same warrant his friend and neighbour the marquis de Rancogne was arrested at the Château d'Herbault. While enjoying a reputation and respect almost equal to that of the Duforts, this family had problems peculiarly their own. The old Marchioness was going out of her mind; she would not have it that there was a Revolution, and so far as she was concerned Louis XVI was still alive. 'Mad on certain counts, she was, for the rest, extremely shrewd in all that concerned her affairs.' Any direct encounter between her and the revolutionaries was bound to be disastrous, and she had to be kept by faithful servants in a state of perfect insulation. Duliepvre had attempted to intrude and had been warned off. He now had his revenge.

Dufort was allowed to go to the Carmelite prison at Blois in his own time in his own coach and to bring his own servants. He was hardly more confined than he had been in his little room at Cheverny. His one complaint was of the fleas. He had at home a cellar filled with the most recherché wines 'none of them less than ten years old'. His wife was allowed to go back to the Château and return with several crates '*remplies des vins les plus précieux*', enough to render the closest imprisonment at least endurable.

But although Dufort's confinement was far from rigorous, there was always the background thought that the Carmelites might be the penultimate position, the ante-chamber to the guillotine.

It was typical of the Revolution that Dufort had the pleasure of sharing his captivity with Hézine, Velu and Arnaud, three of the worst extremists in the area. The execration of the populace for these three men knew no bounds. When they were packed off to the Revolutionary Tribunal a jeering crowd made their departure almost impossible.

There were cheers when handcuffs were produced; '*le peuple les accablait de malédictions et leur souhaitait la mort.'* They were not executed, but when, months later, Velu was recognized in a public vehicle at Orléans, the mob stopped the coach, forced him to get out and kneel down while they poured a bucket full of blood from the nearest abattoir all over him.

The hatred of the people for the extremists was only matched by their respect for Dufort. 'The inhabitants of Cour and of Cheverny wanted to rise in force and petition for my release,' he tells us; 'we opposed the idea, fearing the consequences. Such influence, once known to Robespierre, would be enough to send us to the scaffold.'

His prudence and his patience were in the end rewarded. One day in September 1794, three months after the fall of Robespierre, a slightly tipsy hatter called Avérous entered the Carmelites. Sixteen of the prisoners were summoned to the courtyard and told of their release. 'Citizen Dufort,' said Avérous, 'the people, by unanimous acclaim, have granted you your freedom. I am commissioned to tell you to behave, as you have always behaved, *en honnête homme.'*

Three quarters of an hour later he walked out. *'Il faisait très chaud et le plus beau clair de lune possible.'* With his two children he went to walk, a free man, along the banks of the Loire *'pour respirer un air plus pur'*.

Everywhere he went he was received with such lively tokens of enthusiasm that he was forced to stay indoors. He learned that the villagers of Cour and Cheverny were planning to come *en masse* as far as Clénord and to escort him home in triumph; but he would have none of that. Unobtrusively and after dark he came back to that beloved place from which, a few months earlier, he had thought he was going for ever. *'Ce fut alors que je commençai, pour ainsi dire, à renaître.'*

It was indeed more like a resurrection than a survival. When Laurenceot, the new and more moderate governor of Blois, drove out to Cheverny and found the nobleman still seated in his noble mansion, he could scarcely believe his eyes. As soon as he had seen the beauty of the residence, he exclaimed with a touching artlessness: *'Comment, vous vivez encore?'*

CHAPTER XVI

Restoration

'Guerre aux châteaux, paix aux chaumières!' The slogan was scratched upon the mantelpiece of the gallery at le Plessis-Bourré, where it may still be seen; but the war against the châteaux was never waged. The Revolution did surprisingly little in the way of direct destruction. Only Jarzé, situated in the direct line of country taken by the Vendéen troops in 1792, was sacked and burnt, and with it was lost a precious relic of the architectural genius of Jean Bourré.

At the turn of the century the châteaux of the Loire were mostly in the same condition in which they had been in the last days of the Ancien Régime. When Colonel Thornton, taking advantage of the peace of Amiens to make a sporting tour through France, came to Chanteloup, he could write: 'I was particularly struck by the magnificence of this Château. The bedrooms of the ducs de Penthièvre and Choiseul are splendid in the extreme; the cabinet or boudoir is remarkably elegant.' He observed that there were 'eighty-four gentlemen's bed-chambers with dressing-rooms complete'; he admired the tiny library of the duchesse de Choiseul; he made no complaint about the condition of the house and would have bought it had he not been prevented by currency restrictions.

It is a little difficult to reconcile Thornton's enthusiasm with an official report drawn up in the year 1802. Its list of degradations and despoilings is long, and conjures up a heavy scene of desolation; panelling had been wrenched from the walls, mirrors prized from their frames, even the very locks had been picked from the doors for the enrichment of Citizen Dufaillis, who had 'bought' Chanteloup without ever actually paying for it. Worse still, a large quantity of lead had been stripped from the roof, the weather had got in and the report describes the main block as 'in almost total ruin'.

To this initial damage there succeeded a long period of neglect. In 1812 the Château was visited by another Englishman, Lord Blayney. 'It is at present the property of a M. Chaptal,' he wrote—adding with aristocratic sarcasm, 'a çi-devant Apothecary.' The new owner, however, was seldom in residence and only kept three or four rooms furnished for his use. 'All the rest,' wrote Lord Blayney, 'present the naked walls; even the tapestry hangings have been taken down and the glasses removed.' He wandered from room to room throughout the endless enfilade of the apartments, but it was sorry going; 'the dullness that reigned throughout could not fail to affect us, when we reflected on the scenes of gaiety and pleasure which formerly made these walls resound.' Of these the old concierge did not fail to remind them, recalling with nostalgia how he had often seen fifty guest rooms prepared and thirty or forty carriages on parade before the entrance.

Lord Blayney was a prisoner of war in France during the agony of the first Empire. He gives a lively and often pictorial account of the land of his captivity. Social life had received a severe set-back. Tours, formerly 'one of the most sociable parts of France,' had become one of the dullest, every person being suspicious of his neighbour. It was the situation inevitably produced by a police state, whose system of espionage undermined even the confidence of near relations.

Blayney had little but contempt for French cooking. On two occasions he records having thrown his entire dinner either into the fireplace or out of the window. Thornton also experienced difficulties of a gastronomic nature. On receiving for breakfast 'two brace of beautiful frogs' he commented—'I must do Mr. Bryant the justice to say that he devoured the frogs with the avidity of a real amateur; but they produced so different an effect on Mrs. T and myself that we were under the necessity of quitting the room.'

It is amusing to find outposts of Britannia even at this time solidly planted on French soil. Such was a woman visited by Lord Blayney in the region of Beautois, who told him that 'notwithstanding *tea* was unknown to any other person in the department, and enormously dear, she had not been able to bring herself to forego it, and that she would certainly die if deprived of it.'

Blayney responded, as so many travellers have responded, to the beauties of the Loire valley, but he noticed how few of the châteaux, both here and throughout France, were inhabited by their owners, 'who generally prefer residing in Paris and leave these noble seats in the charge of agents or farmers'. Those who were in possession of confiscated estates were increasingly uneasy about their tenure; 'the still existing fear of their being reclaimed prevents their spending any money in their repairs or embellishments.' Thus to the danger of deliberate destruction there now succeeded a danger of a more insidious nature—the slow erosion of neglect.

It must have been a memorable experience to be one of the first to visit France after the storm was over and to see the downfall of the Ancien Régime reflected in the decay of its architecture. Some of the châteaux had not even been tidied up after the outrages of the Revolution. Blayney describes Menars as 'a magnificent ruin'. He passed through on to the south front and was appalled at the spectacle which met his gaze. 'The gardens are cut into terraces and must have been very grand, but are now totally neglected, and the alleys strewed with the fragments of statues, broken into pieces by the revolutionists.'

It is suggestive of the insignificant role which Menars now played in its village that Blayney was unable even to discover the name of its owner—'doubtless some parvenu,' he concluded, 'who resides in Paris.' It belonged, in fact, to Maréchal Victor, duc de Bellune.

Twenty years later, long after the Monarchy had been restored, another English traveller, Elizabeth Strutt, found the marks of the Revolution still fresh upon the fabric of Ussé. 'The Château itself,' she observed, 'presents a noble exterior, but the interior exhibits a melancholy picture of its former greatness.' The house was full of the most interesting portraits she had ever seen. From their high gilt frames, the Beauties of the Court of Louis XIV looked down from the walls, and 'still exhibited their graces though no admiring eye now turned towards them'. Poets and Philosophers faced them across the Gallery—but

Poets, Philosophers and Beauties had all endured the same fate; 'wanton knives and sabres had been drawn with worse than vandal barbarity across their faces.'

Elizabeth Strutt made her descent of the Loire in June of 1832, and her book, 'originally intended for the amusement of a small circle of friends' and dedicated to the Countess of Euston, is full of interest and charm.

She had the perception which pin-points the significant event and a delightful power of evoking atmosphere. In Tours Cathedral she gives us a glimpse of the Archbishop; 'his countenance was strikingly benevolent, his figure at the same time dignified and humble; it seemed as if it expressed at once his office and himself.' She appears to have been fortunate in her experience of the French Clergy; two Priests at Blois impressed her with their look of piety and sweetness. It was the face of a Church purified by years of persecution. 'I bent my knee to both,' she confessed, 'more lowly than I might have done when their Order was in the full zenith of the power it has so much abused.' Then, with a quick, unflattering comparison between these and the 'ecclesiastical magistrates' of the Church of England, she passed to an inspection of Blois.

Her means of transport was a *patache*—a sort of barge whose progress was as leisurely as its accommodation was comfortable, and the picture is painted from mid-stream. 'The evening was moonlit and serene, and not a ripple of the noiseless Loire interrupted the full concert of the frogs, who seemed imparadised by thousands in the marshy spots reclaimed by the river.' By daylight she found it no less impressive: river, town and countryside combined in one delightful prospect. 'The wooded banks, the winding river with its white sails, stately and still as swans upon its unruffled bosom, the bridge, the town rising above with its ancient Cathedral and once proud Château, all glittering in the sun, formed a picture Claude might have been happy to portray.' Her own portrayal is equally felicitous.

The 'once proud Château' had reached, in 1832, a turning point in its existence. Curiously enough the Revolution had saved Blois. By an edict of February 1788, Louis XVI had decreed the sale and demolition of the Royal residence. A temporary reprieve was effected by military necessity, and two months later the buildings were in use as a barracks. The Revolution came before the demolition order was revived. The Château was stripped of its statues and the insignia of Royalty; it was derided as 'a heap of stones that the emasculated admirers of royal folly regard as superb'—but it was not demolished.

In 1808 a further degradation was envisaged by Napoleon. The Palace of the Valois was to become a beggars' hostel—*un Dépôt de Mendicité*—a condition which must represent the lowest possible ebb in a building's fortune. Nevertheless, the tide of aesthetic opinion was beginning to turn. The value judgments of a revolutionary party are more or less conditioned by the political associations of their objects, and are, as value judgments, worthless. With political emancipation came freedom of thought, and it could be admitted that Blois was 'in its own way a monument of our architecture, which has even some connection with interesting historical memories.'

In 1825, when there was talk of establishing the Prefecture in Gaston d'Orléans's wing, the negotiations revealed a public opinion ready to regard the royal house as *'un monument superbe, riche en souvenirs, dont la conservation est précieuse'*. But it was still the classical age, and its interest was largely confined to Mansart's buildings. Three years later, however, Honoré de Balzac, a great lover of the Loire valley and its architecture represents the full appreciation of Blois for what it is. 'This marvellous monument,' he wrote, 'in which so many styles survive, and where such great things were accomplished, is in a state of degradation which is a disgrace to the country.' He admired the *naïf* of the architecture of Louis XII and the mixture of boldness and delicacy in François I's staircase—'built by giants and decorated by midgets'.

Finally, with the setting up of the Commission des Monuments Historiques, the restoration of Blois—a century and a half overdue—was put in hand by the architect Félix Duban. It was one of the first buildings of France to be thus re-instated. There was, of course, no question of Blois being again inhabited. But for the private châteaux there was a last, late flowering of the taste for country life which secured the restoration of some of the most endangered fabrics.

The Romantic Movement did much to restore the château to a place of honour in the imagination of the age. The eighteenth century had either despised the medieval architecture of which it had so abundant an inheritance, or preserved it proudly as evidence of ancient titles. Now a new interest in things Gothic began to spread.

It was the grimmer side of the medieval castle which captured the imagination first. We have already seen the absurd description by Sir Walter Scott of an imaginary le Plessis-lès-Tours. At about the same time that he was writing there begins to appear in the accounts of travellers a new and almost obsessional interest in *oubliettes*.

Lord Blayney was shown at Amboise a well a hundred feet deep, and was entertained by ghoulish stories of rollers placed at intervals of the descent and armed with two-edged knives which were rotated by machinery. 'The victim being precipitated into the abyss and falling from one roller to another, was minced to pieces before he reached the bottom.' Elizabeth Strutt identified this 'abyss of horror' with the central core of one of the great spiral ramps, the Tour des Minimes or the Tour Hurtault. As she associated these atrocities with the reign of Louis XI, before the towers in question were built, the historical value of the story may be doubted.

Other aspects of the Romantic château—'*Amours secréts des rois et des reines . . . aventures mystérieuses . . . apparitions et fantômes*'—were set before a receptive public by the production, in 1848, of *Mystères des Vieux Châteaux de France* by A. le François. It is obvious that the restoration of medieval castles in the Gothic style under the influence of so inaccurate an inspiration, had much about it that was deplorable. But at least the buildings were repaired and, what is more, inhabited.

Perhaps the most careful and successful restoration was that of Chenonceau by Mme Pelouze. The heavy caryatids imposed upon the entrance front by Catherine de' Medici were removed and the original fenestration re-instated. The high pedimented frontispiece which masked the east façade was likewise taken down and the original appearance of the Château of the Bohiers restored. Mme Pelouze thus takes her place among the long line of ladies who have presided over the fortunes of Chenonceau and played so important a role in the architecture of this region.

Two other ladies, the sisters Jeanne and Marie Say, were to be the restorers of two more of the châteaux of the Loire— Chaumont and Brissac.

Brissac had been abandoned as the result of the Revolution. Augustin, the ninth Duke, built himself a smaller house, the Petit Château, in the park, from which he could observe the decay of his ancestral home. In 1843 his son Timoléon pulled down the new château and took up residence in the old. It is doubtful if he could have carried out the restorations needed had not his son, Roland, married in 1865 the wealthy Mlle Say. In due course the château was made over to the young pair, and she devoted much of her handsome fortune to its restoration. She may be pardoned a few errors of taste which she shared with her generation for having saved this historic mansion for posterity. Thanks to the taste and devotion of the present owners, Brissac has come once more into the front rank of the stately homes of France.

Ten years after the wedding of Jeanne Say came that of her sister Marie to Prince Amédée de Broglie. Their honeymoon was spent in their newly purchased castle of Chaumont-sur-Loire. Their arrival was the scene of the most brilliant reception. Castle and park had been illuminated. The first appearance of their carriage upon the new suspension bridge was to be the signal for an outburst of public rejoicing. '*Les cloches de la vieille église,*' writes an eye-witness, '*sonnent à toute volée; la voiture entre au Château au milieu de la population en délire.*'

There were many advantages to the public in the arrival of a rich and lavish châtelaine, not the least being the improvements of communications by road, and later by telephone, with Blois. When Mme de Staël had been at Chaumont the only road was the levée of the Loire on the opposite bank. '*Il faut arriver par Ecure,*' she instructed her guests, '*et là un petit bateau vous aménera dans le Château de Catherine de Médicis.*'

The new princesse de Broglie found Chaumont in a state in

which we would hardly recognize it today. In the park, close to
the entrance of the Château, there still stood the villages of
Place and Fradillet. The château itself, in which the windows and
doors *'ne joignaient plus'*, was in an advanced state of dilapidation,
and there were trees growing in the courtyard. Both villages
were gradually bought up, their inhabitants rehoused and their
houses demolished. Finally the old Church was pulled down and
rebuilt in the middle of the new village and the high ground
was laid out as a beautiful park *à l'anglaise*. Meanwhile the
architect Sanson was charged with the restoration and moderni-
zation of the château.

The enlargement of the domain was part of the prince de
Broglie's intentions. An anecdote here reveals the character of
the new châtelain of Chaumont. A rich neighbour, from whom
he had refused to buy land at an exaggerated price, was ruined
and had to sell up. *'C'est le moment d'offrir un prix dérisoire de la
propriété,'* the Prince was advised. His answer was truly noble. 'It
is not my custom to speculate on the misfortunes of others,' he
replied; 'this very evening I will offer this unfortunate woman
exactly the price that I was ready to pay for her land last year.'

In later years the Broglies in their turn were faced with
financial embarrassments, which at first were not without their
humorous side. A council of the family was called to consider
retrenchments. It was proposed, as a preliminary economy, to
get rid of the elephant. (An elephant called Miss Pungi had been
presented to them by the Maharajah of Kaputhala; she occupied
a large portion of the stables and ate like twenty horses.) The
idea of dispensing with Miss Pungi was dismissed as grotesque,
and the only economy agreed upon was the suppression of foie
gras sandwiches for tea.

During the nineteenth century Azay-le-Rideau, Luynes and
Le Lude were also restored and rendered habitable. Others
were less fortunate. As early as 1666 Bury, acquired by the
family of Rostaign, had been allowed to fall into irretrievable
ruin. Amboise, badly burnt in the early seventeenth century,
saw more and more of its fabric demolished until, in the days of
the First Empire, it was reduced to its present proportions. Le
Verger, as we have seen, was deliberately destroyed by the

CHAMPIGNY: forecourt
buildings after the
demolition of the main block;
watercolour by Gaignières

CHAMPIGNY:
Sainte Chapelle;
watercolour by Gaignières

RICHELIEU: the main block; engraving by Clarey Martineau

RICHELIEU: garden front, engraving by Marot

CHEVERNY: the south front

CHEVERNY: a set of eighteenth-century engravings;
by courtesy of the marquis de Vibraye

CHANTELOUP: entrance front from the miniature by van Blarenberghe on the snuff-box left by Choiseul to his wife; by courtesy of
Mrs. Charles B. Wrightsman

CHANTELOUP: the garden front; anonymous drawing

MONTGEOFFROY: the Grand Salon

MONTGEOFFROY: the Dining Room

MONTGEOFFROY: entrance front

MENARS: entrance front

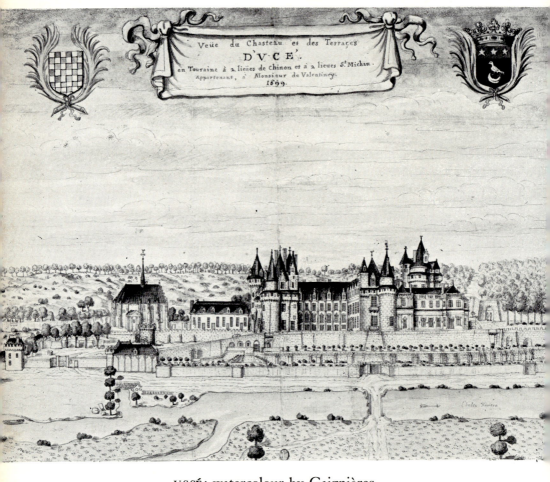

USSÉ: watercolour by Gaignières

CHENONCEAU: east front as altered by Catherine de' Medici; drawing by Félibien, courtesy of the marquis de Vibraye

family that built it. Richelieu, abandoned in the Revolution, and exposed to the pilfering hands of the local inhabitants, was one of the first to succumb to the notorious *Bande Noire*, the profiteers who bought up these priceless relics and sold them for their materials. Napoleon had toyed with the idea of restoring Richelieu for the use of one of his Marshals, but he recoiled before the formidable expense entailed by its repair. In 1805 it was sold to a demolition contractor. In 1823, Chanteloup shared the same fate.

There remained Chambord, temporarily reprieved by Napoleon, who made it over to the prince de Wagram. To his widow posterity owes the destruction of its magnificent forest.

In 1821 the fate of Chambord hung perilously in the balance. The place was a financial millstone round the neck of any owner—'an enormous mass of stones whose upkeep absorbs its revenue'—and its sale was determined upon, a sale that could only have resulted in its piecemeal destruction.

Already the process of decay was far advanced. 'From without,' it was reported in the *Quotidienne*, 'it preserves its imposing architectural character, but within doors its appearance is pitiful.' The rot which had started under the Ancien Régime had been accelerated by the action of the revolutionaries, who had stripped it bare, auctioning the furniture, burning the tapestries and wrenching the chimney pieces from the hearths. In the bedroom of the Maréchal de Saxe only the shattered fragments of the balustrade remained. Now, neglect had accomplished what vandalism had begun; the roofs having let the water through, ceilings had collapsed and falling beams destroyed the floors beneath. Doors without panels and windows without glass exposed the rooms to every inclemency of the weather. In the midst of a devastated park the great château stood—a gaunt and empty carcass.

But the destruction was by no means complete. Much of the carving was still 'in the most perfect state of preservation', and even in François I's old apartment, the worst affected portion of the palace, the Cabinet de Travail could still be appreciated as 'a little masterpiece of sculpture . . . of an astonishing richness of work'. The *fleur de lys* which surmounted the central cupola had survived the buffeting of three centuries; it escaped also the hostility of the Revolution. The architect, M. Marie, convinced the authorities that its removal would cost 100,000 francs, and it remained in place. 'Alone amidst the debris of the Monarchy it seemed for twenty-five years to proclaim to France the return of the descendants of St. Louis.'

The descendants of St. Louis returned in due course, but it needed the eye of a visionary optimist to foresee any possible restoration of Chambord. But such was the enthusiasm of the Royalists that the visionary optimist appeared—Marcellus, the friend of Chateaubriand and devoted partisan of the Bourbons. 'Chambord became to me Versailles,' he wrote; 'I saw already this proud Château resplendent in the magnificence of Royal majesty; I saw its marbles, its galleries, its columns, its gardens, its cascades, its *parterres d'eau*, and in the centre of all its splendours, the Glorious Child, become a great Prince, walking in its superb alleys.'

The 'glorious child' was the duc de Bordeaux, posthumous son of the murdered duc de Berri, the last and almost unlooked-for hope of the Bourbon dynasty. A more practical enthusiast, the comte de Calonne, realized the dream of Marcellus by getting up a subscription to purchase Chambord and present it to this providential child.

Fifty years later this prince, now known as the comte de Chambord, returned to France to be offered the throne as Henri V, and for a few days the Château from which he took his title became the centre of interest to all France. In the summer of 1871 he had returned to Paris and had visited 'with an acheing heart the still smoking ruins of what remained of the Tuileries.' A few days later he left abruptly for Chambord, and from here issued his famous manifesto demanding the white flag of the Bourbons.

'*Je l'ai reçu comme un dépôt sacré du vieux Roi,*' he wrote; '*il a flotté sur mon berceau; je veux qu'il ombrage ma tombe. Français! Henri V ne peut abandonner le drapeau blanc de Henri IV!*' Brave words, but the French were equally zealous in their demand for their '*monarchie tricolore*'. The Bishop of Orléans, who had been with a deputation of anxious Royalists to try and dissuade the

Prince from his folly, declared that 'never had such moral blindness been seen'. Thiers, more sarcastic, suggested that the Prince should be called 'the French Washington', for he had founded the Republic.

Neither side was prepared to separate the symbol from what it stood for, and the beautiful coaches ordered from Binders to carry the King in triumph to Paris were never used. Appropriately enough, they have found their last resting place at Chambord.

Appendix

THE GALLERIES BETWEEN THE DONJON AND
THE CORNER TOWERS AT CHAMBORD

Dr. Frédéric Lesueur, in his article 'Les derniers étapes de la construction de Chambord', published in the *Bulletin Monumental*, 1951, opposes the theory (accepted by Pallustre, Guerlin and Gébelin) that these galleries were an afterthought. He advances two reasons. One, that they tie in perfectly with the pilasters of the donjon towers, providing a split column wherever they meet. But since the blind wall of the ground floor was made to fit the orders of the donjon towers, it would necessarily follow that any storeys subsequently superimposed would also fit.

Secondly he states that the open loggias on the donjon towers could only have been designed to connect with these galleries. I submit that this is going too far. François I was perfectly capable of opening loggias in his façades with the greatest inconsequence. There are loggias on the south front of the donjon which do not lead anywhere.

Finally Dr. Lesueur states that an inspection of the building does not confirm the theory. But this may be questioned. If the visitor will stand with his back to the wing adjoining the Chapel and look at the junction of the top storey of the gallery with the donjon tower, he will see, behind and above the cornice of the gallery, the capital of a pilaster on the drum of the tower. The eaves of the gallery cut right into the capital.

In fact the junction of the top storeys is so awkward as to require the theory that the galleries were later additions. The whole problem results from the fact that the towers of the donjon are half a storey taller than the corner towers. The galleries were built out from the corner towers and continue their proportions, causing this awkward junction when they meet the towers of the donjon. The question must be asked: why were the corner towers not built the same height as those of the donjon? If the connecting galleries had been part of the original design, it would seem obvious to make the towers the same height. But if the original plan was to leave a terrace at first-floor level between the donjon and the corner towers, then the whole design makes sense. The corner towers were deliberately lower and less ornate in order to throw into relief the height and richness of the central block. Chambord as it appears in my drawing makes sense; Chambord with the galleries suggests an afterthought.

General Bibliography

1. *Architectural*

Androuet du Cerceau, J.: *French Châteaux and Gardens in the 16th Century*. Ed. W. Ward. 1909

Anthologies Illustrées: *La Touraine*. Pref: H. Guerlin. 1911

Bever, Ad. van: *La Touraine Vue par les Ecrivains et les Artistes*. 1914

Blunt, Sir A.: *Art and Architecture in France 1500–1700*. 1953

Champigneulle, B.: *Promenades aux Châteaux de la Loire*. 1963

Chevalier, C.: *Promenades Pittoresques en Touraine*. 1869

Colombier, P. du: *Le Château de France*. 1960

Cossé-Brissac, comte P. de: *Châteaux de France Disparus*. 1947

Croy, J. de: *Nouveaux Documents pour l'Histoire de la Création des Résidences Royales des Bords de la Loire*. 1894

Félibien, A.: *Mémoires pour Servir à l'Histoire des Maisons Royales*. 1874

Gébelin, F.: *Les Châteaux de la Renaissance*. 1927

— *Les Châteaux de la Loire*. 1961

Goutel, H. de: *Châteaux de la Loire et du Berry*. 1930

Laborde, comte de: *Les Comptes des Bâtiments du Roi 1528–1517*. 1877

Lesueur, F. *Vues des Châteaux du Blésois au 17ème Siècle*. 1911

Levis-Mirepoix, duc de: *La France de la Renaissance*. 1947

— *François 1er*. 1931

Loiseleur, J.: *Les Résidences Royales de la Loire*. 1863

Rain, P.: *Les Chroniques des Châteaux de la Loire*. 1921

2. *Memoirs, etc.*

Beatis, A.: *Voyage du Cardinal d'Aragon, 1517–1518*. 1913

Brackenhoffer, E.: *Voyage en France, 1643–1644*. 1925

Brantôme, P. de Bourdeille, Seigneur de: *Mémoires Contenant les Anecdotes de la Cour de France*. 1887

Commines, P. de: *Mémoires de Commines, 1524*. Ed. 1747

Cradock, Mrs. A.: *La Vie Française à la veille de la Revolution; Journal Inédit*. 1911

Dubuisson-Aubenay. *Voyage de Dubuisson, 1634*. MSS. in Bibliothèque Mazarine

Dutens, L.: *Memoirs of a Traveller now in Retirement*. Vol. 4. 1806

— *Journal of Travels made through the Principal Cities of Europe.* 1782

Jeckyll, J.: *Correspondence of Mr Joseph Jeckyll with his sister-in-law.* Ed.: A. Bourke. 1894

La Fontaine, J. de: *Œuvres de La Fontaine.* Ed. H. Regnier. 1892

La Roche, S.: *Journal einer Reise durch Frankreich von der Verfasserin von Rosaliens Briefen.* 1787

La Rochefoucauld, F. de: *Voyage en France, 1781–1783.* Vol. 2. 1938

La Valette: 'Un Voyage en Touraine en 1729'. In *Bulletin de la Société Archéologique de Touraine.* Vol. 11. 1898

Locke, J.: *Locke's Travels in France, 1675–1679.* Ed. J. Lough. 1953

Montpensier, Mlle de: *Mémoires.* Ed. A. Cheruel. 1871

Tallemant des Réaux: *Historiettes.* 1854

Wraxall, N.: *A Tour through the Western, Southern and Interior Provinces of France.* 1784

Young, A.: *Travels during the Years 1787, 1788 & 1789.* 1792

INTRODUCTION

Boileau, Abbé: *Vie de Madame la Duchesse de Liancourt.* 1814

Bosseboeuf, L.-A.: *Le Château et la Sainte Chapelle de Champigny.* 1881

Broglie, Prince J. de: *Madame de Staël et sa Cour au Château de Chaumont.* 1936

Liancourt, duchesse de: *Règlement donné par une dame de qualité à sa petite-fille pour sa conduite et celle de sa maison.* 1814

Montalembert, comte de: *The Political Future of England.* 1856

Rabelais, F.: *Pantagruel.* 1533

Rush, R.: *The Court of London from 1819–1825.* 1873

Strutt, E.: *Six weeks on the Loire with a peep into La Vendée.* 1833

Young, A.: *A Six Months' Tour.* 1770

THE HAPPY VALLEY

Alcuin, in C. Chevalier: *Promenades Pittoresques en Touraine.* 1869

Bentivoglio, Cardinal, in C. Chevalier: *Promenades Pittoresques en Touraine.* 1869

Brackenhoffer, E.: *Voyage de Paris en Italie, 1644–1646.* 1927

Evelyn, J.: *The Diary of John Evelyn.* Ed. E. S. de Beer. 1955

Florio, F., in C. Chevalier. *Promenades Pittoresques en Touraine.* 1869

Guerlin, H.: *Anthologies Illustrées. La Touraine.* 1911

La Fontaine, J. de: *Œuvres de La Fontaine.* Ed. H. Regnier. 1892

Lepleigny, T.: *La Décoration du Pays et Duché de Touraine.* 1541. Ed. Prince A. Galitzin. 1861

Vieilleville, F. de Scépeaux, Maréchal de: *Mémoires*. In C. Petitot Collection. Vols. 27 and 28. 1819
Vigny, A. de: *Cinq Mars*. 1845

Talcy

Lesueur, F.: 'Château de Talcy'. In *Congrès Archéologique de France*. 1926
Lognon, H.: 'La Cassandre de Ronsard'. In *Revue des Questions Historiques*. 1902
Martellière, J.: *Pierre de Ronsard, Gentilhomme Vendômois*. 1924
Storelli, A.: *Notice Historique et Chronologique sur les Châteaux du Blaisois*. 1884

THE FORTRESSES
Chinon

Cougny, G. de: *Chinon et ses Environs*. 1898
Crozet, R.: 'Chinon'. In *Congrès Archéologique de France*. 1949
Pépin, E.: *Chinon*. 1925
Vallet de Viriville, M.: *Procès de Condamnation de Jeanne d'Arc*. 1869

Loches

Defourneaux, M.: *La Vie Quotidienne au temps de Jeanne d'Arc*. 1952
Gautier, E.: *Histoire du Donjon de Loches*. 1881
Vallery-Radot, J.: 'Loches'. In *Congrès Archéologique de France*. 1949

Saumur

Bodin, J.: La Cité de Saumur et ses environs
— *Recherches Historiques sur la ville de Saumur, ses monuments et ceux de son arrondissement*. 1812
Landais, H.: 'Le château de Saumur'. In *Congrès Archéologique de France*. 1966

Le Plessis-lès-Tours

Louyrette, W. and Croy, R. de: *Louis XI et Le Plessis-lès-Tours*. 1841
Chevalier, C.: in *Promenades Pittoresques*, op. cit.
Commines, P. de: *Mémoires de Commines, 1524*. Ed. 1747

THE BUILDINGS OF JEAN BOURRÉ
Bricard, G.: *Un Serviteur et Compère de Louis XI. Jean Bourré*. 1893

Le Plessis-Bourré

Dalmatie, duc de: *Le Plessis-Bourré*. s.d.
Port, C.: *Dictionnaire Historique du Maine et Loire*. 1874
Marchegay, P.: 'Le Plessis-Bourré'. In *Le Maine et l'Anjou*. Ed. Baron de Wismes. 1862.

Jarzé

Marchegay, P.: 'Château de Jarzé'. In *Le Maine et l'Anjou*. Ed. Baron de Wismes. 1862

Langeais

Beaumont, comte de: *Le Mariage de Charles VIII et d'Anne de Bretagne*. 1900
Bossebœuf, L.-A.: *Langeais et son Château*. 1894
Lesueur, F.: 'Le Château de Langeais'. In *Congrès Archéologique de France*. 1949

Le Moulin

Aubert, M.: 'Le Château du Moulin à Lassay'. In *Congrès Archéologique de France*. 1926

AMBOISE

Bellay, M. du: 'Mémoires de Messire Martin du Bellay, 1569'. In J. Buchon, *Choix de Chroniques et Mémoires Relatives à l'Histoire de France*. 1875
Bossebœuf, L.-A.: *Amboise. Le Château, la Ville et le Canton*. 1908
Bruneau, Dr.: 'Essai Historique sur le Château d'Amboise'. MSS. in Library of Tours.
Coleman, M.: *Histoire du Clos-Lucé*. 1937
Croy, J. de: 'Documents sur le Château d'Amboise et sur Raymond de Dezest'. In *Bulletin de la Société Archéologique de Touraine*. 1913
Grandmaison, L. de: 'Le Compte de la Construction du Château d'Amboise pour l'Année 1495–1496'. In *Bulletin de la Société Archéologique de Touraine*. 1912
Heydenreich, L.: 'Leonardo, Architect to Francis I'. In *Burlington Magazine*. 1952
Houssaye, A.: *Histoire de Léonard de Vinci*. 1869
Lalanne, L.: 'Transport d'Œuvres d'Art de Naples au Château d'Amboise en 1495'. In *Archives de l'Art Français*. 1853

Lesueur, F.: *Le Château d'Amboise.* 1935
— 'Les Italiens à Amboise au Début de la Renaissance'. In *Bulletin de la Société de l'Art Français.* 1929
Marck, R. de la, Seigneur de Florange: *Mémoires, 1505–1525.* 1913

THREE GREAT BUILDERS

Chaumont

Bosseboeuf, L.-A.: *Le Château de Chaumont dans l'Histoire et les Arts.* 1906
Broglie, Prince J. de: *Histoire du Château de Chaumont.* 1944
Croy, J. de: 'Examen de l'histoire de Chaumont-sur-Loire'. In *Revue de Loir-et-Cher.* 1907, 1908

Gaillon

Chirol, E.: *Le Château de Gaillon.* 1952
Rosci, M. and Chastel, A.: 'Un Château Français en Italie'. In *Art de France.* 1963

Le Verger

Maulde la Clavière, R. de: *Pierre de Rohan, Duc de Nemours, dit le Maréchal de Gié.* 1885
Port, C.: op. cit.

Bury

Anon.: 'Oraison Funèbre sur Florimond Robertet'. In *Recueil de mémoires et documents sur Le Forez.* Vol. IV. 1878
Lesueur, F.: 'L'Hôtel d'Alluye'. In *Congrès Archéologique de France.* 1926
Lesueur, P.: 'Le Château de Bury et Fra Giocondo'. In *Gazette des Beaux Arts.* 1925
Vallière, H. de la: 'Bury en Blésois'. In *Revue de Loir-et-Cher.* 1889

BLOIS

Baillargé, A. and Walsh: *Album du Château de Blois Restauré.* 1851
Betge, M.: 'Les Constructions de Gaston d'Orléans à Blois'. In *Mémoires de la Société de Sciences et Lettres de Loir-et-Cher.* 1935
Bidou, H.: *Le Château de Blois.* 1931
Bernier: *Histoire de Blois.* 1682

Lesueur, F. and Lesueur, P.: *Le Château de Blois.* 1921

Lesueur, F.: 'Les Fouilles du Château de Blois'. In *Bulletin Monumental.* 1908

Roux de Lincy, A. le: *Anne de Bretagne.* 1860

Seyssel, C. de: *Louis XII.* 1558

THE COURT OF FRANCE

Blome, R.: *Hawking and Falconry, 1686.* Ed. 1929

Brézé, L. de: *Les Chasses de François Ier, Racontées par Louis de Brézé Grand Sénéschal de Normandie, 1517–1530.* Ed. 1869

Budé, G.: *Traité de la Vénerie de Budé, traduit du latin en français par Loys Leroy.* 1864

Castiglione, B.: *The Book of the Courtier by Count Baldassare Castiglione, Done into English by Sir Thomas Hoby.* 1561

Cellini, B.: *Memoirs of Benvenuto Cellini written by Himself.* Trans. Thomas Roscoe. 1901

Decrue de Stoutz, F.: *La Cour de France et la Société au 16ème Siècle.* 1885

Fouilloux, J. du: *La Vénerie.* 1561

Tomasseo, M.: *Relations des Ambassadeurs Vénitiens sur les Affaires de France au 16ème Siècle.* 1838

CHAMBORD

Croy, R. de: 'Quelques Renseignements Inédits sur les Maîtres Maçons de Chambord et d'Amboise'. In *Mémoires de la Société Archéologique de l'Orléannais.* 1902

Ganay, comte de: *Le Château de Chambord.* 1950

Jarry, L.: 'Documents Inédits servant à rectifier la date de Construction et le nom des premiers Architectes du Château de Chambord'. In *Mémoires de la Société Archéologique de l'Orléannais.* 1889

Lesueur, F.: 'Les Derniers Etapes de la Construction de Chambord'. In *Bulletin Monumental.* 1951

Merle, J.: *Chambord.* 1832

Paquet, P.: 'La remise en état des communs du Château de Chambord'. In *Les Monuments Historiques de France.* 1937

Raymond, J.: 'Les Premiers réprésentations de "Monsieur de Pourceaugnac" et du "Bourgeois Gentilhomme" '. In *La Nouvelle Revue.* 1933

— 'Le Maréchal de Saxe à Chambord'. In *La Nouvelle Revue.* 1927

Schommer, P.: *Chambord*. s.d.

Vitry, P.: 'Le Château de Chambord'. In *Congrès Archéologique de France*. 1926.

CHENONCEAU

Adhémar, J.: *French Drawings of the 16th Century*. 1955. (For Clouet's drawing of Diane de Poitiers.)
Chevalier, C.: *Archives Royales de Chenonceaux*. 3 vols. 1864
— *Histoire de Chenonceaux*. 1868
— *Restauration de Chenonceaux*. 1878
Ranjard, R.: *Le Secret de Chenonceau*. 1950
Terrasse, C.: *Le Château de Chenonceau*. 1928

FOUR PRIVATE CHATEAUX

Luynes

Bellanger, S.: 'Deux Villes Historiques. Luynes et Amboise'. In Ad. van Bever, op. cit.
Guerlin, H.: *Les Châteaux de Touraine*. 1922
Taralon, J.: *Le Château de Châteaudun*. 1958

Le Lude

Bozo, D.: 'Les Peintures Murales du Château du Lude'. In *Gazette des Beaux Arts*. October 1965
Candé, P.: *Notice Historique sur Le Lude et son Château*. 1964
David, C.: *Le Château du Lude et ses Possesseurs*. 1854

Serrant

Cook, Sir T.: *Twenty Five Great Houses of France*. s.d.
Marchegay, P.: 'Château de Serrant'. In *Le Maine et l'Anjou*. Ed. Baron de Wismes. 1862
Perouse de Montclos, J.-M.: 'Le château de Serrant'. In *Congrès Archéologique de France*. 1966

Azay-Le-Rideau

Auzas, P.-M.: 'Azay-le-Rideau'. In *Congrès Archéologique de France*. 1949
Chevalier, C.: *La Ville d'Azay-le-Rideau aux 15ème et 16ème Siècles*. 1873
Guerlin, H.: *Les Châteaux de Touraine*. 1922

Loiseleur, J.: 'Etude sur Gilles Berthelot'. In *Mémoires de la Société Archéologique de Touraine*. 1859

Maurice, J.: *Azay-le-Rideau et sa Région à travers l'Histoire*. 1946

Sourdeval, M. de: 'Deux Châteaux Historiques; Azay-le-Rideau et Ussé'. In Ad. van Bever, op. cit.

Spont.: *Semblançay*. 1895

THE MANOR HOUSE AND GARDEN

Estienne, C.: *L'Agriculture et Maison Rustique, 1583*. Translated into English by Richard Surflet, Practitioner in Physicke. 1616

Ganay, comte de: *Jardins de France*. 1949

Gouberville, G.: *Le Journal du Sire de Gouberville, 1533–1557*. 1892

Lefranc, A.: *La Vie Quotidienne au temps de la Renaissance*. 1938

Vaissière, P. de: *Gentilshommes Campagnards de l'Ancienne France*. 1904

Wiley, W.: *The Gentleman of Renaissance France*. 1954

Villandry

Fleurent, M.: 'L'Esprit de Villandry'. In *Maison et Jardin*, July/August 1963

Noac'h, P. le: *Histoire de Villandry et son Château*. 1949

Villesavin

Storelli, A.: *Notice Historique et Chronologique sur les Châteaux du Blaisois*. 1884

THE TIME OF TROUBLES

Allart, H.: *La Conjuration d'Amboise*. 1822

Bouillet du Chariol, R. de: *Histoire des Ducs de Guise*. 1849

Cimber, M.: *Archives Curieuses de l'Histoire de France, depuis Louis XI jusqu'à Louis XIII*. Series 1, Vol. 12. 1836

Chevalier, C.: 'Catherine de Médicis et les Fêtes Données à Chenonceaux 1560–1578'. In Ad. van Bever, op. cit.

Forbes, P. (for Throckmorton's Letter): *A Full Review of the Public Transactions in the Reign of Queen Elizabeth*. 1740

Vaissière, P. de: *De Quelques Assassins*. 1912

THE SEVENTEENTH CENTURY

Sully

Loiseleur, J.: *Monographie du Château de Sully*. 1868
Martin, L.: *Histoire de la Ville de Sully*. 1962
Martin, M.-M.: *Sully le Grand, l'Ami du Roi*. 1965

Brissac

Brissac, duc de: *Brissac*. 1957
— *Les Ducs de Brissac*. 1952
Gautier, C.: *Histoire de Brissac et son Château*. 1920
Dauvergne, R.: *Le Château de Brissac au 18ème Siècle*. 1945

Richelieu

Marot, J.: *Le Magnifique Château de Richelieu*. 1660
Sedeyn, E.: 'Richelieu'. In Ad. van Bever, op. cit.
Tallemant des Réaux: *Le Cardinal de Richelieu*. 1920
Vignier, A.: *Le Château de Richelieu*. 1676
Bossebœuf, L.-A.: 'Histoire de Richelieu et ses environs'. In *Mémoires de la Société Archéologique de Touraine*. Vol. 35. 1889

Champigny

Bossebœuf, L.-A.: *Le Château et la Sainte Chapelle de Champigny-sur-Veude*. 1881
Pépin, E.: *Champigny-sur-Veude et Richelieu*. 1928

Cheverny

Aubert, M.: 'Château de Cheverny'. In *Congrès Archéologique de France*. 1926
Blancher-le Bourhis, M.: *Le Château de Cheverny*
Vibraye, comte H. de: *Histoire de la Maison Hurault*. 1929

Domestics

Audiger.: *La Maison Réglée et l'Art de Diriger la Maison d'un Grand Seigneur*. 1700
Babeau, A.: *Les Artisans et Domestiques d'Autrefois*. 1886
Ribbe, Cardinal de: *Une Grande Dame dans son Ménage, d'après le Journal de la comtesse de Rochefort, 1689*. 1889

THE EIGHTEENTH CENTURY

Chanteloup

André, E. and Engerand, R.: *Chanteloup*. 1958
Maugras, G.: *Le Duc et la Duchesse de Choiseul*. 1902
Orliac, J. de: *Chanteloup*. 1929
Snowman, K.: *Eighteenth Century Gold Boxes of Europe*. 1966.
    Appendix on the Chanteloup box by F. Watson.

Montgeoffroy

Anon.: *Louis-Georges-Erasme, marquis de Contades; Notes et Souvenirs.*
    1883
Verlet, P.: *French Furniture and Interior Decoration of the 18th Century.*
    1967

Menars

Chavigny, J.: *Menars*. s.d.
Lesueur, F.: 'Menars'. In *Mémoires de la Société des Sciences de Loir-et-
    Cher*. Vol. 22. 1912

REVOLUTION

Dufort, J.: *Mémoires sur les Règnes de Louis XV et Louis XVI et sur la
    Révolution*. 1886
Pommereul.: *Souvenirs de mon Administration des Préfectures de l'Indre-
    et-Loire et du Nord*. 1807
Ste-Beuve: *Les Causeries du Lundi*. Vol. 14

RESTORATION

Blayney, Lord: *Narrative of a forced Journey through Spain and France
    as a Prisoner of War in the Years 1810–1814*. Vol. 2. 1814
Broglie, Prince J. de: *Mme de Staël et sa Cour au Château de Chaumont en
    1810*. 1936
— *Histoire du Château de Chaumont*. 1944
Merle, J.: *Chambord*. 1832
Thornton, Col.: *A Sporting Tour through various parts of France in the
    Year*. 1802

INDEX

LE MAINE ET ANJOV

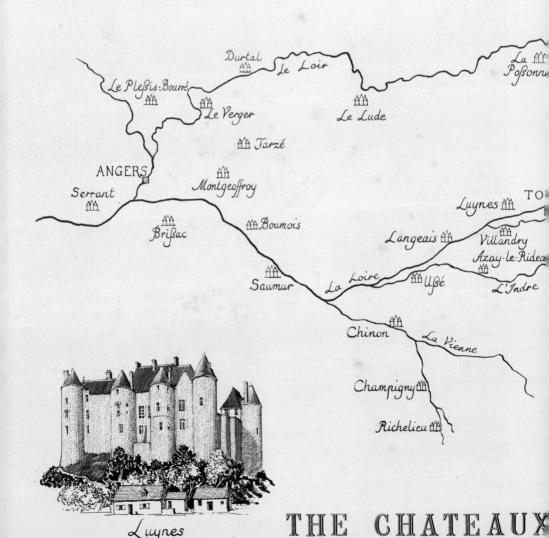

Durtal

Le Loir

La Poßonn

Le Pleßis-Bourré

Le Verger

Le Lude

Jarzé

ANGERS

Montgeoffroy

Serrant

Luynes   TO

Boumois

Langeais

Villandry

Brißac

Azay-le-Ridea

Saumur

La Loire

Ußé

L'Indre

Chinon

La Vienne

Champigny

Richelieu

Luynes

THE CHATEAUX